JOHN HUNTER 1728–1793

JOHN HUNTER (1728-1793)

Portrait of John Hunter by Sir Joshua Reynolds at the Royal College of Surgeons of England

John Hunter
1728–1793

George Qvist

WILLIAM HEINEMANN MEDICAL BOOKS LIMITED · LONDON

to
FRANCES

William Heinemann Medical Books Limited
23 Bedford Square
London WC1B 3HH

First published 1981

Copyright © George Qvist 1981

ISBN 0-433-27095-0

Printed and bound in Great Britain by
Biddles Ltd, Guildford and King's Lynn

CONTENTS

ILLUSTRATIONS

FOREWORD

THIS work has special features that no other of the many biographies of John Hunter possesses. The method of presentation adopted by Mr Qvist enables the reader to appreciate more easily the outstanding qualities that Hunter possessed. He did not limit his interests to surgery but included in his activities a consideration of many other disciplines. In his search for the general principles underlying life and living he studied the whole field of Nature and this is what makes the results of his investigations so convincing.

Here Mr Qvist has discussed and appraised each subject and made ample references to original work and opinions based on fact. For those who have wondered why John Hunter is judged to be the pioneer of scientific surgery when he regarded surgical operations as 'a reflection on the healing art . . . a tacit acknowledgement of the insufficiency of surgery' the answer lies here.

The profound understanding of John Hunter's character and works evident in his account is worthy of the highest respect and the author is to be congratulated most sincerely on this stimulating and scholarly work, bringing to notice John Hunter's unique claims to abiding esteem.

JESSIE DOBSON

PREFACE

ALTHOUGH numerous biographies of John Hunter have been published already, it is at present very difficult to obtain a new or secondhand copy of any of them. It was felt therefore that a new biography might serve a useful purpose.

In compiling this volume an attempt has been made to include only known and established facts relating to John Hunter, with the exclusion of anecdotes about him, many of them apocryphal, for which no sound authenticity can be obtained.

Quotations from John Hunter's works remain ever popular but actual location of their source is often difficult because of the enormous variety of Hunter's interests. It has therefore been one of the objects of this biography to classify the subjects in the hope that quotations can be traced more easily to their source, and to include as many as possible.

In addition to the biographies of John Hunter, there have been thousands of articles, lectures and orations relating to his life and work, many of them in publications of limited circulation. It is hoped that references to the most valuable and original of these publications will be useful.

ACKNOWLEDGEMENTS

I am extremely grateful to many friends for advice and information, especially to Miss Elizabeth Allen, Curator of the Hunterian Museum, Mr E. H. Cornelius and his staff at the library of the Royal College of Surgeons of England, Mr D. W. C. Stewart and the staff of the library at the Royal Society of Medicine, Miss P. Fear and her staff at the library of the Royal Free Hospital School of Medicine, the Librarian South Norwood Library, the Librarian Glasgow University, to Sir Alan Parks, President of the Royal

College of Surgeons of England and Professor A. Harding Rains, editor of the Annals of the Royal College of Surgeons of England for permission to reproduce material from the College and from the Annals, to Dr Edith Gilchrist, to Mr C. Gilson and Mr B. Pike for technical assistance, and to my secretary, Mrs M. Pumphrey for her devoted labours. My most sincere thanks are extended to Miss Jessie Dobson, the world's greatest authority on John Hunter, for valuable advice, for the enormous fund of information available in her books and articles from which I have freely drawn and especially for her kind and generous Foreword.

*   *   *

George Qvist died on the 28th July 1981 a few hours after the page proofs of this book were delivered to his home. He had, therefore, no opportunity to correct the proofs nor to complete the index. He had, however, previously designed the index and left numerous annotations for guidance. His brother, Alfred Qvist, has been largely responsible for correcting the proofs and completing the index and we are sure that the author would wish to thank his brother for his generous help.

PROLOGUE

BEFORE Hunter's time, superstition played a large part in the teaching of medicine. In the seventeenth century Richard Wiseman, the leading surgeon of his time, believed in the efficacy of the Royal Touch in cases of scrofula and even the learned Sir Thomas Browne affirmed that witches did exist.[1] Thomas Sydenham (1624–1689), often referred to as 'the English Hippocrates', was the first prominent physician after Hippocrates who practised essentially clinical bedside medicine.

The practice of medicine in Hunter's day was thus founded partly on time-honoured authority based on the works of Hippocrates, Galen and Celsus, and partly on a rigid concept of diseases as separate specific entities enunciated by Sydenham. John Hunter was the first to attempt a coordination of diseases by a study of their pathology, as for example the different manifestations of the process of inflammation. He approached his study on the Baconian principle of induction, i.e. the process of inferring a general law or principle from the observation of particular instances, or reasoning from particular observed or experimental facts to general principles. Thus John Hunter is rightly regarded as the founder of scientific surgery since he was the first to apply the inductive system of observation and experiment to the study of disease. In these detailed investigations he necessarily also established the foundations of pathology. Furthermore, in order to appreciate correctly the effects of disease, Hunter felt it was necessary to understand the mechanism of the normal healthy body and in the performance of this task he achieved an unrivalled mastery of human anatomy and physiology. When he gave evidence at the trial of John Donellan in 1781, Hunter stated that he had dissected 'some thousands' of human subjects.[2]

In the introduction to his surgical lectures, Hunter said '. . . it is
my intention to begin with the physiology of the animal oeconomy
in its natural or healthy state; and then come to pathology, or the
physiology of disease, which may be called the *perversion of the
natural actions of the animal oeconomy. . . .*'[3] Thus Hunter's
inductive system was a solid structure of observed and experimental
facts of pathology based on a sound knowledge of anatomy and
physiology.

It was chiefly this fundamental factual approach to the study of
disease that alienated John Hunter from his contemporaries who
were mostly still satisfied with the superficialities of their medical
and surgical crafts. This difference in clinical approach is well
illustrated by a case of tetanus described by John Hunter:

> I attended another patient in England, with Sir N. Thomas.
> Assafoetida and opium were given without effect; these were left off,
> and bark given in large quantities. Dr. Warren being called in,
> advised, among other things, a bath prepared of milk and water.
> After this he seemed better, but died soon after.
>
> I discovered, to my amazement, the different modes of different
> physicians. Sir N. Thomas had read much, and knew all the
> antispasmodics from the days of Hippocrates downwards. Dr.
> Warren having just cured his son of locked jaw, implicitly followed
> the same practice in this case, being unable to alter his rules of
> practice in the smallest degree, as occasion might require.[4]

Hunter's inductive philosophy is well exemplified in his most
often quoted words from a letter to Jenner – '. . . why do you ask
me a question, by the way of solving it. I think your solution is just;
but why think, why not trie the Expt. . . .'[5] These words surely
could not imply that Hunter did not advocate thinking. He was
forever thinking. Indeed, his devoted pupil Henry Cline said –
'Much as Mr. Hunter, did, he thought still more. He has often told
me, his delight was to think.'[6] The famous portrait of John Hunter
by Sir Joshua Reynolds stimulated the great physiognomist Johann
Lavater to comment, 'That man thinks for himself.'[7] Hunter's
words to Jenner may best be interpreted, not as a denigration of
thinking, but as an expression of his opinion on the priority of
experiment over speculation in the investigation of problems.

Buckle wrote of John Hunter – '. . . his powers were so
extraordinary, that, among the great masters of organic science, he
belongs, I apprehend, to the same rank as Aristotle, Harvey, and

Bichat, and is somewhat superior either to Haller or Cuvier. . . . in tracing the movements of his most remarkable mind, we shall find, that, in it, deduction and induction were more intimately united than in any other Scotch intellect, either of the seventeenth or eighteenth century.'[8]

It was observed by Buckle that John Hunter's ideas were sometimes confused because they were the product of a mixture of his inductive philosophy with the deductive one of reasoning from general principles to particular facts. 'As a Scotchman, he preferred reasoning from general principles to particular facts; as an inhabitant of England, he became inured to the opposite plan of reasoning from particular facts to general principles . . . I make no doubt that one of the reasons why Hunter, in investigating a subject, is often obscure, is that, on such occasions, his mind was divided between these two hostile methods . . .'[9] Cohen disagreed completely with Buckle's view and pointed out that Hunter applied the deductive method quite deliberately in using a general principle, already established by induction, to the experimental solution of further problems and that Hunter's method was in fact exemplary – observation and experimental establishment of facts, inductive argument to establish a principle, and then deductive reasoning from the general principle applied to the explanation of further problems.[10] An excellent example of this approach is Hunter's study of inflammation where his careful observations and experiments of the pathology led him to establish the general principles of inflammation which he then applied to the explanation of numerous diseases such as osteomyelitis, phlebitis, peritonitis and the complications of gunshot wounds and other injuries.

Hunter's method of investigation founded the scientific approach to surgery, and the few, but admittedly important, occasions in which it led him to false conclusions may be explained by Buckle's suggestion. A similar view was expressed by Babington in his preface to the Treatise on Venereal Disease in 1835 – 'It may even be doubted whether his natural appetite for generalization has not sometimes misled him, and whether, in his desire to ascertain a general law, he has not sometimes abandoned his hold of the acknowledged facts of the disease, and left it even more obscure than before.'[11] Certainly this observation might explain Hunter's erroneous opinions on the nature of the venereal diseases (p. 159), on the viability of the teeth (p. 83), on the function of the red blood corpuscles (p. 102), and on the organisation of coagulated blood (p. 104). In each of these cases it will be found that Hunter made erroneous deductions from a generalisation which he had established on the basis of observations and investigations of which some were themselves erroneous or inconclusive, as for example in venereal disease his opinion that two diseases were not both active at the same time in one subject; on the teeth his experiments failed to demonstrate a circulation; on the blood his opinion that the absence of red blood corpuscles in some animals implied a function of secondary importance to these cells; and in the organisation of coagulated blood a misinterpretation of his observations. In all these cases Hunter seems to have promulgated general laws far too hastily on limited data, and shifted too eagerly from an inductive to a deductive philosophy as Buckle suggested.

Hunter's interminable search for general principles extended throughout the whole of Nature. Indeed he tried to coordinate all the branches of natural and physical science under laws common to them all. He had no doubt that there are in nature such uniform general principles applicable to all matter, animate and inanimate – 'Every property in man is similar to some property, either in another animal, or probably in a vegetable, or even in inanimate matter. Thereby [man] becomes classable with those in some of his parts.'[12] Hunter maintained therefore that the study of man and his diseases starts in fact with a comprehension of the properties of inanimate matter. Accordingly he studied the structure of minerals and he made a valuable collection of crystallizations which he used in his lectures to exemplify the difference between the laws which regulate the growth of organic and inorganic bodies.[13]

Hunter made no apologies for his comprehensive approach to the study of Nature – 'It should be remembered that nothing in Nature stands alone; but that every art and science has a relation to some other art or science, and that it requires a knowledge of those others, as far as this connexion takes place, to enable us to become perfect in that which engages our particular attention.'[14]

John Hunter worshipped Nature with profound humility. He was not just a disciple of Natural History – he was its High Priest. He approached the study of Nature in a humble, almost reverent, attitude, as shown for example in his paper on whales – 'Thus the heart and aorta of the spermaceti whale appeared prodigious, being too large to be contained in a wide tub, the aorta measuring a foot in

diameter. When we consider these as applied to the circulation, and
figure to ourselves that probably ten or fifteen gallons of blood are
thrown out at one stroke, and moved with an immense velocity
through a tube of a foot diameter, the whole idea fills the mind with
wonder.'[15]

Hunter's reverence for Nature and all her works bred in him an
essentially conservative policy to the treatment of disease. His faith
in the healing powers of Nature is expressed frequently throughout
his writings and is well exemplified by his comments on surgical
operations – 'This last part of surgery, namely, operations, is a
reflection on the healing art; it is a tacit acknowledgement of the
insufficiency of surgery. It is like an armed savage who attempts to
get that by force which a civilised man would get by stratagem.'[16]

Undoubtedly the most remarkable facet of Hunter's genius was
his prodigious versatility. His interests in natural history* were
boundless and included anatomy, physiology, botany, geology,
zoology and palaeontology. A remarkable and unusual feature was
that he could contemplate the whole wide field of Nature and yet he
could observe and concentrate on the most minute details of a
subject. At one moment he might be dissecting a bee and at the
next, a whale. On one occasion he might be studying the insect
larva on an oak leaf and the next, speculating on the age of the earth.
No natural phenomenon was too trivial for his attention, as for
example in this observation – 'The powers of digestion may in some
instances be estimated by the appearance of the excrement, in
which, if the food appears not to be much altered, we may conclude
that digestion has had little or no influence on it. Thus, the
excrement of a flea, that has lived on blood, is nearly, to appearance, pure blood, not having even lost its colour.'[17] All this
knowledge and industry in natural history was collateral to his
professional life as a surgeon and indeed constantly applied by him
to the elucidation of surgical problems. An excellent example of this
is seen in his observations on the air-sacs of birds which he demonstrated to be extended into the bones. Hunter used this fact as evidence that air alone does not produce inflammation (p. 147). Many
of his physiological experiments were of immediate application to

---

* Natural history is here used in its broadest sense, as defined in the *Shorter Oxford
English Dictionary* – 'Originally: The systematic study of all natural objects, animal,
vegetable, and mineral.'

the study of human disease as for example his .iimal experiments on absorption by the lymphatics, the res.lts of which were fundamental to his explanation of the phenomena of inflammation. He was undoubtedly the greatest of all surgeon-physiologists.

REFERENCES

1 Guthrie D. *A History of Medicine.* London and Edinburgh, T Nelson. 1945, p. 196.
2 Cornelius E H. John Hunter as an expert witness. *Annals of the Royal College of Surgeons of England.* 1978, vol. 60, pp. 412–418.
3 Hunter J. Lectures on the principles of surgery in *The Works of John Hunter,* ed. JF Palmer. London, Longman. 1835, vol, 1, p, 211.
4 Ibid. p. 589.
5 Editorial. Letters from the Past. *Annals of the Royal College of Surgeons of England.* 1974, vol. 54, p. 149.
6 Abernethy J. *Hunterian Oration.* London, Longman. 1819, pp. 26, 27.
7 Holland Lord. *Further Memoirs of the Whig Party 1807–1821.* ed. Lord Stavordale. London, John Murray. 1905, p. 345.
8 Buckle H T. *History of Civilization in England.* London, Parker Son and Bourn. 1861 vol. 2, p. 550.
9 Ibid. p. 553
10 Cohen Sir Henry (Lord). Reflections on the Hunterian method. *Hunterian Society Transactions* 1955–56, vol. 14, pp. 80–95.
11 Babington G G. Preface to a treatise on venereal disease in *The Works of John Hunter,* ed. J F Palmer. London, Longman. 1835, vol. 2, p. 127.
12 Hunter J. *Essays and Observations on Natural History, Anatomy, Physiology, Psychology and Geology.* ed. R Owen. London, John Van Voorst. 1861, vol. 1, p. 10.
13 Ottley D. Life of John Hunter in *The Works of John Hunter,* ed, J F Palmer. London, Longman. 1835, vol. 1, p. 138.
14 Hunter J. Some observations on digestion in *The Works of John Hunter,* ed. J F Palmer. London, Longman. 1837, vol. 4, p. 83.
15 Hunter J. Observations on the structure and oeconomy of whales in *The Works of John Hunter,* ed. J F Palmer. London, Longman. 1837, vol. 4, pp. 366, 367.
16 Hunter J. Lectures on the principles of surgery in *The Works of John Hunter,* ed. J F Palmer. London, Longman. 1835, vol. 1, p. 210.
17 Hunter J. Some observations on digestion in *The Works of John Hunter,* ed. J F Palmer. London, Longman. 1837, vol. 4, p. 112.

CHAPTER 1

EARLY YEARS
1728–1760

JOHN Hunter was the tenth and last child of John and Agnes Hunter (fig. 1). He was born at Long Calderwood in Lanarkshire, a small estate near the village of East Kilbride, seven miles from Glasgow. The date of John Hunter's birth is given in the parish register as 13th February, 1728 (fig. 2) but it is usually stated that he himself observed the 14th as his birthday.[1] The Royal College of Surgeons of England recognises the latter date as the anniversary while the Hunterian Society celebrates the occasion on the 13th February.

John Hunter had nine elder brothers and sisters, the majority of whom succumbed prematurely to phthisis. The three eldest, *John* (1708–1722), *Elizabeth* (1710–1711) and *Andrew* (1711–1714) died in childhood. Four others, *Janet* (1713–1749), *James* (1715–1745), *Agnes* (1716–1741) and *Isabella* (1725–1742) died young. *William* (23 May 1718 – 30 March 1783) was ten years older than John and died ten years before him. He had a most important influence on John Hunter's career and was responsible for establishing him in London. *Dorothea* (1721–1806) married the Rev. James Baillie in 1785. Their son Dr. Matthew Baillie (1761–1823) became a distinguished physician who published the first English textbook on pathology and from whom are descended the present family links with John Hunter (fig. 1). Dr. Matthew Baillie's two sisters were Agnes (1760–1861) and Joanna (1762–1851). They lived together, to a considerable age, and were well-known in the cultured circles of their time. In their latter days they styled themselves *Mrs.* although they never married.[2] Joanna Baillie achieved fame with her verses and plays and she maintained a close correspondence for many years with Sir Walter Scott.

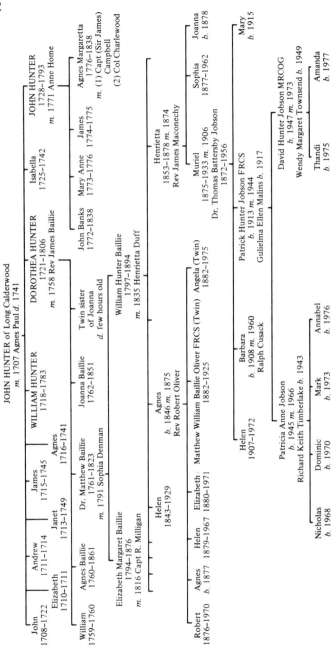

Fig. 1. John Hunter's family tree

EXTRACT OF AN ENTRY

IN A REGISTER KEPT AT THE GENERAL REGISTRY OFFICE. EDINBURGH

John y lawfull son procreat betwixt John Hunter &   Paul
born febr. 13th & baptized March 30th 1728

EXTRACTED from the Register of Births and Baptisms for

the Parish of _____ East Kilbride _____

in the County of _____ Lanark _____ .

GIVEN at the GENERAL REGISTRY OFFICE, NEW REGISTER HOUSE,

EDINBURGH, under the Seal of the said Office, the ___ 4th __

day of _____ November _____ 19 46 .

Fig. 2. Copy of John Hunter's birth certificate, presented to the
Hunterian Society by the president Dr. J. B. Cook, which confirms
the date of birth as February 13th 1728. (*Hunterian Society Transactions* 1957–8. vol. 16, p. 143)

John Hunter went to school in Kilbride but it seems that he was a
bad scholar. His niece Miss Joanna Baillie wrote that he 'could not
be taught to read but with the greatest difficulty . . . he remained an
idle, uneducated Boy upon his Mother's hands . . .'[3] John Hunter's
other niece Miss Agnes Baillie wrote, in a letter to her brother Dr.
Matthew Baillie, 'John Hunter was the youngest son, and his Mother

spoiled him. He would do nothing but what he liked, and neither liked to be taught reading nor writing nor any kind of learning, but rambling amongst the woods, braes, etc., looking after Birds'-nests, comparing their eggs – number, size, marks, and other peculiarities: whilst his two elder brothers had both been to College, and got the same education that the sons of country gentlemen then got.'[4]

Most of John Hunter's biographers have commented on his poor education. But Keith[5] and Wood Jones[6] and others have pointed out that he was in fact not wasting his time as a boy but rather that he taught himself in the study of Nature. His immediate success in anatomical dissection at William Hunter's School suggests that he must have had considerable previous experience in that field. Indeed, in one of William Hunter's lectures upon 'Cleaning of bones and making of Preparations', he remarks that his brother 'prepared a set of bones in the fields which he said was the best method, had we a convenience to do them'.[7]

It is of interest to note that Einstein and Darwin were also poor scholars in their youth. Einstein 'was considered backward by his teachers. . . . his teachers reported to his father that he was mentally slow, unsociable and adrift forever in his foolish dreams. . . . when Hermann Einstein asked his son's headmaster what profession his son should adopt, the answer was simply: It doesn't matter; he'll never make a success of anything.' (Clark)[8] Some years later, Einstein wrote – 'It is nothing short of a miracle that modern methods of teaching have not yet entirely strangled the sacred spirit of curiosity and inquiry; for this delicate plant needs freedom no less than stimulation.'[9]

Charles Darwin wrote '. . . I was considered by all the masters and by my father as a very ordinary boy, rather below the common standard in intellect . . . my father once said to me: You care for nothing but shooting, dogs, and rat-catching, and you will be a disgrace to yourself and all your family.'[10] Obviously, these men of genius by their very nature cannot fit into a standard educational machine. It is doubtful whether any of these great men would have been admitted to a university under modern selective methods.

John Hunter's father died in 1741, when John was thirteen years of age and his mother had little control over him. He made little progress at the school in East Kilbride where his brothers James and William had progressed well, and after his father's death he ceased attending the school. At the age of seventeen he was sent to

Glasgow to stay with his sister Janet who had married a timber-merchant and cabinet-maker named Buchanan. It is probable that John Hunter may have learned some woodcraft in these circumstances – his great contemporary critic Jessé Foot wrote that 'A wheel wright or a carpenter he certainly was, until . . . changed the scheme of his future occupations . . . to lay down the chissel, the rule, and the mallet; and take up the knife, the blow pipe, and the probe.'[11]

John Hunter remained with his sister for only a few months before returning home. His elder brother William was now established teaching anatomy in London and John decided to join him. He left Long Calderwood in September 1748, travelling on horseback with an acquaintance William Hamilton.[12]

William Hunter had originally planned to enter the Church and commenced his studies at Glasgow University. After spending four years in this course his interest was diverted to a career in medicine and he became pupil-assistant to Dr. William Cullen, a medical practitioner in Hamilton seven miles away. Three years later he went to Edinburgh where he studied anatomy under Alexander Monro. In November 1740 he left Scotland and travelled to London by sea. His friendship with Dr. Cullen served him well as he was given introductions to two fellow-Scots, Dr. William Smellie and Dr. James Douglas who were well-established accoucheurs in London, the latter being also an eminent anatomist, famous for his description of the rectovaginal pouch of peritoneum.*

In September 1741, William Hunter became assistant to Dr. James Douglas and entered as a surgical pupil at St. George's Hospital. When Dr. Douglas died in 1742 William carried on his practice and in 1746 he commenced to give private courses of lectures in anatomy at rooms in Covent Garden. It was an eminently suitable time for the establishment of a school for sound anatomical teaching. Prior to 1745 anatomical dissection was limited by Act of Parliament to the public dissection at the Hall of the Barber-Surgeons Company of the bodies of four executed criminals annually. In 1745 the alliance between the Barbers and the Surgeons was dissolved and although the new Corporation of Surgeons retained the privilege of four annual public dissections,

---

* Dr. Douglas was involved in the famous case of the Rabbit Woman of Godalming, when he was the sole consultant who perceived and denounced the deception.[13,14]

the demand for more anatomical teaching was becoming so great that the government, who needed more surgeons for the armed services, made little attempt to interfere with the establishment of the numerous private anatomy schools that sprang up all over the country.

Dr. William Hunter was the most successful teacher of anatomy of his time. His lectures were attended by Edward Gibbon and Adam Smith. In his biography of Gibbon, D. M. Low recounts that – 'In the early part of 1777 variety and relief from historical studies were found in attending Hunter the great surgeon's lectures . . . Attendance at Hunter's lectures on anatomy for two hours in the afternoon "opened a new and very entertaining scene within myself" and lasted from February into April. Gibbon deferred setting out for Paris until they were over. Adam Smith used to go with him. A young student recalled seeing them there together and heard much of the conversation between Gibbon and Hunter:

"for Mr. Gibbon, at the end of every lecture, used to leave his seat to thank the doctor for the pleasure and instruction which he had received. . ."

"Hunter repaid his questioner with the present of a commentary on Thucydides's account of the plague, a quarto of six hundred pages published in Venice in 1603".'[15]

When Gibbon attended Hunter's lectures he was already famous, the first volume of *Decline and Fall* having been published in the previous year with instantaneous success.

In 1753 William Hunter and Percivall Pott were elected Masters of Anatomy at Surgeons' Hall.[16] In 1768 William Hunter built his own school in Great Windmill Street, one which for many years was the most famous of the private anatomy schools in the world.

Meanwhile William Hunter's reputation as an obstetrician had been growing rapidly and in 1748 he had been elected to the staff of Middlesex Hospital. In 1762 he was appointed physician extraordinary to Queen Charlotte whom he attended at the birth of the first of her fifteen children, the future George IV. In 1768 he was appointed by King George III as first Professor of Anatomy at the Royal Academy.[17] In 1774 he published his classic work, *The Anatomy of the Human Gravid Uterus*. William Hunter was an inveterate collector of anatomical specimens, coins, books and works of art, a valuable collection which he bequeathed to the

University of Glasgow.[13] 'That he was a keen collector may perhaps be gathered from a passage of arms that took place one winter's night in William Hunter's home, with one Francis Carter, a traveller in the Orient and a rival collector of coins!

"God grant," writes the latter to a friend "that I may be able to keep my coins from his clutches. He had the impudence to tell me in his own house last winter that he was glad to hear of my loss by capture of the *Grenados*, as it might force me to sell him my Greek coins; an anecdote that should not be forgot when you write his life".'[18]

John Hunter was an immediate success at the Anatomy School. His skill at dissection was obvious and his energy was boundless. He applied himself with enthusiasm to the task of preparation of specimens and to the investigation of anatomical problems. He worked as assistant to William Hunter for twelve years, from 1748 to 1760, when he joined the Army. However during this period he was able to undertake other activities. In 1749 and 1750 he attended Cheselden's surgical practice at Chelsea Hospital. In 1751 he became a surgeon's pupil at St. Bartholomew's Hospital under Percivall Pott. He must have undertaken some clinical work at this period because he says – 'About the year 1752 I attended a chimney-sweeper labouring under a [urethral] stricture. He was the first patient I ever had under this disease.'[19] He also states that 'In the spring of 1753 there was an execution of eight men, two of whom I knew had at that time very severe gonorrhoeas.'[20]

In 1752 Hunter went to Long Calderwood where his sister Dorothea was the sole survivor and he brought her back to London with him. In 1754 he became a surgeon's pupil at St. George's Hospital. In 1755, probably at the suggestion of his brother William, he entered at St. Mary's Hall, Oxford as a gentleman commoner, but it is believed that he left Oxford after less than two months' residence.

In 1756 John Hunter was appointed house surgeon at St. George's Hospital but he resigned the post after only five months tenure. It seems that he was always anxious to return as soon as possible to the study and teaching of anatomy. However even in the short tenure of his house surgeon's post he applied himself to some research problem. He says – 'I put some dark venal blood into a phial, till it was about half full, and shook the blood, which mixed with the air in this motion, and it became immediately of a florid red. These experiments I made in the summer 1755,* when I was house-surgeon at St. George's Hospital, and Dr. Hunter taught them ever after at his lectures.'[21]

In 1759 John Hunter suffered from inflammation of the lungs. In October 1760 he was appointed a staff-surgeon in the Army and in March 1761 he went with the fleet to take part in the siege of Belleisle off the coast of France.

John Hunter's twelve years work from 1748 to 1760 at William Hunter's Anatomy School had been very fruitful. Apart from the acquisition of a profound and accurate knowledge of human anatomy, he had collaborated with William Hunter in the establishment of several new important anatomical and physiological concepts including demonstrations of the human lachrymal ducts, the tubules of the testis, the descent of the testis and congenital hernia, and the absorbent function of the lymphatic system. The importance of all this work was manifest by the ferocity with which the Hunters' claims to originality were attacked by other anatomists. 'Alexander Monro II claimed the lachrymal ducts, Monro I the seminal tubules, Pott the congenital hernia and all three Monros the absorbent system. The quarrels became extremely fierce and provoked many arguments.

'There is however little doubt that much plagiarism existed; manuscript copies of the Hunter lectures were common in Edinburgh and were discussed by the students at the Royal Medical Society† which had been founded there in 1737.'[24]

The happy cooperation between the brothers was never renewed when John Hunter returned from active army service. Indeed they themselves became involved in a severe dispute, ironically a quarrel over the originality of a piece of anatomical research, admittedly an important one, that permanently estranged them – the elucidation and demonstration of the placental circulation (p. 94). A comprehensive account of the professional disagreements involving the Hunters has been given by Paget.[25]

---

* Hunter may have been mistaken in the year which was almost certainly 1756, but the treatise on the blood was of course written many years later.
† This Society was founded by students in 1737 and became the *Royal Medical Society* (of Edinburgh) in 1779 and is still active.[22] Dr. Pitt gives these dates as 1731 and 1778, respectively.[23]

REFERENCES

1 Paget S. *John Hunter*. London, T Fisher Unwin. 1897, p. 20.
2 Poritt Sir Arthur (Lord). John Hunter's Women. *Hunterian Society Transactions* 1958–59, vol. 17, pp. 81–108.
3 Paget S. *John Hunter*. London, T Fisher Unwin. 1897, pp. 31, 32.
4 Ibid. p. 35.
5 Keith A (Sir Arthur). The cradle of the Hunterian school in *Contributions to Medical and Biological Research, Dedicated to Sir William Osler*. New York. 1919, vol. 1, pp. 88–110.
6 Jones F Wood. John Hunter's unwritten book. *Lancet*. 1951, vol. 2, pp. 778–780.
7 Dobson J. *John Hunter*. Edinburgh and London, Livingstone. 1969, p. 22.
8 Clark R W. *Einstein. The Life and Times*. London, Hodder and Stoughton. 1973, pp. 25, 26.
9 Whitrow G J. *Einstein The Man and His Achievement*. London, B.B.C. 1967, p. 4.
10 Darwin F. *Life and Letters of Charles Darwin*. London, John Murray. 1887, vol. 1, p. 32.
11 Foot J. *The Life of John Hunter*. London, T Becket. 1794, p. 10.
12 Home E. A short account of the author's life in Hunter's *A Treatise on the Blood, Inflammation and Gun-shot Wounds*. London, G Nichol. 1794, p. 15.
13 Gunn A L. The inevitable William and the accidental John. *Hunterian Society Transactions* 1967–68, vol. 26, pp. 87–103.
14 Wright A D. The quacks of John Hunter's time. *Hunterian Society Transactions* 1952–53, vol. 11 pp. 68–84.
15 Low D M. *Edward Gibbon 1737–1794*. London, Chatto and Windus. 1937, pp. 255, 256.
16 Dobson J. *John Hunter*. Edinburgh and London, Livingstone. 1969, p. 28.
17 Editorial. Memorial plaque to William Hunter. *Hunterian Society Transactions* 1951–52, vol. 10, pp. 142, 143.
18 Rudolf C R. Hunteriana Part 2. *Hunterian Society Transactions* 1951–52, vol. 10, pp. 120–133.
19 Hunter J. A treatise on venereal disease in *The Works of John Hunter*, ed. J F Palmer. London, Longman. 1835, vol. 2, p. 244.
20 Ibid. p. 159.
21 Hunter J. A treatise on the blood, inflammation and gun-shot wounds in *The Works of John Hunter*, ed. J F Palmer. London, Longman. 1837, vol. 3, pp. 84, 85.
22 Wolstenholme G (Sir Gordon). Societies for the improvement of medical and chirurgical knowledge. *Hunterian Society Transactions* 1974–75–76, vols. 33–34, pp. 124–135.
23 Pitt G Newton. Reflections on John Hunter as a physician and on his relation to the medical societies of the last century. *Lancet*. 1896. vol. 1, pp. 1270–1274.
24 Riches Sir Eric. Example is the school of mankind. *Hunterian Society Transactions* 1966–67, vol. 25, pp. 66–91.
25 Paget S. *John Hunter*. London, T Fisher Unwin. 1897, pp. 56–74.

CHAPTER 2

ARMY SERVICE
1760–1763

In the *Roll of Commissioned Officers in the Medical Service of the British Army*, by the late Colonel William Johnston, CB., published in 1917, Hunter's record reads as follows:

> John Hunter, surgical staff, Great Britain, October 30th 1760. Half pay 1764. Full pay, assistant surgeon-general January 4th, 1786. Surgeon-general and inspector of regimental hospitals March 17th, 1790. Died 1793. Belleisle 1761. Portugal 1762.[1]

It is commonly stated that John Hunter enlisted in the Army for the benefit of his health. This statement was made by Everard Home in his biography of John Hunter in 1794 and repeated by Drewry Ottley and most subsequent biographers. But there is no real evidence for this assertion. Miss Jessie Dobson says: 'I have never come across any evidence to show who, in fact, advised John Hunter about his health . . .'[2]

The explanation of ill-health as an incentive to join the Army is very unsatisfactory because the appalling conditions of service abroad could have been tolerated only by a man in robust health. G. J. Guthrie, Wellington's surgeon, wrote in 1815: '. . . the hardships to which the junior medical officers of the army are unavoidably exposed on service, hardships unknown, even in idea, to those who have not experienced them . . .'[3] Indeed the campaign in Portugal involved John Hunter in a march of 46 miles from Lisbon to Santarum in intensely hot weather, a journey in which 12 men lost their lives.[4]

There are at least three other good reasons why John Hunter may have enlisted in the Army, *viz.* to earn his livelihood, to obtain a medical qualification, or to gain surgical experience. It is probable that all three of these reasons influenced his decision.

John Hunter's economic position at that time was very precarious. He was already aged 32 and still completely dependent financially on his elder brother William in whose School of Anatomy he had been working for twelve years. The prospect of becoming independent and receiving a regular income, however small, by joining the Army, must have been a considerable inducement.

In these days of relatively sound personal economic security, we are apt to underestimate the severe difficulties of earning a livelihood that must have occurred in Hunter's time. Authors, poets, composers and scientists could only survive by means of a private income or by patronage. Even Shakespeare, Chaucer, Haydn and Handel needed patrons. The great Thomas Huxley nearly gave up his scientific career for lack of funds and contemplated emigration to Australia to take up brewing in his fiancée's family business – and this was a century after Hunter. Huxley wrote, in the same year that he received his FRS: 'To attempt to live by any scientific pursuit is a farce . . . A man of science may earn great distinction but not bread. He will get invitations to all sorts of dinners . . . , but not enough income to pay his cab fare.'[5]

The problem of earning a living must therefore have been a major consideration in John Hunter's career. It is of interest to note that his letters from Belleisle and Portugal to his brother William were largely concerned with his pay, e.g.

> If we are order'd home, and a surgeon is to stay here . . . I purpose applying for the deputy parveorship, which is ten shillings a day, and if I get that I can give my Prentice a place of five shillings a day, so that I can make it worth my while . . . *28 September 1761.*
> There is nothing here talkd of but Portugal. . . . I . . . should chuse to stay here, if an Hospital was to be keept, as I suppose that I shall loose my ten shillings by going (but that as it may be). *12 April 1762.*
> . . . the Deputy Directorship, I was in the hopes of getting it; . . . I wish I could get it as it makes a vast difference with me here. *25 July 1762.*[6]

It could never be claimed that John Hunter was avaricious – in later years he spent his money as soon as he earned it, on his Museum and on his household which comprised at least 50 dependents (p. 124). It is very likely that he engaged in dentistry for six years in order to help him earn a living.

A second important reason for John Hunter's enlistment may have been to secure a medical qualification, which was obtainable by military service.

Almost certainly the main reason why Hunter joined the Army was to gain surgical experience. Until the Listerian era of safe surgery and anaesthesia, there was very little surgical experience available in civilian practice. Even Lister's first paper on Antiseptic surgery published in 1867 was based on only 11 cases in a 2-year period in Glasgow.[7] The vast majority of surgeons learned their craft almost entirely from war service.

It is of interest to note that the armorial bearings of the Royal College of Surgeons of England and its predecessor, the Company of Surgeons, include features associated with the fighting services (fig. 3). The figures represent the Greek surgeons Machaon and

Fig. 3. Arms of the Royal College of Surgeons of England granted in 1822, bearing the motto 'The arts which are of benefit to all'.

Podalirius, sons of Aesculapius, the former holding the broken arrow extracted from King Menelaus.[8,9] The Navy is represented by the Anchor and the Army by the Lion and the Portcullis.[10] Among the functions of the old Company of Surgeons was that of examination of surgical recruits for the fighting services and that of assessment of wounded naval personnel among whom the most distinguished was Lord Nelson in 1797.[11]

SURGEONS TRAINED IN THE ARMED SERVICES

The earliest surgeons were no doubt military surgeons. The Greeks and the Roman army had surgeons and injured Crusaders were treated by the Knights Hospitallers. The great majority of famous surgeons whose names are still familiar all gained their experience in military or naval service including:

John Arderne (1307–1390) the first English surgeon of repute, learned his craft in the Hundred Years War. He was present at the battle of Crecy and one of his patients was the Black Prince. He established the treatment of fistula-in-ano on bold surgical principles. He wrote one of the first surgical textbooks, a *System of Surgery*, which is still available in the British Museum.

Thomas Gale (1507–1587) was a leading surgeon of Elizabethan times. He served with the armies of Henry VIII and Philip II. His war experience led him to believe that gunshot wounds were not by their nature poisonous, contrary to the generally accepted view established by di Vigo (1514). Gale published the first English book on this subject entitled *An Excellent Treatise of Wounds made by Gonneshot* (1563).

William Clowes (1540–1604) had a distinguished career in the Army and Navy and was Surgeon to the Fleet at the Armada. He was appointed to St. Bartholomew's Hospital and wrote numerous surgical volumes including an important work on gunshot wounds. Clowes did a lot towards establishing surgery on a sound professional basis and he was forthright in his condemnation of charlatans. He wrote '. . . those who are Masters and Professors, chosen to perform the like operation, ought indeed to have a Lion's heart, a Lady's hand and a hawk's eye . . . It is no afternoon-man's work, as some rake-shames and belly-gods have falsely and slanderously reported.'

Ambroise Paré (1510–1590) was one of the greatest surgeons of all time. His entire surgical training was based on practical experience of war casualties. He was surgeon to four successive kings of France. He was the first to condemn the old practice of cauterisation of wounds and he established the treatment of wounds by non-irritant dressings. He initiated the method of ligature of arteries during amputation instead of sealing off the vessels by cauterisation. Paré's textbook of surgery became the standard surgical work for English surgeons for many years.

John Woodall (1569–1643) was another Elizabethan surgeon who had extensive experience of war surgery. He noted the value of lemon juice for scurvy more than a century before James Lind wrote his treatise (1753). Woodall invented the modern trephine. His textbooks became standard works of surgery for many years. His opinions on gunshot wounds are acceptable even today, *viz.* 'No wound of gunshot can be said to be a simple wound, neither was there any artist that could truly say he healed any gunshot wound by first intention.'

Richard Wiseman (1622–1676) spent most of his lifetime as a surgeon in the Army and Navy. He served with Charles I throughout all his campaigns. He was a prolific writer and his book on 'Severall Chirurgicall Treatises' was the foremost English surgical work that had been written up to his time. Wiseman raised the status of the surgeon from its previously lowly position and became the first truly consulting surgeon seeing patients only by recommendation from another doctor.

Peter Lowe (1550–1612) of Glasgow spent twenty years as a surgeon in the service of the King of France and published a popular textbook on 'A Discourse of the Whole Art of Chirurgerie'. He was a great medical reformer and persuaded King James VI of Scotland to found the College of Physicians and Surgeons of Glasgow in 1599.

Baron Jean Larrey (1766–1842) was a French surgeon who achieved fame in the Napoleonic Wars. He was present at all the battles and took part in the retreat from Moscow and in the battle of Waterloo. He introduced plaster-of-Paris for splinting wounds. He appreciated the importance of early surgery in wounds and invented the 'flying ambulance', a horse-drawn light carriage, to expedite evacuation of the wounded. He believed in early amputation for severe wounds and he was credited with the performance of 200 amputations in one day at the battle of Borodino.

George James Guthrie (1785–1856) was the greatest surgeon of the Peninsular War and was often referred to as 'The British Larrey'. He was born in London of a Scottish family and was apprenticed to a surgeon at the age of thirteen. He entered the army as 'hospital mate' at the age of fifteen at which age he passed the examination for MRCS. The following year, aged sixteen, he was a regimental assistant surgeon treating war casualties in America. He had a distinguished career in the Peninsular War under Wellington and was twice wounded. He was appointed to the staff at Westminster Hospital and was President of the Royal College of Surgeons at the age of forty-eight. His treatise on gunshot wounds (1810) is still well worth reading.

Thomas Spencer Wells (1818–1897) joined the Navy and spent six years at the Naval Hospital at Malta. He rapidly established a splendid reputation so that the FRCS was conferred on him at the age of twenty-six. He served in the Crimea where he first used his forcipressure artery forceps. He was one of the founders of safe abdominal surgery. Although he did not agree with the principle of antiseptic surgery, he did in fact practise aseptic surgery because he was meticulously clean in his operative technique and his results of ovariotomy were unsurpassed.

Many other famous surgeons learned their craft and developed new techniques by their experience of war casualties. They include: Sir James McGrigor (1771–1858); Albrecht von Graefe (1787–1840); Johann Diffenbach (1792–1847); Louis Stromeyer (1804–1876); Joseph Malgaigne (1806–1865); Auguste Nelaton (1807–1873); Nikolai Pirogoff (1810–1881); Karl Thiersch (1822–1895); Friedrich Esmarch (1823–1908); and Richard von Volkmann (1830–1889).

John Hunter's experience in active army service provided him with material on which he built up his profound knowledge of the basic factors of the pathology of inflammation and missile injuries and which he eventually published in the Treatise on Blood, Inflammation and Gun-Shot Wounds. He wrote in the dedication of his work to the King – 'In the year 1761 I had the honour of being appointed by Your Majesty a Surgeon on the Staff in the expedition against Belleisle . . . gave me extensive opportunities of attending to gun-shot wounds, of seeing the errors and defects in that branch of military surgery, and of studying to remove them. It drew my attention to inflammation in general, and enabled me to make observations which have formed the basis of the present Treatise . . .'[12]

In his leisure time abroad, Hunter made observations on the organ of hearing in fishes,[13] regeneration of the lizard's tail,[14] the propagation of eels,[15] the effects of temperature on coagulation of piscine blood,[16] digestion in the hibernating lizard[17] and the geology of Alentejo.[18] Some of these were subjects which Hunter used subsequently as a basis for more extensive investigations which were incorporated into various publications.

John Hunter was commissioned in October 1760 at the age of 32. He was on active service in Belleisle from March 1761 until July 1762 when he was transferred to Portugal. He returned to England in May 1763, at the age of 35, and commenced the hard task of establishing himself in a surgical practice.

REFERENCES

1 Johnston W. Roll of Commissioned Officers in the Medical Service of the British Army. Quoted by Bowlby A. (1919) Hunterian Oration, British military surgery in the time of Hunter and in the Great War. *British Medical Journal*. 1917, vol. 1, p. 205.

2 Dobson J. Personal communication. 1976.

3 Guthrie G J. *On Gun-shot Wounds of the Extremities*. London, Longman. 1815, p. ix.

4 Drew Lieut.-General Sir Robert. John Hunter and the Army. *Hunterian Society Transactions* 1965–66, vol. 24, pp. 97–113.

5 Bibby C. *Scientist Extraordinary. Thomas Henry Huxley*. Oxford, Pergamon. 1972, p. 21

6 Beekman F. John Hunter in Portugal. *Annals of Medical History* ed. F R Packard. New York, Paul Hoeber. 1936, N. S. vol. 8, pp. 288–296.

7 Lister J (Lord). A new method of treating compound fracture, abscess etc. *Lancet*. 1867, vol. 1, pp. 326–329.

8 Wood S. Homer's surgeons: Machaon and Podalirius. *Lancet*. 1931, vol. 1, pp. 892–895.

9 Rains A J Harding. The hand physician. *Annals of the Royal College of Surgeons of England*. 1974, vol. 54, pp. 253–259.

10 Reese A J M. *The Armorial Bearings of the Royal College of Surgeons of England*. Library of the Royal College of Surgeons of England.

11 Dobson J. Lord Nelson and the expenses of his cure. *Annals of the Royal College of Surgeons of England*. 1957, vol. 21, pp. 119–122.

12 Hunter J. To the King. A treatise on the blood, inflammation and gun-shot

wounds in *The Works of John Hunter*, ed. J F Palmer. London, Longman. 1837, vol. 3, p. ix.

13 Hunter J. An account of the organ of hearing in fishes in *The Works of John Hunter*, ed. J F Palmer. London, Longman. 1837, vol. 4, p. 296.

14 Hunter J. *Essays and Observations on Natural History, Anatomy, Physiology, Psychology and Geology*, ed. R Owen. London, John Van Voorst. 1861, vol. 2, p. 364.

15 Ibid. vol. 1, p. 217.

16 Hunter J. A treatise on the blood, inflammation and gun-shot wounds in *The Works of John Hunter*, ed. J F Palmer. London, Longman. 1837, vol. 3, p. 26.

17 Hunter J. Some observations on digestion in *The Works of John Hunter*, ed. J F Palmer. London, Longman. 1837, vol. 4, p. 88.

18 Hunter J. *Observations and Reflections on Geology*. London, Taylor and Francis. 1859, p. 16.

CHAPTER 3

PROFESSIONAL
DOMESTIC AND SOCIAL LIFE
1763–1793

JOHN Hunter embarked on his surgical career in 1763 in most unfavourable circumstances. His main financial support was his Army half-pay of ten shillings a day, he had no hospital appointment, he had ceased to work at William Hunter's School of Anatomy, and the Scots were far from being welcome immigrants in England at that time. However, he took a house in Golden Square and slowly built up a surgical practice, augmenting his income by teaching anatomy and surgery and by his work in Spence's dental surgery (p. 81).

In February 1767 John Hunter was elected a Fellow of the Royal Society. At this time he had no publications to his name but he was well known for his anatomical research and some of his original observations had been published by William Hunter in his Medical Commentaries. In July 1768 John Hunter was admitted a member of the Company of Surgeons (which became the Royal College of Surgeons in 1800), and on 9th December 1768 he was elected Surgeon to St. George's Hospital.

John Hunter's career prospered rapidly from this time. In 1776 he was appointed Surgeon-Extraordinary to King George III. In 1786 he received the Copley Medal, the highest award of the Royal Society. In the same year he was appointed Assistant Surgeon-General to the Armed Forces while in 1790 he became Surgeon-General to the Armed Forces and Inspector-General of Regimental Hospitals. He had meanwhile built up a very large surgical practice, he still attended St. George's Hospital, he was pursuing his many research projects, and he was actively engaged in the establishment of his museum, until his sudden death in 1793.

JOHN HUNTER'S HOMES

On his return from active army service in 1763, John Hunter probably lived in rented rooms in the vicinity of Covent Garden.[1] In 1765 he bought a house in Golden Square and in 1769 he moved to Jermyn Street taking over the house that William Hunter vacated when he moved to Great Windmill Street.

In 1783 he bought a large house on the east side of Leicester Square, together with a house behind it in Castle Street, now part of Charing Cross Road. On the ground between these two houses he built additional rooms, a lecture theatre and a large museum. The house in Castle Street was used for preparation of specimens, dissections and for printing.

In 1765 John Hunter purchased two acres of land at Earl's Court, then a village two miles from London, where he built a small house. It was 'a most complex or heterogeneous structure; a farm, a menagerie, an institute of anatomy and physiology, and a villa decorated in the fashion of the period'.[2] Here he spent many week-ends and prosecuted a large number of physiological experiments and dissections on a great variety of animals. The accommodation seems to have been inadequate for the large staff (p. 22), since Hunter rented part of the Coleherne property in Kensington in 1778.[3]

The house at Earl's Court was bought in 1797 from Hunter's executors by John Hanson, solicitor, who became Lord Byron's attorney and man of business.[4] As a schoolboy Byron spent many of his holidays there.[5]

John Hunter spared no expense in the upkeep of his homes, an account of which was given by William Clift:

> Notwithstanding the very large eating and drinking establishment on the preceding Pages; and the Host of Tradesmen employed, as the Bills hereafter enumerated will show; together with the large outstanding Debts; and money borrowed at Interest, of Gawler; old Mr. Clarke, Cutler, of Exeter Change; of Hannah Apperley; of Mrs. Home; etc., and the great expense of increasing and supporting the Museum, and the large Prices he gave for individual Preparations; - and the large sum he expended in Building the stabling, Conversatione and lecture room, and Museum over them, with an immense Sky-light over the yard to protect the Whale's Skull – of perhaps 500 superficial feet of Glass – with Entrance Galleries etc. – and the expensive but ineffectual *Empyreal* warm Air-Stoves by Jackson & Moser – with the Great Draw-bridge and slope made to let the Chariot down from the Street, and consequent necessary great

alterations of the House, in Windows and Doorways for that purpose, – at more than £6000, – on a lease of about twenty years. – Notwithstanding the expence of keeping up two establishments of Coaches and 6 Horses, Coachmen and Footmen, etc. etc.; Mr. Hunter was always on the look out for bits of Land adjoining to his previous possessions at Earl's Court: – and for Bargains; many of them of *little* use, as an enormous Electrifying apparatus – a splendid but unfinished Air Pump invented by the Earl of Bute, together with a grand Chemical furnace and apparatus by ditto – a magnificent and highly finished Turning Lathe which was made for the Great Duke of Cumberland; several beautiful and large Pieces of Tapestry; – Chinese Ivory puzzle-Balls: Armour of all sorts and kinds – an acre of Landscape and figures painted by Zucarelli as models for Tapestry, which covered the walls and doors of the Conversatione room; as well as a very fine collection of proof prints by Hogarth, Strange, Woolett, Sharpe; – of the latter artist several hundred pounds' worth: besides Chinese Josses and beautiful nodding mandarines; and several original Pictures by Zoffany, Vandevelde, Xuys, Ostade, Teniers, Stubbs, etc., etc. – The large number of Animals both tame and wild that were kept both in London and at Earl's-Court, which consisted not only of presents, but often considerably expensive purchases; serve only to make one Wonder that Mr. Hunter had not died more deeply involved; or that he should have left anything for the support of his family after all his Debts were liquidated.[6]

MARRIAGE. ANNE HOME. CHILDREN

On 23rd July 1771 John Hunter married Anne Home. He was aged forty-three and she was twenty-nine. Anne Home was the eldest daughter of Capt. Robert Boyne Home, an army surgeon whose acquaintance Hunter had made while on active service. She was a handsome, dignified lady with considerable ability in music and poetry. She was a splendid hostess and entertained regularly, her guests being carefully selected from the highest ranks of society and the arts.

John Hunter's engagement to Anne Home lasted about seven years and there can be little doubt that the most important reason for the delayed wedding was John Hunter's meagre income at this time (p. 18). Everard Home stated – 'The expence of his pursuits had been so great, that it was not till several years after his first engagement with this lady, that his affairs could be sufficiently arranged to admit of his marrying.'[7] It was probably not until 1768, after his election to the staff of St. George's Hospital, that Hunter's economic position would have improved sufficiently to allow him to get married.

Anne Hunter was on very friendly terms with Joseph Haydn and she wrote most of the libretto for the dozen canzonettas that he composed while he was in London, amongst which the most popular was 'My mother bids me bind my hair'. A copy of the canzonettas, now in the possession of the Hunterian Society, was signed by Haydn and presented to Mrs. Hunter whose name is stamped on the cover and the verses corrected in ink in her own hand.[8] When the great composer left England in August 1795, Mrs. Hunter wrote him a farewell poem, 'O Tuneful Voice', which he set to music. This little work has been described as 'a great masterpiece in miniature, and a tribute to Anne Hunter, whose verse could unlock such a vein of poetic feeling in the old Haydn; a tribute to England, too, the land that "brought out the best" in the composer and opened the floodgates of his inspiration.'[9]

In the Hunter-Baillie collection of letters and manuscripts there is an autograph copy of the poems of Mrs. Hunter. Written in her own hand is the epitaph to John Hunter which she had intended to place on his tomb at St. Martin's-in-the-Fields, but the Church authorities would not allow it –

> Here rests in awful silence cold and still
>   One whom no common spark of genius fir'd
> Whose reach of thought Nature alone could fill,
>   Whose deep research the love of truth inspir'd.
> Hunter, if years of toil, of watchful care,
>   If the vast labors of a pow'rful mind
> To sooth the ills humanity must share,
>   Deserve the grateful plaudits of Mankind.
> Then, be each human weakness buri'd here
>   Envy would raise to dim a name so bright,
> Those specks which on the Orb of Day appear
>   Take nothing from his warm and welcome light.[10]

It seems that John and Anne Hunter were a happy couple with the mutual respect so essential to a successful marriage. In a letter to his brother-in-law the Rev. James Baillie, John Hunter wrote:

> . . . As to myself, with respect to my family, I can only say that I am happy in a wife . . . it appears to be Anny's enjoyment in seeing me pleasing myself: while all these concurring circumstances go on, I must continue to be one of the happyest men living . . . *Nov. 23rd, 1775.*[11]

Anne Hunter bore four children in the first five years of marriage. She died in 1821, aged 79.

John Banks Hunter (1772–1838) entered the Army. Little is known about him and a letter from his mother in 1804 suggests that he became estranged to her.

Mary Ann Hunter (1773–1776) and *James Hunter* (1774–1775) died in childhood.

Agnes Hunter (1776–1838) was like her mother, handsome and intellectual. She married Captain Campbell, afterwards Sir James Campbell. After his death she married Colonel Charlewood. There were no children by either marriage.

JOHN HUNTER'S HOUSEHOLD

In addition to his wife and children, Hunter supported a large number of other individuals in his homes at Leicester Square and Earl's Court, including assistants, pupils, craftsmen and servants. Three of his most important associates were Everard Home, William Clift and William Bell.

Everard Home (1756–1832) was Anne Hunter's brother. In 1772, at the age of sixteen, he left Westminster School and became apprenticed to John Hunter for six years. In 1778 he was admitted a member of the Corporation of Surgeons and appointed assistant-surgeon to the Naval Hospital at Plymouth. He subsequently served as staff-surgeon in Jamaica and returned home in 1784. In the following year John Hunter's health began to deteriorate while his practice and other commitments had increased considerably so that Everard Home took up residence with him and helped him in his practice, operations and general affairs until 1792 when Home married and settled down in a nearby house. In 1787 Everard Home was elected assistant-surgeon to John Hunter at St. George's Hospital and in 1790 he took over John Hunter's courses of lectures. He was appointed Surgeon to St. George's Hospital when John Hunter died in 1793 and he subsequently became a Baronet, Serjeant-Surgeon to the King and President of the Royal College of Surgeons.

When John Hunter died, Everard Home, in his capacity as acting executor, took charge of all the unpublished papers and manuscripts of his deceased brother-in-law and in 1823 he destroyed them (p. 195).

William Clift (1775–1849) was a simple but intelligent country boy from Bodmin in Cornwall who had a natural talent for penmanship and drawing.[12] He was recommended to Anne Hunter by an old school friend, Mrs. Gilbert, and became apprenticed to John Hunter, arriving on 14th February 1792, on his own seventeenth and John Hunter's sixty-fourth birthday. He settled down rapidly as a devoted amanuensis to John Hunter and was mainly responsible for the survival of many of Hunter's manuscripts and Museum specimens (p. 196).[13]

William Bell (d. 1792) became an assistant and amanuensis to John Hunter in the year 1775. He was an excellent artist and helped considerably in the establishment and organisation of the Museum. In 1783 he obtained the Diploma of the Company of Surgeons. In 1789 he left John Hunter's service to join the Indian Medical Service and he died abroad in 1792.[14]

William André was an excellent anatomist who worked for John Hunter for four or five years.[15]

Robert Haynes was the dissecting-room porter and museum attendant, and he acted also as amanuensis (p. 38).

William Clift gave the following account of Hunter's dependents in 1792:

In Leicester Square.

1. John Hunter, Esq., FRS
2. Mrs. Anne Hunter, his wife, elder Sister to Everard Home, Esq.
3. John Hunter, the Son; from St. John's College, Cambridge.
4. Agnes Hunter, the Daughter (now Lady Campbell).
5. Everard Home, Esq. (afterwards Sir Everard Home. Bt.).
6. Thomas Nicol, Esq., Son of the Rev. Dr. Nicol, Articled Studt.
7. Dr. Edward Bradley, of Alresford, Hants, House Pupil, 1 yr.
8. Mr. Francis Kinloch Huger, N. Carolina, House Pupil, 1 yr.
9. Mr. James Smith, of Ecclefechan, N. Britn, House Pupil, 1 yr.
10. Mr. Henry Jenner, nephew of Dr. Jenner, Berkeley, 1 year.

Servants

11. Robert Adcock, Butler (after Mr. Dewell).
12. Ann Martin, from Southampton, House Keeper.
13. Elizabeth Roby, from Rochester, Lady's Maid.
14. Mr. Hunter's Coachman, Joe.

15. Mr. Hunter's Footman, John.
16. Mrs. Hunter's Coachman, James Goodall.
17. Mrs. Hunter's Footman, George Smith.
18. Mary Edwards, from Llanbeder, cook (Ann Denny, do.).
19. Martha Jones, House-Maid.
20. Little Peggy, do. (*a great laugher*).
21. Mrs. Long (Constant Needlewoman).

In Castle Street House.

22. Robert Haynes, Dissecting room and Lectures.
23. Elizabeth Adam, House and Door-Keeper.
24. William Clift, Museum and Amanuensis.

At Earl's Court, Kensington.

25. Peter Shields, Gardener.
26. Mrs. Shields, House-Keeper and Dairy Woman.
27. Betty, Laundry-maid. (*Butter would not melt in her mouth, but somehow she became enceinte by an equally bashful Kensington sweetheart.*)
28. Tom Barton, Carter.
29. Scotch Willie, Half-witted, employed in the fields.
30. Old David, Head Under Gardener, Hot-houses, etc.
31. Alexander, Out-door Gardener, and Spring-guns.
32. Woman to weed in Garden, and fetch the Cows.
33. Tom Barton's Wife, Assistant-Laundress.

34. Monsieur St. Aubin, Draughtsman, in House, 1 yr.
35. Mr. Dupré, Secretary for Surgeon and Inspector Genl.
36. Mr. Walker, Teacher of Elocution to John.

Outdoor Tradesmen, nearly constant employ.

37. Sawyer Carpenter in London.
38. Sawyer Carpenter at Earl's Court.
39. Piper, Bricklayer and Mason, Earl's Court.
40. Benjamin Harris, Blacksmith, Castle Street.
41. Jas. Weatherall, Cabinet Maker and Joiner, Upholsterer.
42. Painters and Glaziers, Hot and Green Houses.
43.⎫ Printers, nearly constant in Castle Street.
44.⎬ John Richardson, Compositor.
45.⎭ Long, Pressman.
–   Mrs. Hunter's Livery Stable Keeper, Mr. Rand, Golden Sq.
–   Cart, Harness, and Collar-maker, Earl's Court.
–   Farrier, nearly Constant, from Under-ground Stables.
–   Stewardson, *an old Butler, a constant Visitor.*

From the above List, which is but Imperfect, and Several of the Master Tradesmen sending Two or more men, besides occasional helpers to the Coachmen, Gardeners, and in the Grounds, etc., *there were never fewer* than 50 Persons daily provided for at Mr. Hunter's expence, inclusive of the House-pupils, who paid for their Board. [16]

PUPILS

John Hunter's pupils numbered more than one thousand[17] and included Edward Jenner,[18] Matthew Baillie, Sir Everard Home, William Clift,[12,13] Sir Astley Cooper,[19] John Abernethy, Sir William Blizard,[20,21] Sir Anthony Carlisle, Henry Cline, Charles White,[22] William Hewson,[23] William Lynn* and the Americans Philip Syng Physick,[24] William Shippen[22] and John Morgan.[22]

MEDICAL SOCIETIES

John Hunter was associated with Dr. George Fordyce, physician to St. George's Hospital, in the foundation of two medical societies.[25] *The Society for the Improvement of Medical and Chirurgical Knowledge* was founded in 1783 and the *Lyceum Medicum Londinense* in 1785. The former of these was limited in membership to eighteen men of established professional status who met at Slaughter's Coffee House and delivered papers after dinner. The Lyceum Medicum met weekly at John Hunter's house in Leicester Square and its members included undergraduates (fig. 4). Neither of these medical societies survived for more than twenty years after John Hunter's death. Several of John Hunter's papers were published in the Transactions of the Society for the Improvement of Medical and Chirurgical Knowledge. One of these, presented to the Society in 1789, was his classic paper on intussusception (p. 87).

John Hunter was also influential in the establishment of *Guy's Hospital Physical Society* which was founded in 1771 and is still active. His first case of ligature of the femoral artery for popliteal aneurysm was the subject of an address to their society.[26]

John Hunter helped to found the *Royal Veterinary College* of which he became a Vice-President when it was established in 1781.[27]

The *Royal Humane Society* was founded in 1774 by Dr. Thomas Cogan and Dr. William Hawes. John Hunter's name appears in the first list of directors. In 1776 Hunter was requested by Dr. Hawes

---

* William Lynn (1753–1837) was surgeon to Westminster Hospital and President of the Royal College of Surgeons in 1825. He was the latest surviving friend of John Hunter and died aged 84.

REGULATIONS.

THIS Society, under the name of THE LYCEUM MEDICUM LONDINENSE, was instituted for the advancement of medical knowledge, January 25, 1785, under the patronage of Dr. Fordyce and Mr. Hunter, when the following resolutions were unanimously agreed to:

I.

That the society shall consist of honorary, corresponding, and ordinary members.

II.

That the honorary members shall consist of teachers of the different branches of medicine in London; and shall be limited to fix in number.

III.

That the corresponding members shall consist of public teachers, and of physicians and surgeons to public charities.

IV.

That the ordinary members shall consist of the three following classes:

The first class shall consist of such members as have taken a degree in medicine, are settled as practitioners in London, or are members of the company of surgeons. The

REGULATIONS

AND

LAWS

OF THE

LYCEUM MEDICUM LONDINENSE,

HELD AT

Mr. JOHN HUNTER'S

LECTURE-ROOM,

CASTLE-STREET, LEICESTER-SQUARE.

LONDON: PRINTED BY JOHN RICHARDSON, PRINTER TO THE LYCEUM MEDICUM. MDCCLXXXVII.

Fig. 4. Regulations of the Lyceum Medical Society founded by Dr. Fordyce and Mr. John Hunter (Library of the Royal College of Surgeons of England).

to publish his opinion on the resuscitation of drowned persons, which he did in a paper presented to the Royal Society.[28,29]

REFERENCES

1 Dobson J. *John Hunter*. Edinburgh and London, Livingstone. 1969, p. 108.
2 Paget S. *John Hunter*. London, T Fisher Unwin. 1897, p. 86.
3 Hickey W. *Memoirs of William Hickey*, ed. Alfred Spencer. London, Hurst and Blackett. 1913–1925, 5th edn. four vols. vol. IV, p. 486.
4 Marchand L A. *Byron: A Biography. New York, Knopf and London, John Murray*. 1957, vol. 1, p. 53.
5 Ibid. p. 63.
6 Finlayson J. Account of a MS volume by William Clift, relating to John Hunter's household and estate; and Sir Everard Home's publications. *British Medical Journal*. 1890, vol. 1, pp. 738–740.
7 Home E. A short account of the author's life in Hunter's *A Treatise on the Blood, Inflammation and Gun-shot Wounds*. London, G Nicol. 1794, p. 21.
8 Rudolf C R. Hunteriana. *Hunterian Society Transactions*. 1950–51, vol. 9, pp. 84–93.
9 Landon H C Robbins. *Haydn in England 1791–1795*. London, Thames and Hudson, 1976, p. 400.
10 LeFanu W R. The Hunter-Baillie manuscripts. *Hunterian Society Transactions* 1953–54, vol. 12, pp. 88–101.
11 Paget S. *John Hunter*. London, T Fisher Unwin. 1897, pp. 119, 120.
12 Dobson J. William Clift, FRS First Conservator of the Hunterian Museum. *Proceedings of the Royal Society of Medicine*. 1955, vol. 48, pp. 323–325.
13 Rudolf C R. New light on William Clift and his contemporaries. *Hunterian Society Transactions*. 1959–60, vol. 18, pp. 68–97.
14 Dobson J. John Hunter's artists. *Medical and Biological Illustration*. 1959, vol. 9, pp. 138–149.
15 Dobson J. *John Hunter*. Edinburgh and London, Livingstone. 1969 p. 258.
16 Paget S. *John Hunter*. London, T Fisher Unwin. 1897, pp. 158–161.
17 Porritt Sir Arthur (Lord). Hunterian Oration 1967. John Hunter: distant echoes. *Annals of the Royal College of Surgeons of England*. 1967, vol. 41, pp. 1–24.
18 Horder Lord. The Hunterian tradition. *Hunterian Society Transactions* 1936–37, vol. 1, pp. 66–78.
19 Tanner W E. Retrospect and prospect. *Hunterian Society Transactions* 1950–51, vol. 9, pp. 60–75.
20 Cope V Zachary (Sir). Literary surgeons. *Hunterian Society Transactions* 1946–47, vol. 5, pp. 68–84.
21 Riches Sir Eric. Hunterian milestones. *Hunterian Society Transactions* 1968–69, vol. 27, pp. 7–19.
22 Sellors Sir T Holmes. Hunterian Oration 1973. Some pupils of John Hunter. *Annals of the Royal College of Surgeons of England*. 1973, vol. 53, pp. 139–152 and 205–217.
23 Dobson J. John Hunter's microscope slides. *Annals of the Royal College of Surgeons of England*. 1961, vol. 28, pp. 175–188.
24 Dobson J. William Clift to Philip Syng Physick. *Annals of the Royal College of Surgeons of England*. 1964, vol. 34, pp. 197–203.
25 Pitt G Newton. Reflections on John Hunter as a physician and on his relation to the medical societies of the last century. *Lancet*. 1896, vol. 1, pp. 1270–1274.
26 Wolstenholme G (Sir Gordon). Societies for the improvement of medical and

chirurgical knowledge. *Hunterian Society Transactions* 1974–75–76, vols. 33–34, pp. 124–135.

27 Hobday Sir Frederick. John Hunter, the pioneer of veterinary science. *Hunterian Society Transactions* 1937–38, vol. 2, pp. 89–100.

28 Dobson J. John Hunter and the unfortunate Doctor Dodd. *Journal of History of Medicine and Allied Sciences.* 1955, vol. 10, pp. 370–378.

29 Hunter J. Proposals for the recovery of persons apparently drowned in *The Works of John Hunter*, ed. J. F. Palmer, London, Longman. 1837, vol. 4 pp. 165–175.

CHAPTER 4

CHARACTER

JOHN Hunter was described by his brother-in-law Everard Home as a short stocky Scot, 'uncommonly strong and active, very compactly made, and capable of great bodily exertion'[1]. Adams, who knew him well, stated: 'Mr. Hunter's manners were extremely companionable. His wit, or more properly his archness, was always well directed, and the slowness of his articulation enabled him to point and correct it almost as soon as it was uttered.'[2] Abernethy said: 'Mr. Hunter was a man of very considerable humour. His views of subjects in general were quick and peculiar, and when so disposed he could place them in very ludicrous points of view.'[3] Lord Holland wrote – 'John Hunter was neither polished in his manner nor refined in his expression, but from originality of thought and earnestness of mind he was extremely agreeable in conversation; . . . His countenance was indeed full of genius . . .'[4]

Hunter was reputed to suffer from an evil temper, but it is not unlikely that such attacks of irritation could well have resulted from the ill-health from which he suffered during the last twenty years of his life. Adams stated that he 'had a very long conversation with him . . . in which we were . . . led to his complaint . . . Nor did he fail, on this occasion, to revert to the effect it had on his temper.'[5]

It has been asserted that John Hunter was uncultured, ill-bred, and of an uncouth manner. These criticisms have certainly been exaggerated. John Hunter was on the best of terms with the nobility and gentry of his time, many of whom were his friends or patients, including Adam Smith the great economist, Sir Joshua Reynolds, Thomas Gainsborough, Lord Queensberry, Brinsley Sheridan, Lord Eglinton, Joseph Farington, and many others.[6] At his election to the staff of St. George's Hospital on December 9th 1768, one hundred and sixty-one Governors attended including the Bishops

of London and Ely, the Dukes of Bedford, Manchester, Queensberry and Richmond, the Marquess of Granby, Lords Cadogan,
Fortescue, Hardwicke, Hertford, Palmerston, Spencer and Shel-
bourne as well as David Garrick and Sir Joshua Reynolds. The
ballot gave Hunter 114 votes.[7]

Undoubtedly the most reliable assessment of John Hunter's
character would reasonably be expected to have been made by
William Clift who gave such devoted service to his master for the
last two years of John Hunter's life. Dobson wrote – 'As time went
on, Clift became more and more attached to his master and learned
to love and respect him to a degree that, although his association
with him lasted less than two years, his veneration persisted
throughout the whole of his long life. Of Hunter's manner, he says
that he was 'generally, though cheerfully, taciturn – many a morning's labour passing over with scarcely a word of discourse: but
shrewd and witty in his remarks, when he condescended to unbend
and let himself out, as he sometimes did when resting himself, and
standing upright, from his dissection after stooping for hours, as if
nailed to the object. He could relate a professional anecdote very
humourously, concisely and with much point, but with never the
slightest inclination to ill-natured remarks, swearing, or obscenity
for which many of his contemporaries were notorious'. Clift was
well able to judge in these matters, for he, better than almost
anyone else, was in the confidence of his master and spent a good
part of the day working with him. He further remarks that Hunter
was 'mild and kind in his manner, sufficiently but not servilely,
courteous to everybody, and made no distinction between high and
low, great or small; spoke as kindly and familiarly to his gardener or
myself as to his equals or superiors; easily pleased when any about
him shewed an inclination to please; and I believe everyone always
did their best to effect that. Mr. William Bell, who resided so many
years with him and knew him so intimately, did not think of him
according to the adage "that no man is a hero to his valet"; but on
the contrary he absolutely idolized Mr. Hunter and believed him to
be in every thing next to the Almighty for knowledge'. In every
letter written to his brothers and sisters, Clift mentions how happy
he is in his situation . . .'[8]

In a letter referring to the Hunterian Orations, Clift said – 'These
orations are, as you may well believe, highly gratifying to me,
serving as they do to keep alive the memory of one of the best and

honestest men that I can conceive God ever made: one who died too
soon for the world and for me, whilst I was still an urchin in
knowledge and had long been a fatherless and motherless orphan,
when he kindly accepted me as an apprentice without fee, reward or
premium, . . .'[9]

Most of the evidence suggests that John Hunter held a respected
place in the society of his time. Indeed his sedate mode of life and
the cultured salon developed by his wife stand out in sharp contrast
to the general standards of drunkenness, debauchery and licentious-
ness of all classes of society in the eighteenth century. It may be
significant that there is very scanty reference to the Hunter family in
the numerous Journals which were popular at that time and which
relied on society gossip and scandal for their main interest. There
are merely occasional references to the Hunters' professional
activities.[10,11,12,13,14]

John Hunter has been criticised for being ill-read. His contemporary critic, Jessé Foot, stated that John Hunter was illiterate[15]
but he also suggested that Hunter did in fact read surreptitiously[16]
so that he could plagiarise more readily. Hunter himself claimed
that he did not read extensively – 'How far suppuration can be
increased by medicines or applications I do not know . . . hence we
have I think, in the pharmacopoeia, (though I do not read many
books) suppurating cataplasms . . . etc.'[17] However he admits to an
occasional reference, as in discussing the treatment of urethral
stricture – 'I conceived that I might be able to destroy the stricture
by escharotics' to which he has added a footnote – 'Having lately
looked over some authors on this disease, I find that this is not a
new idea.'[18] Indeed, there are numerous references to other authorities throughout his writings, including more than 120 in Palmer's
Works alone, viz. –

Vol. 1. (Palmer's Works, 1835): Dr. Black (p. 279), Dr. Stevenson
(p. 282) and Dr. Fordyce and Dr. Cullen (p. 283) on heat; Dr. Solander
(p. 286) and Dr. Fordyce (pp. 291, 292) on cold; Dr. Blane (p. 295) on
climate; Abbé Fontana (p. 350) on air embolus; Mr. Cline (p. 392) on
wounds; Mr. Douglas (p. 466) and Mr. Else (p. 467) on hydrocele; Dr.
Russell (pp. 507, 508) on bones; Mr. Kirwan (p. 516) on putrefaction;
Cheseldon (p. 540) on haemorrhage; Le Dran and Heister (p. 543), Mr.
Cruickshank (p. 544), Mr. Bromfield (pp. 547, 551), Mr. Pott (pp. 547,
548) and Mr. Martin (p. 551) on aneurism; Mr. Grindle (p. 570) and Mr.
Squire (p. 571) on bone; Mr. Cline (p. 595) on the hip; and Dr. Pitcairn
(p. 610) on carbuncle.

Vol. 2. (Palmer's Works. 1835): Mr. Spence (p. 95) on teeth; Astruc (p. 138), Cook (p. 143), and Mr. Fordyce and Mr. Pott (p. 460) on venereal disease; Abbé Fontana (p. 164) on vipers; Mr. Bromfield (p. 213) on gonorrhoea; Daran (pp. 233, 234), Wiseman (p. 244) and Mr. Van-butchell (p. 271) on urethral stricture; Mr. Tomkyns (p. 282), Dr. Hamilton (pp. 293, 294) and Fleurant and Pouteau (p. 294) on urinary retention; Mr. Pott (p. 312) on testis; and Heister, Astruc, Cowper, Drake and Boerhaave (p. 355), Freke and Gataker (p. 356) and Dr. Fordyce and Lock Hospital (p. 380) on bubo.

Vol. 3. (Palmer's Works. 1837): Hewson (pp. 26, 27, 55, 59) and Malpighi and Van Leewenhoeck (p. 59) on blood; Dr. Black (p. 35) on heat; Dr. Baillie (p. 180) and Dr. W. Hunter (p. 185) on heart; Dr. Hales (p. 182, 224) and Haller (p. 206) on arteries; Taliacotius (p. 256) on transplantation; Mr. Sharp and Mr. Alison (p. 258) on wounds; Dr. Blane (p. 276) on fevers; Mr. Dick (p. 281) on oedema; Boerhaave (p. 304) on inflammation; Mr. Home (p. 447) and Dr. Crawford (p. 455) on pus; Anson's Voyages (p. 487) on ulceration; Le Dran and Mr. Pott (p. 520) on abscess; and Mr. Whately (p. 588), Dr. Ash and Mr. Home (p. 589) and Mr. Smith (p. 592) on intussusception.

Vol. 4. (Palmer's Works. 1837): Leslie (p. 39) on husbandry; Boerhaave, Van Swieten and Mauriceau (p. 78), Bartholinus and Dr. Mead (p. 79) and Dr. Baker and Dr. Clarke (p. 80) on smallpox; Vallisneri (p. 83), Réaumur (p. 84), Spallanzani (p. 86), Bomare (p. 88), Dr. Stevens (p. 115) and Mr. Gosse and Mr. Senebier (p. 116) on digestion; Mr Jenner (p. 87) and Dr. Blagden (p. 131) on heat; Dr. Ingenhousz (p. 100) and Count de Milly and Dr. Pearson (p. 101) on air; Mr. Sieffert and Sir Tobern Bergman (p. 95) on fermentation; Haller (p. 191) on Olfactory nerve; Winslow and Meckel (p. 193) on fifth nerve; Haller, Borelli, Goddard, Glisson and Swammerdam (p. 257) and Boerhaave, Sauvages and Hamberger (p. 258) on muscle; Kiell (p. 276) on optics; Geoffroi and Willoughby (p. 297) and Camper (p. 298) on hearing in fishes; Buffon (pp. 322, 328), Mr. Cameron (p. 328) and Mr. Jenner (p. 329) on dogs; Dale (p. 332) on whales; Swammerdam (p. 422), Réaumur (pp. 432, 435, 439, 442, 446), Riem (pp. 438, 439, 451, 453), Wilhelmi (p. 439), Bonnet (pp. 440, 451), Mr. Schirach (pp. 442, 447–449, 451) and Mr. Debraw (p. 451) on bees; Mr. Cordiner (p. 469) on Terebella; and Spallanzani (p. 472) and Esper (p. 474) on fossils.

Evidence from John Hunter's library suggests that he did actually keep well-informed by reading. The library contents sold at Christie's[19] after his death (fig. 5) comprised a large number of books from a wide field of art and science which included: Haller's works in anatomy, physiology and surgery; in natural history, the classic works of Linnaeus and Buffon as well as books by Da Costa, Willoughby and Swammerdam; in science, works of Newton,

A
CATALOGUE
OF

THE GENUINE AND VALUABLE COLLECTION
OF CAPITAL

PICTURES and DRAWINGS,
OF THE

Italian, French, Flemish, Dutch, and English Schools,
BY THE MOST ESTEEMED ARTISTS,

In the highest State of Preservation; collected, with great Taste, by the late eminent

JOHN HUNTER, ESQ.
DECEASED;

Comprising the Works of the following ADMIRED MASTERS, viz.

TITIAN	RUBENS	VERNET	SIR J. REYNOLDS
PERDONONE	VAN DYCK	LE NAIN	ZOFFANI
SPAGNIOLETTO	TENIERS	CUYP	LOUTHERBOURG
GUIDO	PORBUS	RUYSDAEL	BARRET
ZUCCARELLI	C. JANSEN	BACKHUYSEN	STUBBS
CANALETTI	LARESSE	VAN GOYEN	WRIGHT, &c. &c.

WHICH (BY ORDER OF THE EXECUTORS)

Will be Sold by Auction

By Mr. CHRISTIE,
At his Great Room in Pall Mall,

On WEDNESDAY, JANUARY the 29th, 1794,

AT TWELVE O'CLOCK.

Also on Thursday, will be sold, his Val... ...le Collection o... ...'rints, Books of Prints, &c.
On Friday, his curious Museum, Bronzes, Marbles, &c...
And on Saturday his LIBRARY of SCARCE BOOKS.

To be Viewed on Monday and Tuesday preceding the Sale.

Separate Catalogues may be had in Pall Mall, and at the Rainbow Coffee House.

A
CATALOGUE
OF THE

VALUABLE WELL-CHOSEN SELECT LIBRARY
OF

SCARCE BOOKS,
THE PROPERTY OF THE LATE

JOHN HUNTER, ESQ. Deceased;

AMONG WHICH ARE THE FOLLOWING

QUARTO.	FOLIO.
Philosophical Transactions	Virgilii Opera,
Buffon Histoire Naturelle,	Haller Iconum Anatomicarum.
Brace's Travels,	Bacon's Works,
Hawkesworth's Voyages,	Johnson's Dictionary,
British Zoology,	Swammerdam on Insects, &c. &c.

WHICH WILL BE SOLD BY AUCTION

(BY ORDER OF THE EXECUTORS)

By Mr. CHRISTIE,
At his Great Room in Pall Mall,

On SATURDAY, FEBRUARY the 1st, 1794,

AT TWELVE O'CLOCK.

To be Viewed Two Days preceding the Sale.——Catalogues may be had as above;
and at the Rainbow Coffee House, Cornhill.

Fig. 5. Sale of John Hunter's library and pictures (courtesy of Christie's).

Priestley and the Philosophical Transactions of the Royal Societies
of London and Edinburgh; a large number of medical and surgical
textbooks; the works of Bacon and Virgil, Adam Smith's *Wealth of
Nations* and several books on architecture by Adam and Richardson; a large number of books on travel and geography; several
histories of England and Scotland; and several dictionaries, Johnson's, Latin and others (fig. 6). As might be expected, there are no
examples of romantic literature in the list. The contents of John
Hunter's library surely indicates that he was far from being an
ill-read man.

It is significant that in 1786 Hunter wrote to the Company of
Surgeons to complain about the absence of a library: 'Gentlemen,
At this period, in which the Surgeons of Great Britain have
deservedly acquired the highest reputation in Europe, both by their
practice and publication it appears to be a reflection upon them that
the Corporation of Surgeons of London should not be possessed of
a public Surgical Library, a circumstance so extraordinary that
Foreigners can hardly believe it . . .'[20]

It was stated by d'Arcy Power that 'John Hunter could not
express himself clearly, either in writing or by word of mouth,
when he dealt with the more difficult problems of surgery.'[21] A
study of Hunter's works does not support these assertions and there
are plenty of long but concise and explicit paragraphs to be found in
his writings e.g. in his description of the mechanism of referred pain
(p. 123) and in his letter to the Board of St. George's Hospital
written a few months before his death – 'In whatever way it may be
determined to me is personally immaterial; the good of mankind,
the improvement of the healing art, and the character of the
hospital, are the motives of my conduct, and according to which,
whatever may be the decision of the present question, I shall
continue to do my duty to the hospital as a charity, and confine
myself to the laws of the institution.'[22]

In spite of criticisms of his literacy, Hunter's many scientific
papers were readily accepted by the Royal Society and published in
its Transactions. In 1787, when John Hunter was presented with the
Copley Medal, the highest award of the Royal Society, the President, Sir Joseph Banks said – 'To you, then, Mr. Hunter, I most
willingly deliver this testimony of the regard of the Royal Society;
this regard by which she distinguishes those who are in her opinion,
the most meritorious; . . . and be assured, Sir, that this Society

Anatomy

Haller Opera Anatomica
Collins's Anatomy
Monro's Treatise
System of Blood Vessels and Nerves

Winslow's Anatomy
Haller Iconum Anatomicorum
Dillenius Historia Musculorum
Walter Tabulae Nervorum

Arts

Adam's Architecture
Richardson's Ceilings
Priestley on Oratory
Richardson on Architecture

Richardson's Emblematical Figures
Rymsdycke Museum Britannicum
Inigo Jones's Stone Henge

Dictionaries

Hederici Lexicon
Johnson's Dictionary
Ainsworth's Latin Dictionary

Miller's Gardener's Dictionary
Motherby's Medical Dictionary

Genealogy

Warwick Family

History

Smollett's England
Robertson's Charles V
Robertson's America
Hume's History of England

Guthrie's Scotland
Robertson's Scotland
Dalrymple's Memoirs
Macauley's History of England

Laws of England

Blackstone's Commentaries

Literature

Bacon's Works

Virgilii Opera

Medical and Surgical

Potter's Medical Practice
Fordyce on Food
Blane on Diseases of Seamen
Saunders on the Liver
Celsus on Medicine
Le Dran's Surgery
Medical Observations
Cheselden's Le Dran
Friend's History of Physic
Hunter's Medical Commentaries
Hunter on the Gravid Uterus
Boerhaave's Lectures
Underwood on Diseases of Children

Rymer on Indigestion
Aitken's Elements of Surgery
Baillie's morbid Anatomy
Tiffot on Bilious Fevers
Porterfield on the Eye
Medical Commentaries
Bromfield's Surgery
Haller Bibliotheca Chirurgica
Russell on the Plague
Johnson's Midwifery
Memoires de Chirurgie par Amand
Medical Essays
Pott's Works

Natural History. Biology. Zoology

Linnaeus Opera
Lee on Botany
Dacosta's Shells
Dacosta on Fossils
Willoughby on Birds
Petiveri Historia Naturalem [Birds]

Buffon Histoire Naturelle
Skinner on the Viper
Pennant's British Zoology
Edwards's Gleanings of Natural History
Swammerdam on Insects

Philosophy

Adam Smith's Moral Sentiments

Physiology

Ferris on Milk
Haller Elementa Physiologica
Crawford on Animal Heat

Leslie on Animal Heat
Sheldon on the Absorbent System

Political Economy

Adam Smith's Wealth of Nations

Psychology

Hartley on the Mind

Science

Philosophical Transactions
Falconer on Fixed Air
Macquer's Chemistry
Priestley on Air
Priestley on Electricity
Newton on Fluxions
Price on Minerals

Edinburgh Royal Society Transactions
Home's Chemical Experiments
Isaac Newton by Motte
Cummings on Clock-work
Priestley's History of Electricity
Neumann's Chemical Works
Bion on Mathematical Instruments

Theology

Butler's Analogy

Travel. Geography. Maps

Cordiner's Views
Grant's Greenland
Bruce's Travels
Hawkesworth's Voyages
Cook's second Voyage
Marsden's Sumatra
Hodges's Travels in India
Rocque's Map of London
Cartwright's Journal on the Coast of Labrador
Antiquities of Gloucestershire

Pearson on the Buxton Springs
Robinson's Bath Roads
Lyson's Surrey
Cook's third Voyage
Hunter's Voyages
Paterson's Journey to Caffraria
Bougainville's Voyage round the World
Cellarii Geographia Antiqua
Cary's Atlas
White's Voyage to Botany Bay

Unrepresented

Romantic Literature

Fig. 6. Main contents of Hunter's library, extracted from Christie's catalogue.

will, with gratitude, bear daily testimony to the advantage which Mankind receives from the natural sagacity of your professional and the indefatigable industry of your scientific exertions.'[23]

Furthermore, most of Hunter's work was original and he had to find new words, especially in the field of surgical pathology, a subject which he practically founded, e.g. 'adhesive inflammation', and 'suppurative inflammation'. Hunter's actual handwriting certainly does not appear to be that of an illiterate man, as was pointed out by Cade.[24]

John Hunter did not cultivate the Arts but that may well have been, not because he was not interested but for the simple reason that he just did not have time to do so. Every minute of his life had to be dedicated to his work. He did not disparage the arts. He said, of music:

'Nothing shows the effects of sound upon the body more than music. No man would be inclined to dance without music: the music also determines the kind of dance. Music is universal: the mind immediately feels its effects, and has recourse to it, as much as the body for food.'[25]

There is evidence that Hunter showed interest in the stage. He wrote: 'I went to see Mrs. Siddons's acting. I had a full conviction that I should be very much affected . . .'[26]

Hunter showed a great interest in pictures as can be seen from his great collection sold at Christie's[27] which included all the leading painters (fig. 5). He often refers to pictures in his letters to Jenner, e.g. '. . . Pictures have been very cheap, but the season is now over. There will be but one sale, *viz.* Fordyce's; but I believe all his pictures are exquisite, and will go beyond you or me. Since you wrote to me I purchased up a small landscape of Barrett's, of cattle and herd: I gave five pounds seven shillings and sixpence: it is one of his eight-guinea pictures. You shall have it or not, as you please. I have one of the same size, that I bought of him some time ago.'[28] And again – '. . . I will send you the picture; but by what conveyance? or by what place? I have a picture by Barrett and Stubbs. The landscape by Barrett; a horse frightened at the first seeing of a lion, by Stubbs. I got it for five guineas: will you have it? I have a dearer one, and no use, for two of the same masters; but do not have it excepting you would like it, for I can get my money for it.'[29] Perhaps the collection of pictures was a convenient artistic outlet for Hunter because it occupied little of his valuable time.

In spite of criticisms that John Hunter was arrogant and abrasive, there are numerous passages in his writings that show he was self-critical in his work and that he had that innate modesty and profound humility that are essential in the search for truth in Nature. At the age of forty-seven, he wrote in a letter to his brother-in-law the Rev. James Baillie – '. . . I am following my business as a student . . .'.[30] He frequently admits his own failures in experiments, operations and opinions, e.g.

> Whenever I have seen the dura mater opened, . . . the patients have died. This was the case with a Mr. Cooper, whose dura mater I opened . . . he died, and I think it is probable I killed him, by opening the dura mater.[31]

> . . . where it is found necessary to trepan, . . . We should scalp carefully, lest . . . loose pieces of bone . . . which we cannot see . . . we might plunge into the brain; and yet I own I cannot always call to mind this caution at all times when operating.[32]

> In a woman in whom I performed this [Caesarean] operation, and who died, I found, thirty-six hours after death, . . . the edges of the wound in the uterus had not closed at all, and a good deal of coagulated blood was found in it. I should therefore in future wait until the bleeding had nearly stopped from the uterus before I closed the external wound.[33]

> A gentleman complained of a pain in the hip, running down the outside of the leg and foot. Supposing it rheumatism I gave him . . . Dover's powder . . . but with no good effect . . . He at last perceived a tumour by the os ischii . . . This tumour increased, and the person died.[34]

In the treatment of a patient with gonococcal buboes Hunter said 'I ordered mercurial ointment to be rubbed into both the legs and thighs, to resolve them if possible. . . . I spoke too confidently of my power with respect to the resolution of the buboes, for they both suppurated . . .'[35]

Hunter's relentless pursuit of truth is demonstrated in his tremendous zeal for obtaining an autopsy on any case with which he had been connected, as for example in this letter to the doctor in the case of the Hon. Miss V. aged 13 in whom Hunter had diagnosed congenital heart disease '. . . As this is a case which I think will terminate ill, I wish you would take notes of all the symptoms for probably a time will come when the parts will be inspected by somebody, which will afford valuable information when attended by the history of the case.'[36]

Indeed Hunter demonstrates a deep philosophical humility in his whole outlook to investigations and experiments when he says – 'In pursuing any subject most things come to light as it were by accident, that is, many things arise out of investigation that were not at first conceived, and even misfortunes in experiments have brought things to our knowledge that were not and probably could not have been previously conceived: on the other hand, I have often devised experiments by the fire-side or in my carriage, and have also conceived the result; but when I tried the experiment the result was different, or I found that the experiment could not be attended with all the circumstances that were suggested.'[37]

The foundation of John Hunter's success was his unlimited proclivity for hard work. His day started at 6 o'clock in the morning when he commenced dissection and the preparation of anatomical and pathological specimens. He breakfasted at 9 o'clock and then saw patients at his house until midday. He visited patients and the hospital in the afternoon. He dined at 4 o'clock after which he usually rested for an hour and then settled down to writing, often dictating to his pupils and assistants until midnight or later. He slept for only four or five hours.[38]

William Clift gave an account of John Hunter's system of writing:

> The cabinets which contained these papers stood in Mr. Hunter's study, that he might have ready access to them in the evenings; and scarcely a single evening occurred, except Sundays, during my attendance on Mr. Hunter for the last twenty months of his life, in which something was not added to the contents of these volumes and papers. I wrote for him constantly during that period from seven o'clock till eleven p.m., and sometimes an hour or two later, as did also Mr. Haynes for a great part of that period. The greatest part of these papers was in the handwriting of Mr. Bell, who lived fourteen years in Mr. Hunter's house for the purpose of writing and making drawings.
>
> Mr. Hunter kept an account of the various animals that came under his inspection; and whenever he re-examined an animal, he overlooked his previous account, and corrected or added to it. Also an account of all remarkable and interesting cases that came under his observation, as well as others furnished by his friends.
>
> He generally wrote his first thoughts or memoranda on all subjects on the slips torn off from the ends and the blank pages and envelopes of letters. Thousands of these were copied by Haynes and myself into the different papers and volumes, being generally inserted and frequently pinned into the place where they were to be written

in. He appeared to have no desire for preserving his own handwriting, as we always scored these slips across, and returned them to Mr. Hunter, who usually folded them up, and put them on the chimney-piece to light the candles with; and the rough or waste copies on all subjects, when copied out fair, were taken into his private dissecting room as waste paper to dissect upon.[39]

John Hunter was interested in all Nature's work, animal, vegetable and mineral. He was forever trying to fathom the secrets of Nature and he brought to his investigations a keen and superhuman power of observation, as may be noted in his classic description of the process of sequestration (exfoliation) of bone:

> The first appearance of separation is an alteration in the part round the exfoliating piece. This alteration is first a sponginess; next, its becoming fuller of little holes; then a small groove is produced, a kind of worm-eaten canal about the thickness of a shilling, becoming gradually deeper and deeper; and the depth is irregular, according to the extent of the original cause. The small holes appear at first in the surrounding parts, and these appear more vascular, the more so the nearer the diseased bone. Sometimes parts become dead without any change of colour, dying almost suddenly, perhaps by exposure or a blow, and the surrounding part becomes spongy: the dead portion then looks the soundest; but when killed by previous diseases it is black.

This quotation illustrates well his profound concern with the details of the phenomena of Nature and he sums it up with a final sentence:

> It is astonishing to see what little curiosity people have to observe the operations of Nature, and how very curious they are about the operations of Art.[40]

REFERENCES

1 Home E. A short account of the author's life in Hunter's *A Treatise on the Blood, Inflammation and Gun-shot Wounds*. London, G Nicol. 1794, p. 65.
2 Adams J. *Memoirs of the Life and Doctrines of the late John Hunter, Esq.* London, J Callow and J Hunter. 1817, p. 44.
3 Abernethy J. *Hunterian Oration*. London, Longman. 1819, p. 54.
4 Holland Lord. *Further Memoirs of the Whig Party 1807–1821*, ed. Lord Stavordale. London, John Murray. 1905, p. 345.
5 Adams J. *Memoirs of the Life and Doctrines of the late John Hunter, Esq.* London, J Callow and J Hunter. 1817, pp. 195, 196.
6 Dobson J. Some of John Hunter's patients. *Annals of the Royal College of Surgeons of England*. 1968, vol. 42, p. 124.
7 Dobson J. *John Hunter*. Edinburgh and London, Livingstone. 1969, p. 124.
8 Dobson J. *William Clift*. London, Heinemann. 1954, pp. 10, 11.

9 Ibid. p. 127.
10 Home J A. Ed. *The Letters and Journals of Lady Mary Coke.* Bath, Kingsmead Reprints. 1889–1896.
11 Ellis Annie R. Ed. *The Early Diary of Frances Burney 1768–1778.* London, George Bell and Sons. 1889.
12 Greig J. Ed. *The Diaries of a Duchess* (Elizabeth Percy, 1st Duchess of Northumberland 1716–1776). London, Hodder and Stoughton. 1926.
13 Farington J. *The Farington Diary*, ed. J Greig. Second edn. London, Hutchinson. 1922.
14 Balderston Katharine C. Ed. *Thraliana.* The Diary of Mrs. Thrale 1776–1809. Oxford, Clarendon Press. 1942.
15 Foot J. *The Life of John Hunter.* London, T Becket. 1794, p. 60.
16 Ibid. p. 77.
17 Hunter J. Lectures on the principles of surgery in *The Works of John Hunter*, ed. J F Palmer. London, Longman. 1835, vol. 1, p. 412.
18 Hunter J. A treatise on venereal disease in *The Works of John Hunter*, ed. J F Palmer. London, Longman. 1835, vol. 2, p. 244.
19 Christie's Catalogue. 1st February 1794.
20 Dobson J. *John Hunter.* Edinburgh and London, Livingstone. 1969, p. 287.
21 Power Sir d'Arcy. Hunterian Oration 1925. John Hunter: a martyr to science in *Selected Writings 1877–1930.* Oxford, Clarendon Press. 1931, pp. 1–28.
22 Dobson J. *John Hunter.* Edinburgh and London, Livingstone. 1969, pp. 338, 339.
23 Ibid. pp. 292, 293.
24 Cade Sir Stanford. Hunterian Oration. The lasting dynamism of John Hunter. *Annals of the Royal College of Surgeons of England.* 1963, vol. 33, pp. 8–31.
25 Hunter J. *Essays and Observations on Natural History, Anatomy, Physiology, Psychology and Geology.* ed. R Owen. London, John Van Voorst. 1861, vol. 1, p. 176.
26 Ibid. p. 257.
27 Christie's Catalogue. 29th January 1794.
28 Royal College of Surgeons of England. *Letters from the past. From John Hunter to Edward Jenner.* 1976, p. 7.
29 Ibid. p. 21.
30 Paget S. *John Hunter.* London, T Fisher Unwin. 1897, p. 120.
31 Hunter J. Lectures on the principles of surgery in *The Works of John Hunter*, ed. J F Palmer. London, Longman. 1835, vol. 1, p. 495.
32 Ibid. pp. 495, 496.
33 Ibid. p. 448.
34 Ibid. p. 363.
35 Hunter J. A treatise on venereal disease in *The Works of John Hunter*, ed. J F Palmer. London, Longman. 1835, vol. 2, p. 378.
36 Dobson J. *John Hunter.* Edinburgh and London, Livingstone. 1969, pp. 284, 285.
37 Hunter J. Observations on bees in *The Works of John Hunter*, ed. J F Palmer. London, Longman. 1837, vol. 4, pp. 423, 424.
38 Ottley D. Life of John Hunter in *The Works of John Hunter*, ed. J F Palmer. London, Longman. 1835, vol. 1, pp. 52–55.
39 Paget S. *John Hunter.* London, T Fisher Unwin. 1897, pp. 250, 251.
40 Hunter J. Lectures on the principles of surgery in *The Works of John Hunter*, ed. J F Palmer. London, Longman. 1835, vol. 1, p. 527.

CHAPTER 5

HEALTH

In 1759, after eleven years spent chiefly in the conduct of anatomical dissection, John Hunter suffered from inflammation of the lungs. It is not known whether this was a manifestation of tuberculosis, but several of his brothers and sisters had succumbed to this disease. However in 1760 John Hunter must have been fit again as he went into active service in the Army (p. 10).

In 1773 John Hunter developed symptoms which almost certainly were those of angina pectoris.[1] He experienced a similar attack three years later, in 1776, when he was 'extremely ill'.[2] He convalesced in Bath where he met David Hume (p. 170). He himself described the attack as a severe pain in the epigastrium, associated with pallor and irregular periods of apnoea (p. 48). He stated that during an attack he was unable to feel a pulse in either arm.

In the following year, 1777, he had an attack associated with severe and prolonged giddiness for ten days and he described his symptoms in a letter to Jenner.[3] He spent a few weeks in Bath and was visited by Jenner, who concluded that Hunter was suffering from angina pectoris.[4] In the following years his anginal pains recurred with increasing frequency and in 1785 he spent a few weeks again at Bath with some improvement in his health.

There is a reference to Hunter's illness in a letter written in 1785 by Dr. Lettsom – '. . . Poor Hunter is going from this busy stage: he can scarcely go up stairs, so much is he affected with dyspnoea on the least motion. He declares he was the other day dead for four minutes, not having pulsation in the heart or arteries. He does not look ill; he speaks freely and easily; he thinks it is the gout. I suspect some aneurism. . . .'[5]

Dr. Adams records that Hunter 'was employed in embalming the Princess Amelia [daughter of George II who died in 1786] for three hours in which time he was really fatigued, but had no spasm the whole time: yet, by going the length of Cavendish Square, and on towards Oxford Road, he was seized with a considerable spasm, . . .'[6]

In 1786 there was a recurrence with attacks of pain occurring on the least exertion and E. Home states that 'never afterwards was he entirely free from complaint, or capable of his usual bodily exertions'.[7]

Hunter acknowledged that these attacks could be 'brought on by a state of mind anxious about any event' (p. 127). Hunter's output of work, however, did not diminish. Indeed, in this year he published the *Treatise on the Venereal Disease* and *Observations on Certain Parts of the Animal Oeconomy*, both printed in Castle Street under his supervision. He carried on his private practice and in May 1788 he wrote – 'Dear Jenner, – I have been going to write to you some time past, but business and a very severe indisposition for three weeks past has prevented me; but when two guineas rouse me, I cannot resist . . .'[8]

Farington noted in his Diary that in 1792 John Hunter told him that he himself had some heart trouble 'which he was well assured would cause his death suddenly at some period' (p. 171).

In his last four years, Hunter experienced repeated attacks of pain, giddiness and loss of memory, culminating in a fatal attack at St. George's Hosptial on 16th October 1793 (p. 193).

JOHN HUNTER'S ALLEGED SYPHILIS

The allegation that John Hunter suffered from syphilis was first given wide publicity in 1925 by Sir d'Arcy Power in a Hunterian Oration entitled 'John Hunter: A Martyr to Science'.[9] This allegation had in fact appeared unobtrusively as an unsupported statement in at least three other publications in the previous century (see below). D'Arcy Power stated that John Hunter 'died of syphilitic disease of the arterial system, and . . . , in addition to the angina pectoris due to this cause, he suffered for many years from cerebral syphilis.'[9] He supported this opinion by a misinterpretation of John Hunter's inoculation experiment, suggesting that this was a self-inoculation. D'Arcy Power's statement has been grasped avidly by many subsequent biographers, e.g. Kobler[10] ('he picked up the pus-laden lancet, punctured his foreskin, then the head of his penis'), Gloyne[11] and Gray.[12]

There is no evidence to show that John Hunter ever suffered from venereal disease and there are good reasons to believe that his inoculation experiment was performed not on himself but on some other individual. D'Arcy Power's opinions were completely erroneous and irresponsible. They could not be supported even by the evidence presented in his Oration. It is a sad reflection on human credulity that d'Arcy Power's statements were accepted and promulgated so readily by numerous biographers. Indeed his presentation of John Hunter as a Martyr to Science in the investigation of venereal disease has given his Hunterian Oration more publicity than all the other Orations combined.

Sir d'Arcy Power's numerous publications on medical history have gained well merited success but his facts are not always strictly accurate, e.g. he stated: 'John Hunter wrote a treatise on gunshot wounds. He was in favour of Wisemen's plan of dilating, that is to say, of draining wounds, . . .'[13] This of course is exactly the opposite opinion expressed by Hunter who wrote strongly against dilating wounds.

In addition to d'Arcy Power's Oration, there are at least three other prior references stating that John Hunter carried out an auto-inoculation. One of these occurs in a footnote by G. G. Babington in his edition of Hunter's *A Treatise on Venereal Disease* published in Palmer's Works in 1835 – 'The author inoculated himself with the matter of gonorrhoea, and the consequence was the production of chancres, followed by bubo, and by secondary symptoms. The experiment is related, at length, in Part VI., Chap. ii., Sect. 2, of the present work'.[14]

A second reference occurs in Ottley's Life of Hunter as a footnote – '. . . in relating his own case, where secondary symptoms had ensued on inoculation with the matter of chancre, he repeated over so often, and in so peculiar a tone, "I knocked down the disease with mercury and I killed it," that the whole class at length burst into a loud fit of laughter.'[15]

The third reference is in a volume of manuscript notes on Hunter's lectures on venereal disease.[16] This volume, in the Miner Library of Rochester University New York, consists of notes made after 1800 (as shown by the watermark in the paper) and since Hunter died in 1793 these manuscript notes must have been copied from an earlier exemplar (Weimerskirch). The script follows roughly the order of presentation of Hunter's Treatise but the inoculation experiment is not included. Hunter is quoted as saying: 'It has often been disputed whether the matter of a chancre and gonorrhoea essentially differ – or whether they are the same. But as I have produced in myself a chancre by matter from a gonorrhoea that point is now settled. I am led to conclude that there is no difference . . .' An interesting feature is that this quotation occurs early on in the Miner Library manuscript, in a place corresponding to the section in which Babington appended his note (Weimerskirch).[16]

Several reasons may be presented to question the merit of these three references. The position of Babington's footnote strongly suggests that he gleaned his information from lecture notes similar to those of the Miner Library copy because it would have been far more logical for Babington to have entered the footnote in association with the inoculation experiment in the Treatise which he was editing.

A more important argument concerns the reliability of the Hunterian quotation. Statements in the Lecture notes cannot be regarded as being as authentic as those made on the same subject by the author, especially since the first two editions were printed and published during Hunter's lifetime and at his own press at Castle Street. Furthermore, notes taken down at a lecture would be liable to error even in the first copy and the Miner Library Lectures are second or third hand transcripts written some years after Hunter's decease. It has often been stated by Hunter's biographers that he was a poor lecturer so that it is not difficult to assume an occasional error in the original notes. Indeed if the single word 'in' is omitted from the quotation the whole implication is altered and could well refer to the inoculation of someone other than Hunter himself. It is noteworthy that Hunter has used a similar phraseology referring to himself in other contexts, for example in discussing the treatment of scrofula he wrote – 'From the indolence of scrofula we might *a priori* think that many local applications would be serviceable, especially those of a stimulating kind; but these all prove injurious, as mercury, copperas, balsams, etc.: indeed, few applications are of any service. I have myself only found benefit from cicuta and sea-water. The juice of hemlock made into a poultice is serviceable after suppuration has come on; . . .'[17] It could be implied from this passage that Hunter had treated himself for scrofula.

Finally it must be emphasised that the Treatise was published during John Hunter's lifetime and it contains no statement that he himself suffered from venereal disease – indeed it would have been a remarkable omission for Hunter to leave out a statement of such importance, one that 'settled the point' of the main theme of his Treatise.

The allegations that John Hunter suffered from venereal disease and that he inoculated himself with the disease can be refuted by consideration of his autopsy findings, the clinical features of his illness and Hunter's own description of the inoculation experiment.[18]

John Hunter's autopsy was performed by Everard Home. It showed advanced generalised atherosclerosis, with calcified coronary arteries and ossified internal carotid and vertebral arteries, *viz.*

. . . The coronary arteries had their branches which ramify through the substance of the heart in the state of bony tubes, which were with difficulty divided by the knife, and their tranverse sections did not collapse, but remained open. The valvulae mitrales, where they come off from the lower edge of the auricle, were in many places ossified, forming an imperfectly bony margin of different thicknesses, and in one spot so thick as to form a knob; but these ossifications were not continued down upon the valve towards the chordae tendineae.

The semilunar valves of the aorta had lost their natural pliancy, the previous stage to becoming bone, and in several spots there were evident ossifications.

The aorta, immediately beyond the semilunar valves, had its cavity larger than usual, putting on the appearance of an incipient aneurism: this unusual dilatation extended for some way along the ascending aorta, but did not reach so far as the common trunk of the axillary and carotid artery. The increase of capacity of the artery might be about one-third of its natural area; and the internal membrane of this part had lost entirely the natural polish, and was studded over with opaque white spots, raised higher than the general surface.

On inspecting the head, the cranium and dura mater were found in a natural state. The pia mater had the vessels upon the surface of the two hemispheres of the brain turgid with blood, which is commonly found to be the case after sudden death.

The internal structure of the brain was very carefully examined, and the different parts both of the cerebrum and cerebellum were found in the most natural and healthy state; but the internal carotid arteries as they pass by the sides of the cella tursica were ossified, and several of the ramifications which go off from them had become opaque and unhealthy in their appearance. The vertebral arteries lying upon the medulla oblongata had also become bony, and the basillary artery, which is formed by them, had opaque white spots very generally along its coats.[19]

Professor J. L. Turk states that in his opinion 'there is no evidence in the autopsy report of any pathological changes that might have been caused by syphilis and that there is no doubt that Hunter died as a result of coronary artery disease of atheromatous origin.'[20]

The clinical features of John Hunter's illness were those of myocardial and cerebral ischaemia. In Everard Home's opinion John Hunter suffered from angina pectoris for the last twenty years of his life.[21] This diagnosis had first been made by Dr E. Jenner in 1777 when he had visited Hunter in Bath.[22] An important feature of Hunter's attacks was a weak or absent pulse. It has been suggested by Dr Livesley[23] that John Hunter suffered from a disorder of sinuatrial activity (sick sinus syndrome), a disease of uncertain pathology in the vicinity of the sinuatrial node which may be associated with spasmodic attacks of bradycardia.[24] These attacks of bradycardia in the presence of extensive coronary and cerebral arterial disease would be very likely to precipitate angina and syncope. It is of interest that the sinuatrial node (pacemaker) was first described by Sir Arthur Keith, Conservator of the Hunterian Museum and a keen Hunterian scholar, in 1906 (Keith-Flack node).[25]

John Hunter carried out his famous inoculation experiment in 1767.[26] The suggestion that this was a self-inoculation was strongly supported in 1925 by d'Arcy Power,[9] who presented this view as an explanation of Hunter's alleged terminal syphilitic infection. A careful perusal of Hunter's own account of the inoculation shows that the assumption of self-inoculation is completely unjustified. He did not state that he inoculated himself but the account is presented in a form which can be and has been easily misinterpreted as an experiment in self-inoculation.

John Hunter was the leading authority of his time on venereal disease and his large clinical experience had made him very familiar with the virulent ravages of the disease, for example – 'Gonorrhoea either produces, or is supposed to produce, many disorders besides those already mentioned, and which are totally different from the original disease . . . There is frequently a series of them . . . stricture of the urethra . . . dilatation of the urethra . . . ulceration, fistulae in perinaeo, dilatation of the ureters and enlargement of the pelvis of the kidneys . . . swellings of the testicle and of the glands of the groin'.[27] It is inconceivable that a man of Hunter's intelligence could have even contemplated the idea of inoculating himself with such a disease. What would we think of a doctor or student who inoculated himself with a loathsome disease? We should send him to a psychiatrist. The whole idea of Hunter inoculating himself with a venereal disease is preposterous.

The inoculation experiment is recorded in detail in his famous Treatise, but a careful study of this work shows that the actual subject of the experiment is never identified:

> *Experiments made to ascertain the Progress and Effects of the*
> *Venereal Poison*
> To ascertain several facts relative to the venereal disease, the following experiments were made. They were begun in May 1767.
> Two punctures were made on the penis with a lancet dipped in venereal matter from a gonorrhoea; one puncture was on the glans, the other on the prepuce.
> This was on a Friday; on the Sunday following there was a teasing itching in those parts, which lasted till the Tuesday following . . .
> The time the experiments took up, from the first insertion to the complete cure, was about three years.
> The above case is only uncommon in the mode of contracting the disease.[26]

It will be seen that Hunter has not stated that he inoculated himself. He simply states that two punctures were made. He has used the first person on only two occasions throughout the account, which occupies about two pages, and even these 'I's are not associated with the actual experiment.

The complete absence of the first person in this description of the experiment is a very striking and important fact because Hunter's works abound in the use of the personal pronoun. There are few pages in all his works in which he has not used it. Nearly all his observations were personal. It is very remarkable that this experiment supposed by so many to have been performed on himself should be just the one section in all his works in which he has not bothered to mention himself.

In complete contrast to this impersonal style of description, there are numerous other accounts given by Hunter of observations made on himself and presented in his characteristic personal manner.

Describing the rupture of his Achilles tendon, Hunter wrote –

> . . . happened to myself when I broke my 'tendo Achillis' . . .
> I . . . did not endeavour to act with its muscle; but . . . I found I had
> no power to act . . . even when union had taken place and appeared
> to my senses, and . . . to my reasoning faculty . . . yet I had not the
> least power to raise myself . . . I endeavoured . . . I was convinced it
> arose from a consciousness of the mind . . . all my voluntary powers
> were not able . . . But I found that, in my sleep, I often hurt the
> young union of the tendon . . . And what was the worst, I
> fell . . .[28]

In this account Hunter has used the word 'I' ten times.

Again, Hunter described experiments that he made on himself
with mercury –

> . . . I made the following experiments upon myself. I put some
> crude mercury into my mouth . . . till I tasted it sensibly; I then put
> into my mouth the mercurius calcinatus, and let it remain till I
> perceived the taste of it, which was exactly the same; but I observed
> that it was easier of solution than the crude mercury. I tried calomel
> in the same way, . . . It was some time before I perceived the taste of
> the crude mercury in my mouth. I tasted the calx and calomel much
> sooner. . . . I rubbed in mercurial ointment upon my thighs till my
> mouth was affected, and I could plainly taste the mercury; . . . I
> allowed some time for my mouth to get perfectly well . . . I then
> took calomel in pills . . . I afterwards took mercurius calcinatus, and
> also corrosive sublimate.[29]

In observations on the size of muscles in action, Hunter wrote–

> . . . I made the following experiments . . . in the morning, having
> used my arm as little as possible, I measured . . . of my right
> arm . . . I then bent the forearm . . . I measured it . . . I next
> worked an air-pump . . . my arm became tired . . . I found my
> arm . . . eleven inches and five eighths . . .[30]

Further, Hunter described the first severe attack of his cardiac
lesion, in characteristic words –

> I had the gout in my feet three springs successively, and missed it
> the fourth. In the fifth spring, one day at ten o'clock in the forenoon,
> I was attacked suddenly with a pain nearly about the pylorus: it was a
> pain peculiar to those parts, and became so violent that I tried every
> position to relieve myself, but could get no ease. I then took a
> teaspoonful of tincture of rhubarb, with thirty drops of laudanum,
> but still found no relief. As I was walking about the room, I cast my
> eyes on a looking-glass, and observed my countenance pale, my lips
> white, and I had the appearance of a dead man looking at himself.

This alarmed me. I could feel no pulse in either arm. The pain still
continuing, I began to think it very serious. I found myself at times
not breathing; and being afraid of death soon taking place if I did not
breathe, I produced a voluntary action of breathing, working my
lungs by the power of my will. I continued in this state three quarters
of an hour, when the pain lessened, the pulse was felt, and involuntary breathing began to take place. During this state I took madeira,
brandy, ginger, and other warm things; but I believe nothing did any
good, as the return of health was very gradual. About two o'clock I
was able to go about my business.[31]

These four accounts are written in the personal style characteristic of all Hunter's works. It is surely very significant that an
inoculation experiment supposedly performed on himself should
have been described in a manner which is impersonal and completely
contrary to the style of all the rest of his writings. Indeed there are
numerous passages in the Treatise which would have given Hunter the
opportunity of mentioning his own case if such had existed as in the
following examples:

In the description of the chancre he says 'This . . . begins first
with an itching in the part; . . . a small pimple appears . . . The
itching is gradually changed to pain . . . it is no uncommon thing
for the urethra . . . give a tickling pain, especially in making
water.'[32]

There is a detailed account of the treatment of a chancre without
any mention of a personal experience.[33]

Hunter discusses the use of mercury in the treatment of a bubo in
which he quotes the case histories of soldiers in Belleisle and other
patients but without reference to himself.[34] It is significant that he
has given an account of his own personal experience of mercury
treatment but only as an experiment and without any reference to a
therapeutic effort (p. 48).

There is an account of the consequences of buboes in which
Hunter has described numerous cases but without reference to
himself.[35]

In fact, in the whole Treatise, occupying more than 350 pages
(pp. 131–488), and including dozens of case histories there is not a
single occasion on which John Hunter refers to himself as a subject
of venereal disease.

There is plenty of evidence to suggest that in fact the inoculation
experiment was performed by Hunter on another person. The
Treatise contains several descriptions of inoculation experiments

performed by John Hunter on patients, using 'fresh venereal matter' from chancres or ulcers – e.g.

> A man, who had venereal blotches on many parts of his skin, was inoculated with matter from a chancre . . . The wounds inoculated became chancres . . . Here then was a venereal constitution capable of being affected locally with fresh venereal matter. This experiment I have likewise repeated more than once.[36]
>
> I ordered a person, at St. George's Hospital, to be inoculated with the matter taken from a venereal ulcer on the tonsil, and also with matter from a gonorrhoea . . . The matter from a gonorrhoea produced a chancre but that from the tonsil had no effect.[37]
>
> A woman aged twenty-five . . . St. George's Hospital . . . venereal disease . . . blotches over her body . . . To ascertain whether her secondary ulcers were infectious . . . she was inoculated with some matter from one of her own ulcers and with some matter from a bubo of another person where mercury had not been used.[37]
>
> When the venereal matter has been applied to a sore, so as to irritate, it produces a venereal irritation and inflammation. . . . This experiment I have made several times, . . .[38]
>
> When there are venereal sores on the arms . . . there is no swellings of the glands of the armpit; although much will take place if fresh venereal matter is applied to a common sore on the arm, hand or fingers.[39]
>
> . . . it has been proved that the application of the matter from a gonorrhoea to a bubo does not in the least retard the cure of that bubo; nor does the matter of a chancre applied to a bubo, nor the matter of a bubo applied to a chancre, produce any bad effect; though if venereal matter is applied to a common sore it will often produce the venereal irritation.[40]

Here then is a mass of evidence in John Hunter's own writings to prove that he repeatedly inoculated patients deliberately with venereal matter. There is good reason to assume, therefore, that Hunter performed the crucial experiment on some person other than himself. It must be emphasised that throughout the description of this experiment there is not a single statement that John Hunter himself was the subject of the inoculation. All the observations are completely non-personal. The subject of the experiment could well have been one of the many destitute outcasts of subnormal mentality who roamed the streets of London at that time, and Hunter could have kept him unobstrusively in his large household establishment so that he could make the necessary daily observations.

There is plenty of further evidence throughout Hunter's works that he was quite prepared to experiment on subjects other than himself. In his experiment on heat, Hunter said – 'I put the ball of the thermometer under my tongue . . . I thought the urethra would do still better and I introduced the ball of a thermometer into a man's urethra . . . I procured a dead and a living penis . . . immersed both in water at 50° . . . I repeated the same experiment several times with the same result.'[41] He had no qualms about extracting sound front teeth from young women for transplantation into his own patients. He said that the tooth to be transplanted should be 'a full-grown young tooth, . . . should always be perfectly sound and taken from a mouth what has the appearance of that of a person sound and healthy, . . . should be that of a female . . .'[42]

Hunter's apparent insensitivity towards his experimental human subjects must be judged within the context of his time, when the poorer classes were still in the grip of a patronising feudalism. His animal experiments again bear strong witness to the primitive brutality acceptable in those days. In his experiments on the lacteals, Hunter said: 'I opened the abdomen of a living sheep, which had eat nothing for some days . . . The animal was quite alive all the time of our making these experiments and observations, which lasted from one o'clock till half an hour after three. I chose a sheep rather than a dog . . . because it is much more patient and quiet. . . . I got an ass . . . put him upon his back in an open garden, and tied him fast to four stakes drove into the ground, then opened his abdomen, etc . . . In doing this the animal struggled . . .'[43] In a lecture on the method of making preparations, Dr William Hunter said 'Birds, Little Animals etc. may be best cleaned by Maggots, Ants etc. – their Bones may be freed from grease by gradually starving them to Death.'[44]

It is significant that before Power's publication none of Hunter's many biographers had suggested that the experiment was one of self-inoculation, except Ottley in a footnote (p. 43).* Indeed there is no special mention at all of the experiment in the biographies by Foot (1794),[45] Adams (1817),[46] Butler (1881),[47] Paget (1897)[48] and Peachey (1924).[49] There can be little doubt that these biographers accepted the experiment in its proper context among Hunter's other experiments on venereal disease.

---

* References to self-inoculation were made also by Babington (p. 43) and in the Miner manuscript notes (p. 43) but these were not biographies.

However, a most important account of the inoculation experiment has been given by Foot in a book especially written as a critical commentary on Hunter's *Treatise on Venereal Disease*. In a detailed account of the experiment occupying twelve pages Foot refers throughout to the subject of the experiment as 'the case'. Further, he says, 'The person upon whom the Professor tried the experiment amused him, if he told him that he had been chaste; and that if he told him to the contrary, the fable is all at an end'.[50] Foot was a contemporary and a great critic of John Hunter, but he makes no adverse comments here except about Hunter's opinions on venereal disease.

There can be little doubt that experimental inoculations of this kind were not regarded as unethical in Hunter's time. The history of smallpox is replete with examples of experimental inoculations in John Hunter's time. In 1721, following Lady Mary Montagu's introduction into this country of smallpox inoculation, Dr. Maitland inoculated six condemned prisoners in Newgate Prison with active smallpox virus in exchange for granting them pardons.[51] The experiment was successful and this method of smallpox inoculation became fashionable in the latter half of the eighteenth century. John Hunter described several such inoculations that he performed, e.g. 'On Thursday, March 16, 1775, I inoculated a gentleman's child, in whose arms it was observed I made large punctures . . . The smallpox appeared at the regular time, went through its usual course, and terminated favourably.'[52] In 1802 Dr. Benjamin Waterhouse, who had introduced the practice of vaccination against smallpox into the United States, persuaded the Boston Board of Health to conduct a convincing public experiment.[53] Nineteen volunteers were vaccinated with cowpox virus and one week later they were inoculated with fresh smallpox virus; in addition two non-vaccinated volunteer controls were inoculated to prove the activity of the smallpox matter. The test was a complete success but the fate of the two controls is not recorded. Clearly, although the eighteenth century was the age of elegance, it was also the age of brutality, when lunatics were flogged, children were sent up chimneys, and executions were public celebrations.[54]

It is suggested therefore that John Hunter's inoculation experiment was not in fact a self-inoculation and that he used another subject for the experiment. There is incontrovertible evidence that Hunter made repeated experiments of this kind on patients. His description of the crucial experiment does not actually state that he inoculated himself, but the account is presented in a form which can be and has been easily misinterpreted as an experiment in self-inoculation.

It is significant that Hunter's mental clarity and cerebration suffered no deterioration with age. During the last three years of his life his output of work was unabated, as shown by his case records, his administration as Surgeon-General to the Army, and his correspondence. There is not the slightest evidence of the mental deterioration that would be expected with cerebral syphilis. The neurological features of John Hunter's illness were studied by Brain, who found no evidence of syphilis in the nervous system.[55]

It is commonly stated that Hunter postponed his marriage for several years until he had cured his syphilitic infection. This statement is completely without foundation and the delay was almost certainly due to Hunter's restricted income at that time (p. 20).

D'Arcy Power stated that 'the consequences of his action were visited upon his children' and he quotes in evidence the loss in infancy of two of Hunter's four children.[9] There is no evidence of congenital syphilis in any of Hunter's descendants and d'Arcy Power's statement must be regarded as completely irresponsible.

It is suggested that John Hunter's illness was due to non-specific atherosclerosis, that he never contracted syphilis, and that the 'self-inoculation' experiment was not in fact an inoculation on himself but on another subject. The suggestion that John Hunter was a 'martyr to science' is sheer romantic sentimentality and it is to be hoped that a dispassionate scientific reappraisal of all the facts will result in the complete eradication of the stigma of syphilis from his image.

REFERENCES

1 Paget S. *John Hunter*. London, T Fisher Unwin. 1897 p. 101.
2 Home E. A short account of the author's life in Hunter's *A Treatise on the Blood, Inflammation and Gun-shot Wounds*. London, G Nicol. 1794, p. 27.
3 Ottley D. Life of John Hunter in *The Works of John Hunter*, ed J F Palmer. London, Longman. 1835, vol. 1, p. 63.
4 Baron J. *Life of Edward Jenner*. London. 1827, p. 38.
5 Pettigrew T J. *Memoirs of the Life and Writings of the late John Coakley Lettsom*. London, Nicholls, Son and Bentley. 1817, vol. 3, p. 295.
6 Adams J. *Memoirs of the Life and Doctrines of the late John Hunter, Esq*. London, J Callow and J Hunter. 1817, pp. 170, 171.

7 Home E. A short account of the author's life in Hunter's *A Treatise on the Blood, Inflammation and Gun-shot Wounds.* London, G Nicol. 1794, p. 33.

8 Ottley D. Life of John Hunter in *The Works of John Hunter*, ed. J F Palmer. London, Longman. 1835, vol. 1, p. 110.

9 Power Sir d'Arcy. Hunterian Oration 1925. John Hunter: a martyr to science in *Selected Writings 1877–1930.* Oxford, Clarendon Press. 1931, pp. 1–28.

10 Kobler J. *The Reluctant Surgeon.* New York, Doubleday. 1960, p. 154.

11 Gloyne S. *John Hunter.* Edinburgh, Livingstone. 1950, p. 72.

12 Gray E A. *Portrait of a Surgeon.* London, Robert Hale. 1952 p. 67.

13 Power Sir d'Arcy. Early books on naval and military surgery in *Transaction of the Medical Society of London*, ed. Gask. London, Harrison. 1915, vol. 38, pp. 157–160.

14 Babington G G. Preface, *The Works of John Hunter*, ed. J F Palmer. London, Longman. 1835, vol. 2, pp. 146, 147.

15 Ottley D. Life of John Hunter in *The Works of John Hunter*, ed. J F Palmer. London, Longman. 1835, vol. 1, p. 47.

16 Weimerskirch P J. Hunter and venereal disease. *Lancet.* 1979, vol. 1, p. 503.

17 Hunter J. Lectures on the principles of surgery in *The Works of John Hunter*, ed. J F Palmer. London, Longman. 1835, vol. 1, p. 600.

18 Qvist G. John Hunter's alleged syphilis. *Annals of the Royal College of Surgeons of England.* 1977, vol. 59, pp. 205–209.

19 Home E. A short account of the author's life in Hunter's *A Treatise on the Blood, Inflammation and Gun-shot Wounds.* London, G Nicol. 1794, pp. 62–64.

20 Turk J L. Personal communication. 1976.

21 Home E. A short account of the author's life in Hunter's *A Treatise on the Blood, Inflammation and Gun-shot Wounds*, London, G Nicol. 1794, p. 14.

22 Baron J. *Life of Edward Jenner.* London. 1827, p. 38.

23 Livesley B. The spasms of John Hunter: a new interpretation. *Medical History.* 1973, vol. 17, pp. 70–75.

24 Editorial. Sick sinus syndrome. *British Medical Journal.* 1977, vol. 1, p. 4.

25 Keith A and Flack M W. The auriculo-ventricular bundle of the human heart. *Lancet.* 1906, vol. 2, pp. 359–364.

26 Hunter J. A treatise on venereal disease in *The Works of John Hunter*, ed. J F Palmer. London, Longman. 1835, vol. 2, p. 417.

27 Hunter J. *A Treatise on the Venereal Disease.* London, 13 Castle Street. 1786, p. 109.

28 Hunter J. *Essays and Observations on Natural History, Anatomy, Physiology, Psychology and Geology.* ed. R Owen. London, John Van Voorst. 1861, vol. 1, p. 255.

29 Hunter J. A treatise on venereal disease in *The Works of John Hunter*, ed. J F Palmer. London, Longman. 1835, vol. 2, p. 453.

30 Hunter J. Croonian lectures on muscular motion in *The Works of John Hunter*, ed. J F Palmer. London, Longman. 1837, vol. 4, p. 221.

31 Hunter J. Lectures on the principles of surgery in *The Works of John Hunter*, ed. J F Palmer. London, Longman. 1835, vol. 1, p. 244.

32 Hunter J. A treatise on venereal disease in *The Works of John Hunter*, ed. J F Palmer. London, Longman. 1835, vol. 2, pp. 319–321.

33 Ibid. pp. 328–336.

34 Ibid. pp. 372–375.

35 Ibid. pp. 375–380.

36 Ibid. p. 386.

37 Ibid. p. 387.

38 Ibid. p. 150.

39 Ibid. p. 386.
40 Ibid. p. 164.
41 Hunter J. Lectures on the principles of surgery in *The Works of John Hunter*, ed. J F Palmer. London, Longman. 1835, vol. 1, pp. 288, 289.
42 Hunter J. A treatise on venereal disease in *The Works of John Hunter*, ed. J F Palmer. London, Longman. 1835, vol. 2, p. 99.
43 Hunter J. On absorption by veins in *The Works of John Hunter*, ed. J F Palmer. London, Longman. 1837, vol. 4, pp. 303–306.
44 Hunter W. Anatomical lectures: on the method of making preparations. *London MS.* (Royal College of Surgeons of England Library). Lecture 71st. 1763, pp. 591–609.
45 Foot J. *The Life on John Hunter*. London, T Becket. 1794.
46 Adams J. *Memoirs of the Life and Doctrines of the late John Hunter, Esq.* London, J Callow and J Hunter. 1817.
47 Butler F H. John Hunter. *Encyclopaedia Britannica*. Edinburgh, Adam and Charles Black. 9th edn. 1881, vol. 12, pp. 385–391.
48 Paget S. *John Hunter*. London, T Fisher Unwin. 1897.
49 Peachey G C. *A Memoir of William and John Hunter*. Plymouth, William Brendon and Son. 1924.
50 Foot J. *Observations upon the New Opinions of John Hunter on the Venereal Disease*. London, T Becket. 1786, pt. 3, pp. 124–135.
51 Dixon C W. *Smallpox*. London, Churchill. 1962, p. 227.
52 Hunter J. A treatise on venereal disease in *The Works of John Hunter*, ed. J F Palmer. London, Longman. 1835, vol. 2, p. 133.
53 Blake J B. *Benjamin Waterhouse and the Introduction of Vaccination*. Philadelphia, University of Pennsylvania Press. 1957, pp. 46, 47.
54 Ashton J. *Social England under the Regency*. London, Ward and Downey. 1890.
55 Brain Sir Russell (Lord). The neurology of John Hunter's last illness. *British Medical Journal*. 1952, vol. 2, pp. 1371–1373.

CHAPTER 6

PUBLICATIONS

It is important to distinguish between John Hunter's own publications and those edited and published by others after his death. Hunter wrote:

> . . . I may venture to say that those who are only able to publish / the works of others, are themselves not fit to publish anything in that way; for they never can be a Judge of what should be taken away or what should be added; for if they were perfectly master of the subject, then they certainly could make a better book upon the Subject themselves.
>
> It is much easier for a man of real knowledge to make a new work than to mend an old one; it is clear they can only in real knowledge be Coblers, and indeed there are few works that deserve a New edition when they require additions, except by their Original Author.[1]

Obviously the most reliable statements made by Hunter occur in those of his manuscripts in his own handwriting or in those written at his dictation by his amanuenses. Next in reliability would be those of his writings published during his lifetime, but even with these publications subsequent editions have perpetrated errors which fully endorse Hunter's opinion that new editions should be written by their original author. Babington states in his preface to the Treatise on Venereal Disease in Palmer's Works (1835) – 'The third edition [of the Treatise] was published [in 1794] after his death by Sir Everard Home, who has in general followed the text of the first edition, and has introduced some passages which were never written by John Hunter.'[2]

Those writings reprinted or edited after John Hunter's death cannot be regarded as being completely free from error or misrepresentation. The Surgical Lectures published in Palmer's *Works of John Hunter* were not written by Hunter and there are other editions of Hunter's lectures still extant which were written by various of his pupils and copied by others. This is an important consideration in relation to some statements allegedly made by John Hunter, the most significant being those concerning his supposed syphilitic infection (p. 44).

Similar reservations may be made concerning other parts of Palmer's edited *Works of John Hunter*. William Clift was critical of several items in this publication. He wrote to Palmer, who had sent him a copy of the book in 1837 – '. . . I should have been happy to have given more than an opinion on some of the doubtful points and corrected some of the dates and some of the statements which I am convinced are as unfounded in truth as that they are unphilosophical and, consequently un-Hunterian . . .' He criticised the 'worn-out recollections when none such appear in any of Mr. Hunter's writings . . .' and he disagreed completely with Ottley's account of an occasion when, on arriving home to find Mrs. Hunter giving a party, Hunter was alleged to have dismissed the guests angrily. Clift said – 'Nor could I believe him capable of the gross rudeness palmed upon him respecting Mrs. Hunter's party – I do not believe it – because Mrs. Hunter's Wednesday evening parties never interfered or could interfere with his studies; he always went upstairs for a short time to shake their mutual friends by the hand and returned to me and to his labour of thought without further interruption for the rest of the evening and great part of the night.'[3]

Another type of misquotation has occurred as the result of confusing Palmer's extensive additional notes with Hunter's text in his edition of *The Works*. For example, in relation to arteries, the statement that '. . . in general when large vessels are obliterated their office is vicariously performed by the enlargement of others which had previously existed' is often attributed to Hunter but, although it may express Hunter's opinion correctly, it in fact appears in a footnote written by Palmer.[4]

JOHN HUNTER'S OWN PUBLICATIONS

John Hunter published three books during his lifetime, *viz.* *Treatise on the Natural History of the Human Teeth* (Part 1 in 1771; Part 2 in 1778); *A Treatise on the Venereal Disease* (1786); and *Observations on Certain Parts of the Animal Oeconomy* (1786), a second edition of which was published in 1792. In addition, Hunter had prepared the manuscripts of three more books which were published posthumously, *viz. A Treatise on the Blood, Inflammation and Gun-shot Wounds* (1794); *Observations and Reflections on Geology* (1859); and *Memoranda on Vegetation* (1860).

Hunter presented a large number of original papers on a great variety of subjects to the Royal Society which were published in their Philosophical Transactions. Most of these papers were subsequently included in *Observations on Certain Parts of the Animal Oeconomy*. Some of Hunter's papers were published elsewhere, chiefly in the *Transactions of the Society for Improvement in Medical and Chirurgical Knowledge*. A few of his manuscripts were presented on his behalf by Everard Home during Hunter's lifetime and also posthumously.

POSTHUMOUS PUBLICATIONS EDITED BY OTHERS

In 1835 James F. Palmer edited and published *The Works of John Hunter* in four volumes.* This contained the three books published in John Hunter's lifetime together with the Treatise on the Blood, Inflammation and Gun-shot Wounds. The Animal Oeconomy section in the Works was edited by Richard Owen and he included some previously unpublished papers by Hunter. In addition, the Works included John Hunter's Lectures on the Principles of Surgery which were prepared from notes taken by Mr. Nathaniel Rumsey of Chesham in 1786 and 1787.[5]

In 1861 Richard Owen edited some of Hunter's previously unpublished notes and manuscripts in *Essays and Observations on Natural History, Anatomy, Physiology, Psychology and Geology*.

CLASSIFICATION OF JOHN HUNTER'S WORK

John Hunter's field of interest was boundless and covered the whole of the natural sciences. It is therefore difficult to classify his work since his contributions to anatomy, physiology and other subjects were often expressed in the same article. An excellent example of this is to be seen in a profound geological opinion he has inserted as a footnote in *General Principles of the Blood* – 'The distribution of water from the sea is similar to the arterial system, and the rivers returning to it have an analogy to the veins; . . . The

---

* Vol. 3 of *The Works* was re-issued and vol. 4 was published in 1837.

waters are continually carrying away the land from one situation, and depositing it in another, taking down continents, and leaving the ocean in their place; whilst at the same time they are raising continents out of the sea . . ."[6] Thus a classification of John Hunter's writings and lectures can only be broad and imperfect. It is usually made on a chronological system[7] but one based on the main interest of each subject may be of more practical value and is presented below.

Digestive system

Treatise on the natural history of the human teeth	1771 1778 1835	Part One Part Two *Works*. Palmer. Vol. 2.
Some observations on digestion	1786 1837	*Animal Oeconomy* *Works*. Palmer. Vol. 4. pp. 81–116
On the digestion of the stomach after death	1772 1786 1837	*Phil. Trans*. 62, 447 *Animal Oeconomy* *Works*. Palmer. Vol. 4. pp. 116–121
Observations on the Gillaroo trout, commonly called in Ireland the Gizzard trout	1774 1786 1837	*Phil. Trans*. 64, 310 *Animal Oeconomy* *Works*. Palmer. Vol. 4. pp. 126–130
Anatomy of the camel's stomach by Mr. Hunter	1794	Included in *Natural History of Aleppo* by Alexander Russell, 2nd Edition. Vol. 2. p. 419
A case of paralysis of the muscles of deglutition cured by an artificial mode of conveying food and medicines into the stomach	1790 1835. 1837	*Trans. Soc. Improv. med. chir. Knowl*. 1793. Vol. 1. p. 182 *Works*. Palmer. Vol. 3. pp. 622–624

On introsusception	1789	*Trans. Soc. Improv. med. chir. Knowl.* 1793. Vol. 1. p. 103.
	1835.1837	*Works.* Palmer. Vol. 3. pp. 587–593

Reproductive system

Observations on the State of the Testis in the Foetus, and on the Hernia Congenita	1762	*Medical Commentaries* by Dr. William Hunter. Part I. p. 75
	1786	*Animal Oeconomy*
	1837	*Works.* Palmer. Vol. 4. pp. 1–15 [Included in *A description of the situation of the testis etc.*]
A description of the situation of the testis in the foetus, with its descent into the scrotum	1786 1837	*Animal Oeconomy* *Works.* Palmer. Vol. 4. pp. 1–19
Observations on the glands situated between the rectum and bladder, called vesiculae seminales	1786 1837	*Animal Oeconomy* *Works.* Palmer. Vol. 4. pp. 20–33
On the structure of the placenta	1786 1837	*Animal Oeconomy* *Works.* Palmer. Vol. 4. pp. 60–73
An experiment to determine the effect of extirpating one ovarium upon the number of young produced	1787 1792 1837	*Phil. Trans.* 77, 233 *Animal Oeconomy*, 2nd Ed. *Works.* Palmer. Vol. 4. pp. 50–54

On a secretion in the crop of breeding pigeons for the nourishment of their young	1786 1837	*Animal Oeconomy* *Works*. Palmer. Vol. 4. pp. 122–125
An account of the free-martin	1779 1786 1837	*Phil. Trans.* 69, 279 *Animal Oeconomy* *Works*. Palmer. Vol. 4. pp. 34–43
An account of an extraordinary pheasant	1780 1786 1837	*Phil. Trans.* 70, 527 *Animal Oeconomy* *Works*. Palmer. Vol. 4. pp. 44–49
Observations tending to show that the wolf, jackal, and dog are all of the same species	1787 1792 1837	*Phil. Trans.* 77, 253 *Animal Oeconomy*, 2nd Ed. *Works*. Palmer. Vol. 4. pp. 319–330
Supplement to the paper on the wolf, jackal and dog	1789 1792 1837	*Phil. Trans.* 79, 160 *Animal Oeconomy*, 2nd Ed. *Works*. Palmer. Vol. 4. pp. 319–330
Account of a woman who had the smallpox during pregnancy, and who seemed to have communicated the same disease to the foetus	1780 1837	*Phil. Trans.* 70, 128 *Works*. Palmer. Vol. 4. pp. 74–80
The case of a young woman who poisoned herself in the first month of pregnancy, by Thomas Ogle; to which is added an account of the appearances after death, by the late J. Hunter	1794 1837	*Trans. Soc. Improv. med. chir. Knowl.* Vol. 2. p. 63 *Works*. Palmer. Vol. 4. pp. 55–59

Circulatory system

An account of	1789	*Trans. Soc. Improv.*
Mr. Hunter's method		*med. chir.*
of performing the		*Knowl.* 1793. Vol. 1.
operation for the cure		p. 138. 1800, Vol. 2
of popliteal aneurism,		p. 235
by Everard Home,	1835.1837	*Works.* Palmer. Vol. 3.
Esq., from materials		pp. 594–621
furnished by		
Mr. Hunter		
Observations on the	1784	*Trans. Soc. Improv.*
inflammation of the		*med. chir.*
internal coats of veins		*Knowl.* 1793. Vol. 1.
		p. 18
	1835.1837	*Works.* Palmer. Vol. 3.
		pp. 581–586
On absorption by veins	1762	*Medical Commentaries*
		by Dr. William
		Hunter. Part I. p. 42
	1837	*Works.* Palmer. Vol. 4.
		pp. 299–314

Nervous system and special senses

A description of the	1786	*Animal Oeconomy*
nerves which supply the	1837	*Works.* Palmer. Vol. 4.
organ of smelling		pp. 187–192
A description of some	1786	*Animal Oeconomy*
branches of the fifth	1837	*Works.* Palmer. Vol. 4.
pair of nerves		pp. 193–194
On the colour of the	1786	*Animal Oeconomy*
pigmentum of the eye in	1837	*Works.* Palmer. Vol. 4.
different animals		pp. 277–285
Some facts relative to the	1793	*Phil. Trans.* 84, 21
late Mr. J. Hunter's	1837	*Works.* Palmer. Vol. 4.
preparation for the		pp. 286–291
Croonian lecture, by		
E. Home, Esq.		

The use of the oblique muscles	1786 1837	*Animal Oeconomy* *Works*. Palmer. Vol. 4. pp. 274–276
An account of the organ of hearing in fishes	1782 1786 1837	*Phil. Trans.* 72, 379 *Animal Oeconomy* *Works*. Palmer. Vol. 4. pp. 292–298
Anatomical observations on the torpedo	1773 1837	*Phil. Trans.* 63, 481 *Works*. Palmer. Vol. 4. pp. 409–413
An account of the Gymnotus electricus	1775 1837	*Phil. Trans.* 65, 395 *Works*. Palmer. Vol. 4. pp. 414–421

Musculoskeletal system

Croonian lectures on muscular motion [six lectures]	1776.1782 1837	Not printed *Works*. Palmer. Vol. 4. pp. 195–273
Experiments and observations on the growth of bones, from the papers of the late Mr. Hunter, by Everard Home, F.R.S.	1798 1837	*Trans. Soc. Improv. med. chir. Knowl.* Vol. 2. p. 277 *Works*. Palmer. Vol. 4. pp. 315–318

Metabolism

Experiments and observations on animals and vegetables with respect to the power of producing heat	1775 1786 1837	*Phil. Trans.* 65, 446 *Animal Oeconomy* *Works*. Palmer. Vol. 4. pp. 131–155 .
On the heat of animals and vegetables	1777 1786 1837	*Phil. Trans.* 68, 7 *Animal Oeconomy* *Works*. Palmer. Vol. 4. pp. 131–155 [Included in above publication]

| Experiments and observations on vegetables with respect to the power of producing heat | 1775 1837 | *Phil. Trans.* 65, 450 *Works.* Palmer. Vol. 4. pp. 156-164 |

Comparative anatomy

Invertebrates

| Observations on bees | 1792 1837 | *Phil. Trans.* 82, 128 *Works.* Palmer. Vol. 4. pp. 422-466 |
| Description of a new marine animal, in a letter from Mr. Everard Home to J. Hunter, containing anatomical remarks upon the same [Serpula gigantea] | 1785 1837 | *Phil. Trans.* 75, 333 *Works.* Palmer. Vol. 4. pp. 467-469 |

Amphibians

| An account of an amphibious bipes, by John Ellis, with supplement by John Hunter [Siren lacertina] | 1766 1837 | *Phil. Trans.* 56, 189 *Works.* Palmer. Vol. 4. pp. 394-397 |

Birds

| An account of certain receptacles of air in birds, which communicate with the lungs and Eustachian tube | 1774 1786 1837 | *Phil. Trans.* 64, 205 *Animal Oeconomy* *Works.* Palmer. Vol. 4. pp. 176-186 |

Mammals

| Observations on the structure and oeconomy of whales | 1787 1837 | *Phil. Trans.* 77, 371 *Works.* Palmer. Vol. 4. pp. 331-392 |

General observations on the mode of collecting and sending home animals, and on the nomenclature and classification of animals. Description of the kangaroo [and other Australian animals]	1790 1837	Included in *Journal of a Voyage to New South Wales* by John White, Esq. *Works*. Palmer. Vol. 4. pp. 481–493
Notes on the anatomy of the jerboa by Mr. Hunter [Dipus sagitta]	1794 1837	Included in *Natural History of Aleppo* by Alexander Russell, 2nd Ed. Vol. 2. p. 419 *Works*. Palmer. Vol. 4. p. 393

Surgery and clinical subjects

Treatise on the Blood, Inflammation and Gun-shot Wounds	1794 1835.1837	*Works*. Palmer. Vol. 3.
Treatise on the Venereal Disease	1786 1835	*Works*. Palmer. Vol. 2.
Lectures on the Principles of Surgery	1835	*Works*. Palmer. Vol. 1.
Some observations on the loose cartilages found in joints, and most commonly met with in that of the knee, by Everard Home, Esq., from materials furnished by Mr. Hunter	1790 1835.1837	*Trans. Soc. Improv. med. chir.* *Knowl.* 1793. Vol. 1. p. 229 *Works*. Palmer. Vol. 3. pp. 625–630
Proposals for the recovery of persons apparently drowned	1776 1786 1837	*Phil. Trans.* 66, 412 *Animal Oeconomy* *Works*. Palmer. Vol. 4. pp. 165–175

| Observations on certain horny excrescences of the human body, by Everard Home, F.R.S., from materials furnished by Mr. Hunter | 1791 1835.1837 | *Phil. Trans.* 81, 95 *Works.* Palmer. Vol. 3. pp. 631–638 |

Geology and palaeontology

Observations and Reflections on Geology	1859	
Observations on the fossil bones presented to the Royal Society by the Margrave of Anspach, by the late Mr. J. Hunter	1794 1837	*Phil. Trans.* 84, 407 *Works.* Palmer. Vol. 4. pp. 470–480
Memoranda on Vegetation	1860	

Natural history in general

| Essays and Observations on Natural History, Anatomy, Physiology, Psychology and Geology. Ed. Richard Owen. 2 vols. | 1861 | |

REFERENCES

1 Hunter J. *MS Catalogue of the Museum 1800 Gallery.* Library, Royal College of Surgeons of England. p. 40.

2 Babington G G. Preface, a treatise on venereal disease in *The Works of John Hunter*, ed. J F Palmer. London, Longman. 1835, vol. 2, p. 124.

3 Dobson J. *John Hunter.* Edinburgh and London, Livingstone. 1969, p. 109.

4 Hunter J. A treatise on the blood, inflammation and gun-shot wounds in *The Works of John Hunter*, ed. J F Palmer. London, Longman. 1837, vol. 3, p. 531.

5 Paget S. *John Hunter.* London, T Fisher Unwin. 1897, p. 110.

6 Hunter J. A treatise on the blood, inflammation and gun-shot wounds in *The Works of John Hunter*, ed. J F Palmer. London, Longman. 1837, vol. 3, p. 15.

7 LeFanu W R. *John Hunter: A List of His Books.* London. Royal College of Surgeons of England. 1946.

CHAPTER 7

MUSEUM

THE Hunterian Museum is 'one of the most remarkable monuments that any man has ever raised to perpetuate his memory . . . it is John Hunter's great unwritten book.'[1]

John Hunter started his collection of specimens while working at William Hunter's Anatomy School and his first catalogue was prepared after his return from Army service in 1763.[2] The expansion of this collection was one of his main occupations throughout the remaining thirty years of his lifetime and when he died in 1793 the museum contained more than 13,000 specimens.

Prior to Hunter's time, museums of natural history were mostly collections of curiosities exhibited without any underlying biological principle. In those museums which were arranged systematically, classification was based on a rigid static concept that devolved from the generally accepted theory of the immutability of species supported by Linnaeus and Cuvier. Hunter set up his museum as a dynamic concept illustrating function and adaptation throughout the whole of animate nature. It was devised 'to demonstrate, in terms of anatomical preparations, how function determined structure, how a like physiological goal might be attained by diverse morphological arrangements and how the morphological (expressive of Nature's own experimentation with living organs and tissues) provided the key to understanding of function and behaviour.' (Cave).[3]

Hunter arranged the specimens in three main groups, *viz.* to demonstrate structures developed for the survival of the individual, those for the preservation of the race, and a third group demonstrating a great variety of pathological conditions. In addition there was a large collection of animal and vegetable fossils which numbered nearly 3000 at the time of Hunter's death.[4] In the majority the site of origin was noted and in many cases the fossil specimen was demonstrated with a similar part of the recent form to which it was most akin.[5]

The demonstrations were arranged under the various body systems and in each system the coordinating affinity was one of function. The section on *organs for locomotion* demonstrates the great variety of adaptations which serve this function, e.g. the foot pads serving rapid locomotion in the horse, ostrich, camel and dog; the numerous mechanisms for grasping and climbing such as plant tendrils, the prehensile tail of monkeys, opposable digits of mammals and the sucking disc of fish; and the varieties of anatomical design serving aerial locomotion in the bird, bat and flying lemur.

The *organs of motion* are demonstrated by specimens of muscle and bone which again illustrate elegantly the principle of adaptation of function and structure. Hunter said of muscles – 'fibres are differently arranged according to the mechanical advantage required, so that the smallest quantity of contraction shall produce the greatest effect.'[6]

The specimen of an arm with a fracture of the humerus united with considerable shortening shows an adaptive shortening of the associated biceps muscle. The classic specimen of the neck of the femur demonstrating its internal architecture shows 'the columnar cancelli arranged in decussating curves, like the arches in Gothic architecture, where they transfer the weight sustained by the head and neck of the bone upon the strong and compact shaft' (Owen).[7]

The section on *organs of digestion* demonstrates the great variety of adaptations for the digestion of different types of food throughout the alimentary canal, arranged from the most simple to the most complex. The numerous mechanisms for the capture of food are demonstrated in the series on the mouth, the tongue and beaks. A splendid example of adaptation is shown in the specimen of a woodpecker. The specimens of stomach illustrate a great variety of mechanisms serving the purpose of digestion. The grinding function of the stomach in fish is demonstrated in the Mullet. The stomach of a seagull which Hunter had fed for one year on grain shows a greatly increased muscle layer – one of the best demonstrations of Hunter's concept of the museum, the interdependence of structure and function.

The *nervous system* is demonstrated in a large series of dissections extending from the simplest invertebrates up to the mammals. The specimens indeed illustrate an evolutionary series commencing with the simple nerve chain of the earthworm and passing up through the more highly organised brain and spinal cord of the fish, amphibia, reptiles, birds and mammals.

A section on *regeneration* illustrates the power of some animals to regenerate organs. This is demonstrated by the chelae of lobsters and by the tails of lizards, which, Hunter wrote 'are so tender as to be easily pulled off by the strength of the animal when held by the tail; but this tenderness is only confined to the part of the tail beyond the bed of the penis, for there the tail is very strong. The reason why the tail should be so brittle, is perhaps to allow the animal to make its escape when caught by the tail, for it is generally broken in that way.'[8]

The tail vertebrae of the lizard are cleft transversely at which area the tail can be detached from the rest of the body. This faculty (autotomy) enables it to escape as suggested by Hunter.[9]

STRUCTURES FOR THE PRESERVATION OF THE RACE

'This section remains much as it was in Hunter's lifetime and as a demonstration of Hunter's original plan or arrangement it is the most interesting and valuable section of the museum. It contains several preparations still in their original jars, with the pig's bladder and lead foil luting probably just as Hunter left them.'[10]

The various stages in the metamorphosis of insects are demonstrated in moths and bees. Reproductive stages in the eel, pipe fish and dogfish are demonstrated. The development of the human embryo is shown in specimens ranging from the age of four weeks to the full term fetus. A good example of Hunter's insistence on the priority of function in his museum demonstrations is apparent in the specimens of toad and opossum associated because of their similar mode of carrying their young on their backs. There is a remarkable specimen of a crocodile emerging from its egg.

PATHOLOGY SERIES

John Hunter is rightly regarded as the founder of surgical pathology and the museum demonstrates some of the specimens on which he made his careful observations and experiments. The first group of preparations illustrates general principles in pathology including inflammation, absorption, repair and transplantation. The results of several successful grafting experiments are demonstrated – an autograft, the spur of a cock transplanted into its comb; a homograft, the testis of a cock grafted into the peritoneum of a hen; and a heterograft, a human tooth grafted into a cock's comb.

The second group of pathological specimens demonstrates various specific diseases and diseases of individual organs and tissues. The former include tuberculosis, syphilis, smallpox and cancer while the latter illustrate diseases of bone and of the teeth and popliteal aneurysm. The section on bone disease is one of the best examples of Hunter's profound appreciation of the basic elements in the aetiology of disease – the specimens are arranged to demonstrate deformities, fractures with non-union and false joints, and various stages of osteomyelitis and sequestration of bone. The condition of acromegaly is demonstrated by the skeleton of Charles Byrne, the Irish Giant, a specimen that was acquired by John Hunter at considerable expense.[11] There are two specimens of popliteal aneurysm on which Hunter had performed his high ligation operation, in one case fifty years previously.

John Hunter's museum was built up by hard work and at considerable expense. Two of the most expensive items must have been the alcohol and jars for the 'wet' specimens of which there were more than 5000 of the total collection of over 13,000 specimens in the collection at his death. 'The duty on alcohol in the early 18th century rose to 20 shillings a gallon; specimen jars had to be made of flint glass which likewise was subject to duty, nearly 10 shillings a hundredweight in this period.'[2]

After Hunter's death in 1793 the museum collection was offered to the British government for purchase, in compliance with Hunter's instructions in his will which stated: 'I also give to the said Matthew Baillie and Everard Home all my collection of natural history, and the cases, and other things belonging thereto, or used therewith, upon trust that they offer the same to sale in one entire lot to the Government of Great Britain.'[12] However, Parliament, with Pitt as prime minister, was unable to supply the funds and the collection remained at Hunter's house in Leicester Square under the sole care of William Clift. The purchase was eventually made as the result of the determined efforts of Lord Auckland (William Eden) who had been on friendly terms with John Hunter for many years, and on June 13, 1799 Parliament voted £15,000 for the purchase of the Hunterian collection. The custody of the collection was offered to the Company of Surgeons under the guardianship of a board of sixteen trustees and on December 23, 1799 the Court of Assistants voted unanimously to accept the collection. It was moved from Castle Street to the College in Lincoln's Inn Fields in 1806.

The request to Parliament for the custodianship of the Hunterian Collection made by the Company of Surgeons, subsequently the Royal College of Surgeons of England, was first made in April 1799 and is recorded in the minutes:[13]

> At a Special Court of Assistants summoned by order of The Master and holden at the Company's House in Lincoln's Inn Fields on the 26th day of April 1799
> Present
>   Messieurs Earle Hawkins Long Warner Lucas Howard S Cooper Chandler Blicke Forster Birch Howard J Blizard Cline Keats [Keate] . . . . the Court . . . . unanimously came to the following Resolutions viz.
>   . . . . That if Parliament shall think proper to purchase this valuable Collection for the benefit of the Public and Honour this Corporation by Entrusting it to their Care This Court will be highly gratified in receiving the same and will use their utmost endeavours to render it conducive to the Advancement of Anatomical and Surgical Science.

Great credit is due to the members of the Court of Assistants for this unanimous decision. It was a bold step because custodianship of the collection would involve the Company in an enormous expense for the housing and preservation of the specimens for many years ahead. In the event the costs for maintaining and augmenting the collection up to August 1833 were not less than £36,000. The College of Physicians had already refused the offer to receive the collection since it would have been too expensive to house without an extra grant.[14]

As a result of this decision by the Company of Surgeons it was essential to try and establish a more certain means of economic stability. The Company therefore applied for a new Charter as the Royal College of Surgeons, with a licence for the granting of diplomas by examination. The new Charter was obtained in March 1800. In the first two years applications for diplomas were less than 300, but they increased to 770 in 1833 when the average receipts to the College from this source alone were £11,116 per annum.

Thus the acquisition of the Hunterian Collection and the new Charter brought the College valuable public recognition, an improved professional status and a sound economic position. The Museum rapidly established an international reputation and the College benefited from its association with the museum. Among Clift's manuscripts is a note, written in 1833, to the effect that, since 1800, thirty-two thousand, two hundred and eight visitors had been conducted round the Museum.[15]

The visitors included the Prince Regent, the Grand Duchess of Oldenburgh, General Wiebel, Physician to the King of Prussia, Sir James Wylie, Surgeon to the Emperor of Russia, Dr. Hamel of St. Petersburg, the Archdukes John and Lewis of Austria, the Duke of Sussex, the Grand Duke Nicholas of Russia, Dr. Pockels, Chief Surgeon to the Brunswick Troops, Dr. Savenko of the Academy of St. Petersburg, the Archduke Maximilian of Austria, the Archbishop of York, the Earl and Countess Spencer, the Duke of Northumberland, Lord Prudhoe, the Bishop of Ely, the Most Reverend Gregorio Petro Giarve, Syrian Bishop of Jerusalem, Lord George Seymour, Lord Dunsany, Prince Christian of Denmark, Count Orloff and Countess Meerfeldt,[16] as well as Prince Louis Napoleon, Lord Walpole, the Rajah Rammohum Roy and Clot Bey, Surgeon to Ibrahim Pasha.[17]

Eminent foreign scientists who visited the Museum included Professor Retzius of Stockholm and Professor Jacobson of Copenhagen[17] and Camper, Poli, Scarpa and Blumenbach,[18] as well as Du Fresne, Parmentier, Abbé Gregoire, Jean Baptiste Huzard, Dr. Gärtner, Dr. Stöll, Professor Aldini, Dr. Frank and Cuvier who made several visits to the Museum.[19]

. Charles Darwin contributed a number of the specimens collected on The Beagle to the Museum. He wrote:

> I have disposed of the most important part of my collections, by giving all the fossil bones to the College of Surgeons; casts of them will be distributed, and descriptions published. They are curious and valuable: one head belonged to some gnawing animal, but of the size of a hippopotamus. Another, to an ant-eater of the size of a horse.[20]

Darwin visited the Hunterian Museum on Tuesday, January 22nd, 1839, as described by Asa Gray* – 'This morning we

---

* Asa Gray (1810–1888) was professor of natural history at Harvard and became the chief protagonist of Darwinism in America.

breakfasted with Richard Taylor in the city and went afterwards to the College of Surgeons, by appointment Sir Wm. Hooker had made, to see Prof. Owen and the fine museum of the College under his charge (John Hunter's originally); a magnificent collection it is, in the finest possible order, and the arrangement and plan of the rooms is far, very far, prettier and better and prettier than any I have seen. I shall make some memoranda about it. We there met Mr. Darwin, the naturalist who accompanied Captain Fitz-Roy in the Beagle . . . .'[21]

The acquisition of custodianship of the Hunterian Collection was one of the most important landmarks in the history of the Royal College of Surgeons of England because, during the early years of its development, the College gained far more credit, both at home and abroad, from the excellence of the Museum than from the activities of the surgeons. Indeed, the surgeons and their management of the College were under constant criticism by a large section of the medical profession and also by the public, as for example in a typical editorial from the Lancet in 1824:

> The COLLEGE of SURGEONS constituted as it is at present, is not likely to pass any measure calculated to benefit the profession[22] . . . . Who hold the reins of government at the College we know not; but this we know, that they are taking the most decided steps to bring the whole of the practitioners of surgery into the utmost contempt . . . . surgeons are . . . . . bringing themselves into the most humiliating and contemptuous dilemma by quietly submitting to the iniquitous imbecile and injurious laws enacted by such men as Sir *Fretful* BLIZARD, *Cantwell* CHEVALIER, and *Mesdames* FORSTER and LYNN.[23]

The Examiners were the subject of virulent criticism:

> As a scientific body, we do not believe that a more contemptible one exists than the Court of Examiners. Some of them have been politely declared incompetent to fulfil their duties as hospital surgeons, and all have proved themselves unworthy of the trust which is reposed in them.[24]

The aims of the College were summarised in an editorial:

> 'To increase expence, to diminish competition, and thus to retard the progress of science in order to put money into the pockets of the Aristocracy of the College, are the only effects of many, perhaps of most of the bye-laws of the College.[25]

Thus the reputation of the College, in its early formative years, was built up on the solid foundation of the Hunterian Museum, a foundation established securely by William Clift and his son-in-law Sir Richard Owen.[26,27] The great debt owed to these two men by the College, and indeed by British surgery, has probably never been fully appreciated. Through them, the results of John Hunter's prodigious labours were organised to become the most important factor in the early years of establishment of the Royal College of Surgeons of England.

REFERENCES

1 Jones F Wood. John Hunter's unwritten book. *Lancet.* 1951, vol. 2, pp. 778–780.

2 Dobson J. The place of John Hunter's museum. *Annals of the Royal College of Surgeons of England.* 1963, vol. 33, pp. 32–40.

3 Cave A J E. A constellation of conservators. *Annals of the Royal College of Surgeons of England.* 1980, vol. 62, pp. 66–70.

4 Owen R. in Hunter's *Essays and Observations on Natural History, Anatomy, Physiology, Psychology and Geology,* ed. R Owen. London, John Van Voorst. 1861, vol. 1, p. 295.

5 Jones F Wood. John Hunter as a geologist. *Annals of the Royal College of Surgeons of England.* 1953, vol. 12, pp. 219–245.

6 Editorial. *Hunterian Museum Guide.* Royal College of Surgeons of England, ed. E Allen. 1974, p. 4.

7 Owen R. Descriptive catalogue of the physiological series in the Hunterian Museum of the Royal College of Surgeons of England. Part 2. Specimen no. 207, pp. 198, 199.

8 Hunter J. *Essays and Observations on Natural History, Anatomy, Physiology, Psychology and Geology,* ed. R Owen. London, John Van Voorst. 1861, vol. 2, p. 364.

9 de Beer G R. *Vertebrate Zoology.* London, Sidgwick and Jackson. 1966, p. 281.

10 Editorial. *Hunterian Museum Guide.* Royal College of Surgeons of England, ed. E Allen. 1974, p. 30.

11 Dobson J. *John Hunter.* Edinburgh and London, Livingstone. 1969, pp. 262–264.

12 Dobson J. *William Clift.* London, Heinemann. 1954, p. 97.

13 Royal College of Surgeons of England. *Minute Book. Court of Assistants of Company of Surgeons.* 1799.

14 Ottley D. Life of John Hunter in *The Works of John Hunter,* ed. J F Palmer. London, Longman. 1835, vol. 1, p. 142.

15 Dobson J. *William Clift.* London, Heinemann. 1954, p. 94.

16 Ibid. pp. 38–41.

17 Ibid. p. 94.

18 Owen R. Preface, *The Works of John Hunter,* ed. J F Palmer. London, Longman. 1837, vol. 4, p. xxxviii.

19 Ottley D. Life of John Hunter in *The Works of John Hunter,* ed. J F Palmer. London, Longman. 1835, vol. 1, p. 146.

20 Keith Sir Arthur. Memorable visits of Charles Darwin to the Museum of the

Royal College of Surgeons. *Annals of the Royal College of Surgeons of England.* 1952, vol. 11. p. 362.

21 Gray A. *Letters of Asa Gray.* 1893, vol. 1, p. 117. Quoted by A Keith in *Annals of the Royal College of Surgeons of England.* 1952, vol. 11, p. 362.

22 *Lancet.* 1824, vol. 3–4, p. 205.

23 Ibid. p. 116.

24 Ibid. p. 206.

25 Ibid. p. 270.

26 Rudolf C R. Hunteriana Part 4. *Hunterian Society Transactions* 1957–58, vol. 16, pp. 141–167.

27 Dobson J. The Conservators of the Hunterian Museum. II Richard Owen. *Annals of the Royal College of Surgeons of England.* 1962, vol. 30, pp. 117–224.

ADDITIONAL BIBLIOGRAPHY

Brock Sir Russell (Lord). Museum, research and the inspiration of Hunter. Hunterian Oration 1961. *Annals of the Royal College of Surgeons of England.* 1961, vol. 29, pp. 1–27.

Dobson J. Curiosities of natural history as illustrated in John Hunter's museum. *Annals of the Royal College of Surgeons of England.* 1970, vol. 47, pp. 233–242.

Dobson J. John Hunter's microscope slides. *Annals of the Royal College of Surgeons of England.* 1961, vol. 28, pp. 175–188.

Dobson J. The architectural history of the Hunterian Museum. *Annals of the Royal College of Surgeons of England.* 1961, vol. 29, pp. 113–126.

Fleurent C H. Early visitors to the Museum of the Royal College of Surgeons of England. *Annals of the Royal College of Surgeons of England.* 1958, vol. 23, pp. 47–52.

Jones F Wood. John Hunter and his museum. *Annals of the Royal College of Surgeons of England.* 1949, vol. 4, pp. 337–341.

Turner G Grey. *The Hunterian Museum Yesterday and Tomorrow.* Hunterian Oration 1945. London, Cassell and *Lancet.* 1945, vol. 1, pp. 359–363.

Walker D Greer. John Hunter – order out of variety. *Annals of the Royal College of Surgeons of England.* 1961, vol. 28, pp. 238–251.

Wall Cecil. *The History of the Surgeons' Company 1745–1800.* London, Hutchinson. 1937.

CHAPTER 8

INFLAMMATION

JOHN Hunter recognised the process of inflammation as one of the most important phenomena in pathology. He said – 'The operation in the body called inflammation is one of the most common and most extensive in its effects . . . producing abscesses, fistulas, diseased bones, etc., and in many diseases is the first step towards a cure; so that it becomes a first principle in surgery.'[1]

Prior to Hunter's time, it was generally believed that the most favourable outcome of inflammation was the development of 'laudable pus'. This concept arose principally from the theory that all diseases were the result of a disturbance of the 'humours' of the body. Hunter recognised that suppuration is not an inevitable or advantageous result of inflammation but that it represented a failure in the onset of resolution. He said – 'The cure of inflammation is resolution, . . .'[2] and '. . . it does not appear to me necessary that it should suppurate, for suppuration is only a consequence of the inflammation, . . .'[3]

Hunter described three main types of inflammatory reaction, viz. adhesive, suppurative and ulcerative inflammation. Adhesive inflammation caused adherence of contiguous parts with localisation of disease. Suppurative inflammation resulted in the formation of pus with generalised spread or abscess formation. In ulcerative inflammation there was loss of tissue due to the 'action of the absorbents' [lymphatics]. He used this simple classification as a basis of surgical pathology which he then applied to the explanation of many disease processes throughout the body, as in the following examples:

(a) *Injuries*

Perhaps the most important application of Hunter's basic pathology of inflammation was to the understanding of injuries. He recognised the essential difference in prognosis between closed and open injuries in relation to their liability to inflammation and classified injuries accordingly – 'The injuries of the first division, in which the parts do not communicate externally, seldom inflame, while those of the second commonly both inflame and suppurate.' Hunter went further and subdivided open injuries into those made with 'sharp-cutting instruments' and those with 'contusions producing death in the injured parts' – the 'clean' and 'dirty' wounds of modern traumatic surgery.[4]

Hunter's application of the principles of inflammation to the pathology of missile wounds was of fundamental significance. He criticised the contemporary opinion 'that gun-shot wounds have a something peculiar to them, and of course are different from all other wounds . . .'[5] While Hunter's conservative treatment of missile injuries has been the subject of considerable controversy (Chapter 15), there can be no doubt that his clear exposition of the underlying pathology of wounds is irrefutable. He said: 'Violence done to parts is one of the great causes of suppuration . . .'[6] and . . . 'gun-shot wounds being contused obliges most of them to suppurate, because in such cases there is more or less of a slough to be thrown off . . .'[7]

In discussing penetrating wounds of the abdomen, he said: '. . . although the ball has passed with such velocity as to produce a slough, yet that wound shall do well, for the adhesive inflammation will take place on the peritoneum all round the wound, which will exclude the general cavity from taking part in the inflammation . . .'[8]

In penetrating wounds of the chest, Hunter made the important observation of the favourable prognostic significance of previous pleural adhesions. He said: 'The lungs immediately collapse . . . when a wound is made into the chest . . . the cavity of the thorax . . . must be filled either with air or blood, or both, so that adhesion cannot readily take place: but it very often happens that the lungs have previously adhered, which will frequently be an advantage.'[9]

(b) *Transplantation*

Hunter explained transplantation of organs and tissues on the basis of adhesive inflammation. He said: 'By adhesive inflammation different parts of the body may be united to another by coming into contact; but the most extraordinary union is that of removing parts from one body and uniting them to another. Here is the testicle of a cock, separated from that animal, and put through a wound, made for that purpose, into the belly of a hen; . . . The hen was afterwards killed, and the testicle was found adhering to the intestines, . . . Here is another preparation, in which the spur of a cock has been inserted into the comb of another; and here a human tooth, inserted into the same part, and united by means of vessels . . . from one to another. These living bodies thus applied to each other produce adhesive, not suppurative inflammation.'[10]

(c) *Bones*

Hunter pointed out that there is no difference in principle between the pathology of inflammation in bone and that in the soft tissues – 'Bones are subject to the adhesive, suppurative, and ulcerative inflammation, as the soft parts are.'[11] He gave an accurate description of the stages of osteomyelitis (p. 39).

(d) *Serous cavities*

The gross pathological changes in peritonitis and pleurisy were described simply and effectively by Hunter – '. . . we find this [adhesive] inflammation produced; which either prevents the suppurative altogether, or if it does not, it unites the parts . . . and confines the suppuration to that point . . . so that the general cavity is excluded. . . .'[12] If an abscess developed, it would tend to progress by ulcerative inflammation, i.e. localised absorption of tissue so that 'the matter is led on to the external surface of the body, where it is at last discharged.'[13]

Hunter noted that the umbilicus is a common site of presentation of abdominal abscess, especially in chronic cases – '. . . most abdominal suppurations open at the Navel, especially . . . extraneous bodies [foreign bodies], . . . slow suppuration [tuberculosis], . . . Most children who have died in the Abdomen [ectopic gestation], . . . Ovarian cases [malignant ovarian cyst]. From these facts it would appear that ulceration more readily takes place there than in any other part.'[14]

Appendicitis – Hunter described the autopsy on a patient with peritonitis.[15] The account is clearly that of a gangrenous appendicitis with perforation and peritonitis. The history was that of a week's abdominal pain and distension and absolute constipation. Autopsy showed recent peritonitis maximal in the lower part . . . 'The appendix caeci was vastly large, and on squeezing the Colon, the air escaped through the coats of the appendix caeci. On feeling the appendix caeci, I found hard bodies in it, which proved to be hard chalky faeces; some as large as a nut. . . . the appendix caeci . . . was vastly inflamed, ulcerated, and in some places mortified.' A large faecolith from the appendix is still preserved in the Hunterian Museum.

Cope states: '. . . This is the earliest record, in English, of such a case . . . Heister had noted a gangrenous appendix in 1711 and had described it in his "Observations", and Mestivier in 1759 and Lamotte in 1766 had published somewhat similar accounts of a diseased appendix, but no English or American account appeared before that of Parkinson in 1812.'[16]

Neurogenic ileus – The case described above had been incorrectly diagnosed as one of acute intestinal obstruction. Hunter noted at autopsy that '. . . There was a good deal of air in the Stomach and the whole of the intestines: . . . The reason for his want of stools must have arisen from a paralysis of the intestines, as no obstruction was observable, even to the Anus . . .'[17] This surely must be one of the earliest records of the concept of a non-mechanical, paralytic type of intestinal obstruction.

Perforated gall bladder – John Hunter's Case-Books include a report on the autopsy findings in a man who died with general peritonitis after a short illness – '. . . Winter 1763/4. . . . I examined the gall-bladder and found . . . two holes at its fundus . . . Was the gall-bladder become rotten in this short time, or was it just burst as the pain came on, and was the cause of this universal inflammation in the abdomen? This is somewhat reasonable, as the inflammation seemed to be more on the external surface of the viscera than on the internal.'[18]

Puerperal sepsis – Hunter criticised the generally held view that pelvic peritonitis was a consequence of a puerperal fever of unknown cause. He believed that the inflammation arose in the pelvic organs with the fever only 'a sympathetic symptom'. Although he suspected a uterine cause he could find no evidence of this but he came near to the correct conclusion – 'Sometimes . . . a circumscribed abscess will be formed in the lateral and lower part of the belly, and probably the inflammation was chiefly in the round or broad ligament . . . [when] there is . . . fluctuation . . . it may be safely opened.'[19]

REFERENCES

1 Hunter J. Lectures on the principles of surgery in *The Works of John Hunter*, ed. J F Palmer. London, Longman. 1835, vol. 1, p. 265.
2 Hunter J. A treatise on the blood, inflammation and gun-shot wounds in *The Works of John Hunter*, ed. J F Palmer. London, Longman. 1837, vol. 3, p. 368.
3 Ibid. p. 371.
4 Ibid. p. 240.
5 Ibid. p. 548.
6 Ibid. p. 404.
7 Ibid. p. 549.
8 Ibid. p. 559.
9 Ibid. p. 567.
10 Hunter J. Lectures on the principles of surgery in *The Works of John Hunter*, ed. J F Palmer. London, Longman. 1835, vol. 1, p. 391.
11 Ibid. p. 505.
12 Hunter J. A treatise on the blood, inflammation and gun-shot wounds in *The Works of John Hunter*, ed. J F Palmer. London, Longman. 1837, vol. 3, p. 400.
13 Ibid. p. 484.
14 Hunter J. *Case-Book. Transcript by W Clift.* vol. 4, p. 115.
15 Ibid. vol. 3, pp. 125–127.
16 Cope V Z (Sir Zachary). John Hunter's account of a 'mortifyd' appendix caeci. *Annals of the Royal College of Surgeons of England.* 1949, vol. 4, pp. 142, 143.
17 Hunter J. *Case-Book. Transcript by W Clift.* vol. 3, pp. 125–127.
18 Ibid. pp. 61, 62.
19 Hunter J. Lectures on the principles of surgery in *The Works of John Hunter*, ed. J F Palmer. London, Longman. 1835, vol. 1, pp. 446, 447.

CHAPTER 9

DIGESTIVE SYSTEM

TEETH

JOHN Hunter engaged in dental surgery for six years at the commencement of his professional career, almost certainly as a means of augmenting his very small income (p. 18). He worked with an established dentist, James Spence, a fellow Scot who had an excellent reputation and appears to have recognised and appreciated Hunter's great capabilities, for Hunter wrote: 'I must do Mr. Spence the justice to say . . . that he is the only operator I ever knew who would submit to be instructed, or even allow an equal in knowledge; and I must do the same justice to both his sons.'[1] At that time the practice of dentistry occupied a very low status and was largely in the hands of self-trained quacks. Little respect was paid to any medical man who associated with dentists. However, Hunter brought science and skill to dentistry and was instrumental in raising it to a respectable profession. Dentistry formed the subject of Hunter's first book, the *Treatise on the Natural History of the Human Teeth* and he sold the first edition for one thousand pounds. Prior to Hunter's publication there had been some half a dozen books on the subject written in English[2] but John Hunter's was the first to present a study of the teeth in a logical scientific and useful practical manner.

Hunter's experience in dental surgery, even though it may have been undertaken as a temporary economic and grudging necessity, was in fact a most important episode in his career. Apart from the economic return from the practice, the sale of his book and his influence in the establishment of the dental profession, it gave him the initial ideas about three of his most fruitful biological concepts, *viz.* on the subjects of the absorbents, transplantation and referred pain.

Absorbents – Hunter's first appreciation of the concept of absorption of tissue arose from his observations on this process in connection with the teeth and jaws. He wrote – 'The removal of a solid part of our body . . . by means of the Absorbent system is a process that has not been . . . even suspected . . . that any solid part should be totally absorbed is a New Doctrine . . . This use of the Absorbents . . . first suggested itself to me in observing the waste of the Sockets of the Teeth, as also in the fangs of the shedding Teeth, which was in the Year 1754 and 1755 . . . the change is not produced by a mechanical pressure but is a particular process in the Animal Oeconomy.'[3]

This fundamental concept of the absorption of solid tissue gave Hunter the basis for an understanding of many physiological and pathological processes throughout the body, especially the modelling and exfoliation of bone, the shedding of antlers, and perhaps the most important, the ulcerative stage of inflammation and extrusion of pus and gangrenous tissue (p. 76).

Transplantation – The practice of transplantation of teeth from one person to another, although popularised by John Hunter, had in fact been practised a century earlier.[2] Even in Hunter's hands the results were extremely poor, although two of his cases of transplantation that could be regarded as successful are recorded by James Gardette in the Medical Recorder in 1827.[2] Hunter's experience of transplanting teeth gave him an insight into the power of union of different tissues. He wrote – 'Of Transplanting the Teeth. The success of this operation is founded on a disposition in all living substances to unite when brought into contact with one another, although they are of a different structure, and even although the circulation is only carried on in one of them.'[4] He demonstrated this concept by his successful autograft of the spur of a cock transplanted into its comb. Hunter extended the principle of union of different tissues to the trial of heterografts. He wrote – 'I have hitherto explained unions as taking place only in the division of corresponding parts of the same living body, but it is equally possible to unite different parts of the same or of different bodies, by bringing them into contact under certain circumstances.'[5] His classic success in this field is in his Museum, a human tooth grafted into a cock's comb.

Thus Hunter's work on transplantation of teeth, although of little clinical value, led him to the study of the union of tissues and thence to an explanation of the adhesive stage of inflammation with its significance in the pathology of peritonitis and disease of other body cavities (p. 77, 78).

Referred pain – The concept of pain referred to the teeth from a distant site was described by Hunter in his Treatise on the Teeth as 'Nervous Pains in the Jaws'.[6] It demonstrates his appreciation of the principle of referred pain which he subsequently described in an authoritative manner (p. 123).

Viability of teeth – As a result of his investigations, Hunter concluded that the teeth are not truly organised bodies and had to be considered as extraneous bodies, chiefly because he was unable to demonstrate a circulation by his injection experiments and because madder feeding experiments showed permanent retention of the dye in the teeth, implying the absence of absorbents. However, he believed that teeth 'have most certainly a living principle' because he found from the result of transplantation experiments that they 'are capable of uniting with any part of a living body.'[7] Hunter was thus driven to the unsatisfactory conclusion that an organ can be an extraneous body and yet at the same time possess a living principle rendering it capable of uniting with a living body.

This erroneous conclusion reached by Hunter relative to the viability of the teeth is perhaps another example of Hunter's anxiety to argue from deduction rather than from induction as suggested by Buckle (p. xiii). Hunter's initial inaccurate experiments on the teeth led him too hastily to the generalisation that the teeth are unorganised bodies. He then found evidence of a living principle in the teeth, but rather than abandon his already established general principle he would merely acknowledge that these extraneous bodies could yet possess a living principle allowing them to unite with a living body.

OESOPHAGUS

Dysphagia – In 1790 Hunter was called upon to treat a patient suffering from acute dysphagia due to a nerve disorder of unknown aetiology which had caused paralysis of the muscles of deglutition.[8] A tube was passed into the stomach by which the patient was fed for three weeks after which time normal deglutition returned. The tube was made of a fresh eel-skin, supported by whalebone, through which food was squeezed by means of an attached bladder.

Hunter described this case in a paper entitled *A case of paralysis of the muscles of deglutition cured by an artificial mode of conveying food and medicines into the stomach*. This was presented in 1790 and published in 1793. The purpose of intubation was 'to adopt some artificial mode of conveying food into the stomach, . . . and such medicines may be administered as are thought conducive to the cure.'[9] Although this appears to be the first case of dysphagia treated by Hunter by gastric intubation, he had in fact advised the use of a gastric tube, to 'convey any stimulating matter,' fourteen years previously, in 1776, in his paper on resuscitation of the drowned (p. 107).[10] It seems remarkable that Hunter had not had occasion to employ this method on other cases during this long interval.

Richardson recounts that in 1799, at Alexandria, one of Napoleon's generals, Murat, sustained a gunshot wound of the neck which caused complete dysphagia for several days. Larrey overcame this problem by feeding him through a gum-elastic stomach tube. Richardson remarks that Larrey may well have been only the second person to adopt this method.[11]

Spontaneous rupture of oesophagus – Under the title of 'Ruptured Oesophagus' Hunter has given a classic picture of a spontaneous rupture – 'Captain Sir James Pettigrew, of the 10th Regiment Aged 50, at Kingston in the Island of Jamaica, on the morning of the First of December 1787, was seized with cholicky pain, nausea and retching to vomit, . . . by his own account, he had the sensation of something giving way within him, attended with a rushing noise . . . a difficulty of breathing and sense of suffocation. . . . Mr. Menzies, Surgeon of the Regiment, saw him . . . The lower part of the neck, and upper part of the sternum (thorax) was puffed; and the crackling of air could be felt in the cellular membrane . . .'

At autopsy 'a laceration was found in the oesophagus, running longitudinally in its posterior parts, about an inch and a half long, and about an inch above the Cardia. Through this opening the contents of the Stomach had been evacuated into the right and left cavities of the Pleura; measuring in all, about a gallon and a half, the greatest quantity in the left side.'[12]

Carcinoma of oesophagus – Hunter recorded this case as an ulcer in the oesophagus. The description is typical of carcinoma. 'Ulcer in the Oesophagus. February 27th 1802* John Dennis. Forty-two years of age.' There was a history of increasing dysphagia for a few weeks with a fatal termination. At autopsy '. . . the obstruction was found to have been formed by the upper cartilaginous edge of a very extensive ulcer which had destroyed the whole of the internal membrane of the oesophagus for the space of three inches: the distance between the stricture and the Cardia. The passage was so completely obstructed, that the smallest sized probe could not be made to pass.'[13]

STOMACH

'The stomach is the distinguishing part between an animal and a vegetable; for we do not know any vegetable that has a stomach nor any animal without one.'[14] This aphorism of Hunter's is far more subtle than at first appears. It is not merely a pithy contrast of animal and plant, but rather it epitomises his fundamental concept of the unique origin of animal life by a process of assimilation, animalisation and vivification of inanimate matter – 'The conversion . . . of vegetable and animal matter into animals, which is animalization . . . is effected by the actions of the . . . animal.'[15] And the essential agent in this conversion is the stomach – 'It is the converter of the food by hidden powers into part of ourselves, and is what may be called the true animal, . . . A polypus is little more than stomach. An animal can exist without any senses, brain or nervous system, without limbs, heart or circulation, in short without anything but a stomach.'[16]

Thus, in Hunter's view, the stomach is the most important organ in the body, because it is the vitalising link in the chain of development of animal life. Commencing with common mineral matter – 'Animal and vegetable matter has certainly arisen out of the matter of the globe . . . Vegetables alone appear to have a power of immediately converting common matter into their own kind. Animals probably have not that power, therefore are removed further from common matter; so that a vegetable seems to be an intermediate step between common matter and animal matter.'[17]

---

* This date is obviously erroneous and may have been a mistake in transcription by Clift.

Finally the vital stage in the production of animal life is brought about by the action of the stomach.

In his *Observations on Digestion* Hunter gave an account of contemporary physiological views. Such an exhaustive account of the work of others is indeed a very unusual feature in Hunter's writings, as was pointed out by Owen.[18] Although he acknowledged the validity of much of the work of Réaumur and Spallanzani, he criticised them for being merely 'experiment-makers' whose ignorance of natural history rendered them incapable of applying their experimental results correctly.[19]

Hunter discussed various possible mechanisms of digestion and gave sound reasons for dismissing a mechanical explanation of the process and also those based on chemical means and fermentation. He concluded that digestion 'neither depends on a mechanical power, nor contractions of the stomach, nor on heat, but something secreted in the coats of the stomach, and thrown into its cavity, which there animalizes the food, or assimilates it to the nature of the blood.'[20]

There seems to be some doubt about Hunter's views on the acid content of the gastric juice. He said 'I am not inclined to suppose that there is any acid in the gastric juice as a component or essential part of it, although an acid is very commonly discovered . . .'[21] However Hunter also stated that 'As we find stomachs possessed of a power of dissolving the whole substance of a bone, it is reasonable to suppose that its earth [Calcium phosphate], is destroyed by the acid in the stomach.'[22] Moreover it has been pointed out by Owen that in Hunter's original paper he had stated 'In all the animals . . . upon which I made observations . . . to discover whether or not there was an acid in the stomach . . . I constantly found that there was an acid, but not a strong one, in the juices . . . in a natural state.'[23]

Postmortem digestion – Hunter's correct interpretation of the digestive powers of the gastric juice was developed largely as the result of his important and original observations on postmortem digestion of the stomach – 'observing that the half-digested parts of the stomach were similar to the half-digested food, it immediately struck me that it was the process of digestion going on after death; and that the stomach, being dead, was no longer capable of resisting the powers of that menstruum which itself had formed for the digestion of food.'[24] He described one such lesion in a female aged about 18 –' '. . . large hole in the great end of the stomach . . . all round the hole the stomach was very slimy as if it had been steeped for a little while in a Caustic Alcali . . . Here then was a dissolving power that first dissolved the stomach, and then the Cellular Membrane of other parts, but was not sufficient to dissolve muscular fibres.'[25]

Peptic ulcer – There is evidence that Hunter was not unfamiliar with peptic ulcer. In describing a case of perforation of the stomach he said '. . . if it took place before death [i.e. not postmortem digestion] it is probable that it was owing to ulceration, which I have sometimes seen.'[26]

Hunter's Case-Books include autopsies on two patients with the pathological features of chronic peptic ulcer. In a case of haematemesis, there was a large chronic ulcer extending up from the pylorus for three inches.[27] A second case showed the features of peritonitis associated with a perforated duodenal ulcer – 'Autopsy on the Right Hon[ble] the Earl of Morton . . . an universal inflammation on all the external surface of the bowels . . . close by the Pylorus I found a round hole about the diameter of a large Pea in which there was a plug formed of a bit of some solid aliment, which his Lordship had swallowed sometime . . . This hole . . . must have been forming for some time before Death, . . . Perhaps it arose at first from an ulcer . . .'[28]

INTUSSUSCEPTION

In 1789 John Hunter presented to the Society for the Improvement of Medical and Chirurgical Knowledge a paper on the subject of intussusception. He gave a classic description of the condition with clinical and autopsy details in a fatal case of an infant.[29]

ACUTE APPENDICITIS p. 78

NEUROGENIC ILEUS p. 79

GALL BLADDER

Gallstones – Among Hunter's records are the histories of three patients who suffered from the complications of gallstones.

'Case of Gall-stones passing by the Anus.' Mrs. Smith aged thirty-three experienced several attacks of acute upper abdominal pain which eventually resolved completely after passing numerous gallstones *per anum*.[30]

Mrs. G. aged 54 had an abscess of the gallbladder presenting in the skin which was incised and ten gallstones were discharged. She also passed one stone *per anum*.[31]

'The Case of Mr. Appleby who had an Abscess formed in the Gall-Bladder, which opened into the Gut, as also externally.' This was undoubtedly a case of cholecystocolic fistula. John Hunter diagnosed a gas-containing abscess in the right subcostal area – 'I began to conceive there might have been an inflammation between the liver, gall-bladder and colon probably owing to some disease in the gall-bladder from Stones etc which I have often seen . . .' The abscess discharged spontaneously through the skin – 'several gallstones came through the wound . . .', and '. . . in the Stools there was found a vast quantity of matter, from which it was pretty evident that the matter had found its way into the gut, probably through the passage that had admitted the air from the gut . . .'[32]

Perforated Gall bladder p. 79

HERNIA

Inguinal hernia – Hunter gave a full account of the anatomy of congenital inguinal hernia in his paper on descent of the testis (p. 91). He described the autopsy findings in a case of strangulated inguinal hernia associated with incompletely descended testis (p. 92).

Sliding hernia – Hunter observed that the peculiarity of descent of the testis carrying the peritoneum with it often takes place in the intestines in old ruptures. – '. . . The caecum has sometimes been found to have descended into the scrotum . . . The same thing has happened to the sigmoid flexure of the colon . . . Such herniae cannot be reduced; and in case of strangulation, which may be brought on by a fresh portion of intestine coming down, are not to be treated in the common way . . .'[33]

Diaphragmatic hernia – Among the unidentified cases in Hunter's Case-Books is one in which the autopsy findings record the presence of a diaphragmatic hernia – 'November 1757. I dissected the body of a Marine who died at St. George's. He was in there only for a carious Tibia . . . [which] was cauterized . . . but (it)* threw him into a fever of which he died . . . the Epiploon . . . seemed to

---

* This insertion in the *Case-Book* was probably made by Clift in transcribing the manuscript.

come through the Diaphragm from the Thorax . . . a large portion of the Epiploon lying loose in the Cavity of the Thorax . . . It adhered to the edge of the hole in the Diaphragm . . .'[34]

REFERENCES

1 Hunter J. Treatise on the natural history of the human teeth in *The Works of John Hunter*, ed. J F Palmer. London, Longman. 1835, vol. 2, p. 95.
2 Dobson J. John Hunter and the dentists. *The Dental Magazine and Oral Topics*. 1964, pp. 1–6.
3 Hunter J. *MS. Catalogue of the Museum 1800. Gallery*. p. *32, 33*. Royal College of Surgeons of England Library.
4 Hunter J. Treatise on the natural history of the human teeth in *The Works of John Hunter*, ed. J F Palmer. London, Longman. 1835, vol. 2, pp. 55, 56.
5 Hunter J. A treatise on the blood, inflammation and gun-shot wounds in *The Works of John Hunter*, ed. J F Palmer. London, Longman. 1837, vol. 3, p. 255.
6 Hunter J. Treatise on the natural history of the human teeth in *The Works of John Hunter*, ed. J F Palmer. London, Longman. 1835, vol. 2, pp. 84, 85.
7 Ibid. p. 18.
8 Hunter J. A case of paralysis of the muscles of deglutition cured by an artificial mode of conveying food and medicines into the stomach in *The Works of John Hunter*, ed. J F Palmer. London, Longman. 1837, vol. 3, p. 622.
9 Ibid. p. 623.
10 Hunter J. Proposals for the recovery of persons apparently drowned in *The Works of John Hunter*, ed. J F Palmer. London, Longman. 1837, vol. 4, p. 174.
11 Richardson R G. *Larrey: Surgeon to Napoleon's Imperial Guard*. London, John Murray. 1974, p. 74.
12 Hunter J. *Case-Book. Transcript by W Clift*. vol. 5, pp. 90, 91.
13 Ibid. pp. 91–93.
14 Hunter J. Lectures on the principles of surgery in *The Works of John Hunter*, ed. J F Palmer. London, Longman. 1835, vol. 1, p. 247.
15 Ibid. p. 218.
16 Ibid. pp. 247, 248.
17 Ibid. pp. 214, 215.
18 Owen R. in *The Works of John Hunter*, ed. J F Palmer. London, Longman. 1837, vol. 4, p. 84.
19 Hunter J. Some observations on digestion in *The Works of John Hunter*, ed. J F Palmer. London, Longman. 1837, vol. 4, p. 86.
20 Hunter J. On the digestion of the stomach after death in *The Works of John Hunter*, ed. J F Palmer. London, Longman. 1837, vol. 4, pp. 120, 121.
21 Hunter J. Some observations on digestion in *The Works of John Hunter*, ed. J F Palmer. London, Longman. 1837, vol. 4, p. 105.
22 Ibid. p. 97.
23 Hunter J. On the digestion of the stomach after death in *The Works of John Hunter*, ed. J F Palmer. London, Longman. 1837, vol. 4, p. 121.
24 Ibid. p. 120.
25 Hunter J. *Case-Book. Transcript by W Clift*. vol. 3, p. 99.
26 Hunter J. Some observations on digestion in *The Works of John Hunter*, ed. J F Palmer. London, Longman. 1837, vol. 4, p. 116.
27 Hunter J. *Case-Book. Transcript by W Clift*. vol. 3, pp. 100–102.
28 Ibid. pp. 138, 139.

29 Editorial. An interesting document. *British Medical Journal.* 1897, vol. 2, p. 300.

30 Hunter J. *Case-Book. Transcript by W Clift.* vol. 4, pp. 43, 44.

31 Ibid. pp. 97–99.

32 Ibid. pp. 38–41.

33 Hunter J. A description of the situation of the testis in the foetus, with its descent into the scrotum in *The Works of John Hunter*, ed. J F Palmer. London, Longman. 1837, vol. 4, pp. 10, 11.

34 Hunter J. *Case-Book. Transcript by W Clift.* vol. 3, pp. 26, 27.

CHAPTER 10

REPRODUCTIVE SYSTEM

JOHN Hunter placed the function of generation next after that of digestion in order of importance in the animal economy. Indeed he stressed that these two functions alone are the only ones absolutely essential to sustain animal life. Referring to the simple polypus 'as little more than stomach,'[1] he said – 'Nothing more is necessary to complete an animal than the power of continuing the species, which power is superadded to this bag in many.'[2] Investigation of the system of generation was therefore a very great interest to Hunter and he wrote numerous papers on the subject.

TESTIS

Descent of the testis. In 1755–56 John Hunter made a series of dissections to demonstrate congenital hernia and the descent of the testis. An account of these observations was published in 1762 by Dr. William Hunter.[3] This was John Hunter's first published paper and it includes the first description of the gubernaculum – 'At this time of life the testis is connected in a very particular manner with the parietes of the abdomen, at that place where in adult bodies the spermatic vessels pass out, and likewise to the scrotum. This connection is by means of a substance which runs down from the lower end of the testis to the scrotum, and which at present I shall call the ligament, or gubernaculum* testis, because it connects the testis with the scrotum, and directs its course in its descent.'[4] A further account of the descent of the testis was given by John Hunter in 1786.[5]

Hunter demonstrated by means of dissections of the fetus the various stages of descent of the testis from its high abdominal

---

* Gubernance = Governance (OED)

position down into the scrotum. He showed that it was accompanied by a peritoneal sac and was thus able to explain the circumstance of the intestine and testis being both present in a common peritoneal sac in some cases of congenital hernia – 'for when there is a hernia congenita there is no other cavity than that of the hernial sac; and that cavity communicates with the general cavity of the abdomen . . . There are besides two circumstances peculiar to a rupture of this kind, the intestine being always in immediate contact with the testis, and there being no tunica vaginalis propria testis.'[6]

Hunter then demonstrated that the early abdominal position of the testis as well as the early transient state of the tunica vaginalis in the human fetus remain as permanent structures in lower mammals – '. . . the elongation of the peritoneum, which contains the testis in the scrotum, must at first communicate with the general cavity of the abdomen . . . Thus it is in the human body when the testis is recently come down; and thus it is, and continues to be through life, in every quadruped which I have examined where the testis is in the scrotum; but in the human body the communication between the sac and the cavity of the abdomen is soon cut off.'[7]

The priority of these observations was the subject of much angry debate. The suggestion that a 'congenital' hernia was essentially the result of a persistent embryonic condition was first made by Haller in 1755. John Hunter demonstrated his dissections in the following year. A few months later Percivall Pott described a similar account of the condition in his book on hernia. It seems that Pott had in fact seen John Hunter's specimens but he answered the Hunters' criticisms by stating that he had made the original observations himself at St. Bartholomew's Hospital.

Hydrocele. Hunter's account of the descent of the testis contains a reference to the anatomy of hydrocele – '. . . the mouth and neck only of the sac close up . . . the lower part . . . makes the tunica vaginalis propria. Whence it is plain . . . that the hernia congenita and the true hydrocele cannot exist together . . . For when there is a hernia congenita there is no other cavity than that of the hernial sac . . .'[8]

Incompletely descended testis with strangulated hernia. Hunter described an autopsy on a male aged 24 with gangrenous ileum in a congenital type of right inguinal hernia with the testis lying just below the abdominal inguinal ring. He added – 'This case proves that a Hernia congenita can take place even where the Testicle is not come down into the Scrotum, if it has but passed the ring, by the process of the peritonoeum being elongated into the Scrotum beyond the Testis, . . .'[9]

Torsion of testis. Hunter gave an account of bilateral acute swellings of the testis in a man aged 18, in which the lesion was certainly torsion. The patient developed an acute spontaneous attack of painful swelling of the left testis in February 1776, followed 8 months later by a similar attack in the right testis. On each side the swelling subsided slowly and 'continued to decrease till not a vestige was left.' The patient was seen also by Mr. Adair and Mr. Pott 'but nothing could be thought of that could give any hopes of success.'[10]

Torsion of the testis was first described by Delasiauve in 1840.[11]

VESICULAE SEMINALES

It was commonly believed that the seminal vesicles functioned as reservoirs for the semen. Hunter was not satisfied with this opinion and he conducted experiments and observations to prove that it was erroneous. His publication on the subject is a good example of the thoroughness and energy with which Hunter carried out his investigations. He obtained fresh samples of the content of human vesicles from autopsy and showed that the fluid was not semen. He then obtained similar results in the examination of vesicles in different animals including the horse, boar, rat, beaver, guinea-pig and hedgehog. He concluded – 'From the facts which I have stated respecting the organs of generation, the observations which I have made, and the series of actions which I have considered as taking place in the copulation of animals, I think the following inferences may be fairly drawn:

'That the bags, called vesiculae seminales, are not seminal reservoirs, but glands secreting a peculiar mucus; and that the bulb of the urethra is, properly speaking, the receptacle in which the semen is accumulated previous to ejection.

'Although it seems to have been proved that the vesiculae do not contain the semen, I have not been able to ascertain their particular use; we may, however, be allowed upon the whole to conclude that they are, together with other parts, subservient to the purposes of generation.'[12]

It has been pointed out by Owen that others prior to Hunter had noted the absence of semen from the vesicles but no one before

Hunter had established the fact with the incontrovertible evidence with which he presented it.[13]

It is accepted now that in fact the seminal vesicles do not contain spermatozoa but 'subservient to the purposes of generation' they produce seminal fluid containing fructose which imparts motility to the sperm.[14]

PLACENTA

In 1774, William Hunter published *The Anatomy of the Human Gravid Uterus*. This was the result of many years work and in its preface William Hunter put on record the help in its preparation he had received from his brother John – 'whose accuracy in anatomical researches is so well known, that to omit this opportunity of thanking him for that assistance, would be in some measure to disregard the future reputation of the work itself.'[15]

In 1780 John Hunter presented a paper to the Royal Society, *On the Structure of the Placenta*, in which he claimed priority, in association with a Dr. Mackenzie, for the discovery of the circulatory relationship between the placenta and the uterus. He stated 'The connexion between the mother and foetus . . . . . . and the structure of the parts which form the connexion, were unknown till about the year 1754 . . . it is my intention . . . to give such an account of it . . . while, at the same time, I establish my own claim to the discovery.'[16]

John Hunter then described his dissection and demonstration of a specimen obtained for him by Dr. Mackenzie, Dr. Smellie's assistant, in May 1754. He took Dr. William Hunter to see the specimen – 'Some of the parts were given to him, which he afterwards showed at his lectures, and probably they still remain in his collection . . . The facts being now ascertained and universally acknowledged, I consider myself as having a just claim to the discovery of the structure of the placenta, and its communication with the uterus, together with the use arising from such structure and communication. . . .'[17]

He refers to William Hunter's *Anatomy of the Gravid Uterus* '. . . that very accurate and elaborate work which he has published on the Gravid Uterus, in which he has minutely described and accurately delineated the parts, without mentioning the mode of discovery.'[17]

John Hunter's paper was not published in the Transactions of the Royal Society but it is included in Animal Oeconomy (1786). Following the delivery of this paper in 1780 Dr. William Hunter wrote a letter to the Secretary of the Royal Society denying his brother's claim, while John Hunter wrote and suggested that, as three people had been primarily concerned, the honours should be divided between them.[18] However the Society wisely refused to take sides in the dispute or to publish the paper. Dr. William Hunter died three years later but their quarrel was never made up.

OVARIES

Hunter was anxious to determine the factors which influence the length of the breeding period in the female. He questioned whether these factors were local, in the ovaries, or constitutional, with secondary effects on the ovaries. In his experiment of extirpation of one ovary, Hunter's object was to determine whether each ovary has a fixed alloted number of ova, or whether the number is influenced by the constitution or other circumstances. If the former, extirpation of one ovary would either diminish the number of offspring at each birth in those animals whose nature it is to bring forth more than one at a time or it would shorten the breeding period of the animal. If the number of ova is influenced by the constitution, then extirpation of one ovary would result in the same number of offspring at each birth as would have been produced by both ovaries.

This simple physiological experiment was organised in a modern exemplary fashion, *viz.* a statement of the two conflicting hypotheses to be tested, careful documentation and quantitative observations, the employment of controls at each stage, and an unbiased assessment of the results.

Hunter conducted the experiment over a period of seven years using pigs, '. . . two females of the same colour and size, and likewise a boar-pig, all of the same farrow . . .'[19] He removed an ovary from one female and labelled the animal by means of a slit in one ear. The spayed pig bred for nearly four years and had 76 offspring while the control pig bred for six years and had 162 offspring. Hunter concluded that 'it seems most probable that the ovaria are from the beginning destined to produce a fixed number, beyond which they cannot go, . . . but that the constitution at large has no power of giving to one ovarium the power of propagating equal to both; for in the present experiment the animal with one ovarium produced ten pigs less than half the number brought forth by the sow with both ovaria.'[20]

Hunter admitted that a single experiment may not be 'justifiable to draw conclusions'[21] but he pointed out that 'the difference in the number of pigs produced by each was greater than can be justly imputed to accident,' with a footnote – 'It may be thought by some that I should have repeated this experiment; but an annual expense of twenty pounds for ten years, and the necessary attention to make the experiment complete, will be a sufficient reason for my not having done it.'[20]

HERMAPHRODITES

Hunter's two papers, on an extraordinary pheasant and on the free-martin, are a study of hermaphroditism. He pointed out that every species of animal and every part of an animal is subject to deviation, which 'may not improperly be called monstrous.'[22] This tendency to monstrosity applies also to the organs of generation so that male and female organs may be combined in one animal as in the free-martin which is a monstrous hermaphrodite peculiar to black cattle, being to appearance a cow-calf but unfit for propagation, one of twins, the other being a normal bull-calf.

Hunter noted that each species of animal is disposed to have nearly the same sort of defects which also tend to be uniform in each part, a disposition that applies again also to the organs of generation, as exemplified by the free-martin. This uniformity of deviation suggested to Hunter that congenital malformations exist in the original germ cells – '. . . each part of each species seems to have its monstrous form originally impressed upon it.'[23]

Perhaps the most important observation in these papers is Hunter's clear exposition of the distinction between primary and secondary sexual characters, a subject to which Darwin ascribed considerable significance and wrote – 'With animals which have their sexes separated, the males necessarily differ from the females in their organs of reproduction; and these afford the primary sexual characters. But the sexes often differ in what Hunter has called secondary sexual characters, which are not directly connected with the act of reproduction; for instance, in the male possessing certain organs of sense or locomotion, of which the female is quite destitute, or in having them more highly-developed, in order that he may readily find or reach her; or again, in the male having special organs of prehension so as to hold her securely.'[24]

Hunter's account of the pheasant exemplified his observation 'that there is often a change of the natural properties of the female sex into those of the secondary of the male; the female . . . assuming the secondary peculiarities of the male.'[25] He described the appearances in several hen pheasants who developed the feathers of a cock and in one case also formed spurs resembling those of a cock.

Hunter concluded that this change of the female towards a male type 'is merely the effect of age, and obtains to a certain degree in every class of animals. We find something similar taking place even in the human species . . .'[26]

It may seem a little surprising that Hunter has presented this account of a sex change in a pheasant as an extraordinary event since the reversal of female to male in birds had been common knowledge for years. 'From pre-Christian times, men have regarded a hen's assumption of male plumage, and of an ability to crow, tread, and fight as a portent of disaster . . . It would seem that after a hen assumes some male characters it may occasionally still lay a malformed egg . . . In Basel, as late as the 15th century, a cock was solemnly tried for witchcraft after laying an egg . . . the cock and its egg were . . . burnt at the stake. Post-mortem examination showed that it contained . . . three more unlaid cock's eggs.'[27] The facility of this sex reversal is probably associated with the rudimentary state of the right ovary in almost all avian species and indeed Hunter refers to this anatomical fact in another paper – 'In all animals of distinct sex, the females, those of the Bird-kind excepted, have, I believe, two ovaria, and of course the oviducts are in pairs.'[28]

ARTIFICIAL INSEMINATION

John Hunter made numerous experiments on the impregnation of sheep and he accumulated a series of specimens of the genitalia of ewes at various stages of pregnancy (Hunterian Museum).

In 1799 Everard Home reported that John Hunter had carried out with success artificial insemination on a woman whose husband suffered from hypospadias.[29] Hunter had advised him to collect the fresh seminal emission in a syringe and inject it immediately into the vagina. Home included this case in a paper delivered to the Royal

Society entitled 'An Account of the Dissection of an Hermaphrodite Dog. To which are prefixed, some Observations on Hermaphrodites in general.' It seems remarkable that this important case, the first recorded pregnancy and delivery of a child conceived by artificial insemination (AIH), should have been presented in this surreptitious fashion, and further that Hunter himself had not reported the case at an earlier date. It is possible that fear of severe criticism on ethical or religious grounds may have been the responsible factor.

REFERENCES

1 Hunter J. Lectures on the principles of surgery in *The Works of John Hunter*, ed. J F Palmer. London, Longman. 1835, vol. 1, p. 247.
2 Ibid. p. 248.
3 Hunter J. Observations on the state of the testis in the foetus and on the hernia congenita in *Medical Commentaries* by Dr. William Hunter. London, A Hamilton. 1762, Part I, pp. 75–90. (Also in *The Works of John Hunter*, 1837, vol. 4, pp. 1–15.)
4 Ibid. p. 78. (Also in *The Works of John Hunter*, 1837, vol. 4, pp. 6, 7.)
5 Hunter J. A description of the situation of the testis in the foetus, with its descent into the scrotum in *The Works of John Hunter*, ed. J F Palmer. London, Longman. 1837, vol. 4, pp. 1–19.
6 Ibid. pp. 14, 15.
7 Ibid. p. 11.
8 Ibid. p. 15.
9 Hunter J. *Case-Book. Transcript by W Clift*. vol. 5, p. 101.
10 Ibid. vol. 2, pp. 312, 313.
11 Delasiauve L J-F. Descente tardive du testicule gauche, prise pour une hernie étranglée. Rev. Méd. Fr. Etrang. 1840, vol. 1, 363–75. Quoted by R E May and W E G Thomas in Recurrent torsion of the testis following previous surgical fixation. *British Journal of Surgery*. 1980, vol. 67, pp. 129, 130.
12 Hunter J. Observations on the glands situated between the rectum and bladder, called vesiculae seminales in *The Works of John Hunter*, ed. J F Palmer. London, Longman. 1837, vol. 4, p. 33.
13 Owen R. in *The Works of John Hunter*, ed. J F Palmer. London, Longman. 1837, vol. 4, p. iv.
14 *Gray's Anatomy*. Edinburgh and London, Churchill Livingstone. 1980, 36th edn. p. 1417.
15 Hunter W. Preface, *The Anatomy of the Human Gravid Uterus*. London, S Baker and G Leigh. 1774.
16 Hunter J. On the structure of the placenta in *The Works of John Hunter*, ed. J F Palmer. London, Longman. 1837, vol. 4, p. 60.
17 Ibid. p. 62.
18 Dobson J. John Hunter's anatomy. *Annals of the Royal College of Surgeons of England.* 1967, vol. 41, pp. 493–501.
19 Hunter J. An experiment to determine the effect of extirpating one ovarium upon the number of young produced in *The Works of John Hunter*, ed. J F Palmer. London, Longman. 1837, vol. 4, p. 51.
20 Ibid. p. 54.

21 Ibid. p. 53.
22 Hunter J. An account of an extraordinary pheasant in *The Works of John Hunter*, ed. J F Palmer. London, Longman. 1837, vol. 4, p. 44.
23 Ibid. p. 45.
24 Darwin C. *The Descent of Man and Selection in Relation to Sex*. London, John Murray. 1871, vol. 1, p. 253.
25 Hunter J. An account of an extraordinary pheasant in *The Works of John Hunter*, ed. J F Palmer. London, Longman. 1837, vol. 4, p. 46.
26 Ibid. p. 49.
27 Parker T J and Haswell W A. *A Text-Book of Zoology*. London, Macmillan. 1962, 7th edn. vol. 2, p. 645.
28 Hunter J. An experiment to determine the effect of extirpating one ovarium upon the number of young produced in *The Works of John Hunter*, ed. J F Palmer. London, Longman. 1837, vol. 4, p. 50.
29 Home E. An account of the dissection of an hermaphrodite dog. To which are prefixed, some observations on hermaphrodites in general. *Philosophical Transactions*. 1799, vol. 89, pp. 157–178.

CHAPTER 11

CIRCULATORY SYSTEM METABOLISM

BLOOD

'BLOOD is the material out of which the whole body is formed and out of which it is supported'[1]; '. . . it would seem to be the most simple body we know of endowed with the principle of life.'[2] This concept of the importance of the blood in the animal economy was fundamental to Hunter's philosophy of animate structures. It was not an original concept and had been enunciated especially by Harvey – '. . . the blood is the first engendered part, whence the living principle in the first instance gleams forth, and from which the first animated particle of the embryo is formed; that it is the source and origin of all other parts, both similar and dissimilar, which thence obtain their vital heat and become subservient to it in its duties.'[3]* But Hunter's physiological investigations on the blood went much further than Harvey's and he established the concept of the vitality of the blood by a mass of accurate observations and experiments.

Hunter's arguments follow a logical sequence. He first of all establishes that organisation of animal matter is not essential to life and therefore that 'fluidity is no objection to the blood being alive,'[4] the evidence being his observations on the developing chick. By means of simple experiments he shows that a fresh egg 'has a power of resisting heat, cold and putrefaction; and similar results are come to by similar experiments on some of the more imperfect animals . . .'[5] He observes that the blood 'appears to carry life to

---

* An even earlier reference of course is *Leviticus* (11.17):
'For the life of the flesh is in the blood'.

every part of the body, for whenever the whole or a part is deprived of fresh blood it very soon dies.'[4] Furthermore he remarks that 'If the blood had not the living principle, it would be, in respect of the body, as an extraneous substance.'[6]

Hunter's next observation is one of the most important in his study of the blood, viz. that 'whilst circulating, or in useful motion, it is always in a fluid state.'[7] This lack of disposition to coagulate inside the vessels does not arise from the motion of the blood since in cases where the circulation is very slow coagulation does not necessarily occur. Hunter found that 'the blood of a fish, which had the actions of life stopped for three days, and was supposed to be dead, did not coagulate in the vessels; but upon being exposed or extravasated, soon coagulated'.[8]

Hunter carried out extensive investigations of the conditions and behaviour of the blood and blood vessels in inflammation. His studies were nearly all made by simple naked-eye observation. He distrusted microscopic findings; he reasoned that the naked eye has a power of adaptation 'to the different distances of the parts of an object within its compass, making the object always a whole; but a magnifying glass has no such power'.[9]

It was in the course of these relatively crude test-tube experiments that Hunter was led to the discovery of the elevated erythrocyte sedimentation rate in inflammation – '. . . I took the serum of inflammatory blood, with some of the red part, and also some serum of blood free from inflammation, with nearly the same quantity of the red part, . . . allowed them to stand quiet, and observed that the red globules subsided much faster in the inflammatory blood than in the other'.[10]

During his investigations into the formation of the constituents of the blood, Hunter made the discovery that the vessels in the embryo of red-blooded animals originally contain colourless blood, as in the permanent circulation of invertebrates. The red globules 'seem to be formed later in life than either of the other two [constituents]; thus we see, while the chick is in the egg, and the heart beating, it then contains a transparent fluid before any red globules are formed, which we may suppose to be the serum, and the lymph.'[11] This Hunterian observation was rediscovered some fifty years later, as recounted by Owen – 'I well remember the feelings of surprise with which I listened while at Paris in 1832 to a memoir read before the Academy of Sciences . . . as a novel and important discovery . . . without its being suspected that our great physiologist had half a century before embraced it . . . in . . . his investigations'.[12]

Despite his comprehensive investigations of the blood, Hunter seems never to have fully appreciated the function of the red blood corpuscles. He wrote – 'The red part of the blood I choose to consider last, . . . because I believe it to be the least important . . .'[13] He gave good reasons for this view – 'the red globules . . . are not to be found in all animals [e.g. insects], nor so early in those that have them [e.g. developing chick]; nor are they pushed into the extreme arteries [e.g. cartilage]; . . . neither do they appear to be so readily formed [e.g. after haemorrhage]'.[14] Hunter was fully aware of the fundamental importance of respiration – 'the time that we can live without air, or breathing, is shorter than that in which we die from a defect in any other natural operation; breathing, therefore, seems to render life to the blood'.[15] Hunter made numerous experiments in dogs using a pair of double bellows of his invention placed in the trachea, and observed the effects on the heart of varying degrees of pulmonary insufflation. He demonstrated the deleterious effects on the heart which occurred on decreasing the inspiratory inflow – '. . . when I left off blowing the whole blood . . . was of a dark colour . . . it was curious to see the coronary arteries turn darker and darker . . . and on blowing again resume gradually a brighter colour, till they became a florid red. As respiration was . . . prevented . . . the blood was . . . of a dark colour, and the heart large and hardly acting; but on throwing into the lungs fresh air, the heart began to act . . .'[16]

But Hunter did not associate the vital respiratory process with the change of colour of the blood during respiration. He gave reasons for this opinion – 'it was not necessary for the blood to undergo this [colour] change to render it fit for every purpose in the animal oeconomy, for we find that venal blood answers some purposes; thus, the blood from the intestines, spleen, etc., going to the liver, as we suppose for the secretion of the bile, shows that venal blood will do for some secretions, . . .'[17] And he pointed out that 'in animals which have no red globules of any kind respiration is as essential to their existence as in any other . . .'[18] He observed that the change in colour takes place out of the circulation as readily as when in it and does not therefore depend upon life. It seems that even in the light of all these accurate observations and experiments

Hunter came to an erroneous conclusion on the function of the red blood corpuscles. This could well be an example of Hunter's inductive method of investigation being overtaken by an inherent inclination towards the deductive approach, as suggested by Buckle (p. xiii). Certainly this impression is gained from a significant sentence – '. . . if we suppose the change in colour in the red globules to be all that respiration is to perform, we shall make the red globules the most essential part of the blood, whereas they are the least so'.[19] In other words, Hunter had come to an erroneous conclusion on the function of the red cells, influenced perhaps especially by his important observations on the embryonic circulation, and his further opinions on the subject would be deduced from this erroneous conclusion.

Organisation of coagulated blood – Hunter was firmly of the opinion that extravasated coagulated blood can become vascularised and organised into a tissue 'according to the stimulus of the surrounding parts which excites this coagulum into action, and makes it form within itself, blood, vessels, nerves, etc.'[20]

Hunter formed this opinion chiefly as the result of observations made on organised fibrinous coagula which occurred in the tunica vaginalis after incisional evacuation of a simple hydrocele. Hunter noted these coagula at subsequent orchidectomy and he demonstrated by injection that they had been vascularised from the tunica – 'That the blood becomes vascular is clearly shown in the case of the blood extravasated on the testicle.'[21]

He was further convinced in this opinion by a comparison with his observations in the developing chick – '. . . I compare these again with the progress of vascularity in the membranes of the chick; where one can perceive a zone of specks . . . similar to the above extravasation, and which in a few hours become vascular, . . .'[22]

This concept was of great importance to Hunter since it provided him with a general principle from which he deduced an explanation of union by first intention and of the formation of loose bodies in serous and synovial cavities.

In describing the adhesion of two divided surfaces he said – '. . . the union of the ruptured vessels is produced by the coagulation of the extravasated blood of this part, which becomes vascular.'[23]

In the formation of loose bodies, Hunter said – '. . . the blood . . . when it is extravasated into a cavity, adheres to the cavity, and is not absorbed . . . but becomes vascular, and afterwards membranous, cartilaginous, or bony, . . .'[24]

In spite of his opinion in this matter, Hunter makes several other observations which fail to support this view. Indeed he makes it clear that blood is not necessary for the union of tissues and that the effusion of plasma (coagulable lymph) is the usual method of adhesion in the union of parts – 'If the divided parts . . . remain till . . . the divided vessels are . . . shut [i.e. till bleeding has ceased], inflammation will . . . follow, and will furnish . . . materials for union . . . by throwing out the coagulated lymph . . . This inflammation I have called the adhesive . . .'.[25] 'In inflammations of the pleura . . . the adhesive inflammation takes place, and the surfaces are united . . . The cellular membrane everywhere in the body is united exactly in the same manner; . . . the cells throw out . . . the uniting matter, which . . . unites the whole into one mass.'[26]

In addition, Hunter gives examples of the lack of union in the presence of extravasated blood in some fractures, as in the formation of false joints[27] and of non-union,[28] as well as examples of failure of organisation of simple haematomas throughout the body. However, despite these observations, Hunter still regarded union by means of the organisation of extravasated blood as an important concept, as for example in discussing the non-union of a fractured femur, Hunter wrote – 'Here the parts had lost two chances of being united, the one by the extravasated blood, the other by the coagulable lymph thrown out by the adhesive inflammation . . .'[28]

Hunter's erroneous view on the organisation of coagulated blood, in which he persisted despite considerable evidence to the contrary, is probably another example of his anxiety to establish a general principle from which to make deductions, as suggested by Buckle (p. xiii). Hunter was strongly impressed by the evidence of his own observations on the vascularisation of the coagula in the tunica vaginalis and on the tissues in the developing chick, although in describing the former he seemed a little doubtful – '. . . I think I have been able to inject what I suspected to be the beginning of a vascular formation in a coagulum . . .'[29] There is little doubt that these were erroneous observations and they led him on too hastily to the promulgation of a false generalisation from which he would not be moved and from which he made erroneous deductions.

Hunter made frequent references to the importance of the heart in the animal economy. He said – '. . . the heart exerts its influence upon the different parts of the body in proportion to their vicinity to it; and the more distant that the parts are, the weaker are their powers. . . . In diseases we see mortification arising . . . in the extremities oftener than in other parts, . . . the heart not propelling the blood to these distant parts with equal force.'[30]*

There can be no doubt about the association of peripheral gangrene and a poor vascular supply. But Hunter applies a similar argument to the healing of wounds – '. . . the situation . . . in the body makes a material difference both in the powers of resistance to injuries, and of reparation when injuries have taken place. This difference seems to arise in proportion to the distance of the parts from the heart, or source of the circulation. Thus we see muscles, skin, etc. becoming more readily diseased in the legs than anywhere else, and more slow in their progress towards a cure; . . .'[31] These observations of Hunter's are simple and are not often quoted but in fact they enunciate a fundamental principle of clinical practice. Wounds and operations on the heart are very rarely complicated by infection, inflammation of the internal coats of arteries is rare, and wounds of the head and neck commonly heal without infection. But sepsis is still common in wounds of the abdomen and limbs, and there is good reason to associate this with the factor of blood supply. The initial overwhelming success of Listerian surgery focussed the attention of surgeons almost exclusively on exogenous factors in the management of wounds and the vitality of the tissues is still regarded by many as of relatively minor importance in comparison with bacterial contamination. Evidence is accumulating that endogenous factors are of more importance in wound infection than exogenous causes (p. 153). A subnormal blood supply is one of the most important endogenous factors contributing to wound infection (p. 148). Experience has shown that prophylactic and therapeutic antimicrobial measures have not in practice eliminated wound infection. Hunter's observations on the beneficent influence of an adequate blood supply in wounds are eminently applicable to

---

* Hunter in fact stated that gangrene of the lower extremity occurs more commonly in tall people (*The Works*: vol. 1, p. 274; vol. 2, p. 134; vol. 3, p. 272), an observation which it should be possible to confirm or refute.

modern surgery because they emphasise the priority of host resistance over bacterial contamination in the management of wound infection (p. 154).

Heart disease – Hunter appreciated that a patent ductus arteriosus and an atrial septal defect are compatible with life. He said – 'These passages, however, are shut up almost immediately after birth, or at least the canalis arteriosus, which immediately prevents the foramen ovale from producing its former effects; therefore it is not so necessary it should be shut up in the adult. I have seen it, to common appearance, as much open as in a foetus. There have been instances of the canalis arteriosus being open in the adult.'[32]

Fallot's tetralogy – Hunter described a case of Fallot's tetralogy: 'I was . . . consulted about . . . a young gentleman's health . . . From his infancy, every considerable exertion produced a seeming tendency to suffocation . . . change from the scarlet tinge to the modena or purple . . . in the face, . . . at the finger-ends, . . . He lived to the age of between thirteen or fourteen.' Autopsy showed '. . . a canal, or passage, was found communicating with both ventricles, . . . so large as to admit the end of the finger from the aorta with equal facility into either ventricle, the septum of the ventricle appearing to terminate with this canal. . . . the entrance of the pulmonary artery within the ventricle . . . was much smaller, and more firm than common.'[33]

Aortic valve incompetence – Hunter gave an account of a case of aortic valve incompetence: 'A. B. when a boy . . . could not run upstairs without being out of breath . . . he grew to be a well-formed . . . man; but still he retained those defects which indeed rather increased . . . often . . . seized so ill with palpitations and almost a total suffocation. . . . At such times he became black in the face. . . . my opinion was that there was something very wrong about the construction of the heart, . . . that the blood did not flow freely through the lungs . . .' Autopsy revealed – '. . . The heart was very large . . . I found the valves of the aorta thicker and harder than usual, having at the same time the appearance of being very much shrivelled. . . . the blood, therefore, must have fallen back into the cavity of the ventricle again at every systole of the artery. . . . This produced a stagnation . . . of the blood almost in every part of the body; first, in the left ventricle, . . . left auricle; pulmonary veins, pulmonary arteries, right ventricle, right auricle, and all the veins of the body . . .'[34]

In discussing this case, Hunter makes the remarkably astute observation that the ultimate cause of cardiac failure may be in the myocardium rather than in an associated valvular lesion – a concept that Sir Thomas Lewis promulgated over a century later. Hunter said – 'It may be difficult to account for the increased size of the heart; whether it was a mechanical effect, as the blood would be thrown back into it at every systole of the aorta and diastole of the heart, or whether it arose from a particular affection of that viscus. The first idea is the more natural; but it is not necessary that the cause should be of this kind, for we see every day enlarged hearts, where the symptoms have been somewhat similar, and yet no visible mechanical cause existed; and indeed it is a common effect where there is an impeded circulation.'[35]

Aneurysm of Ventricle – John Hunter found this lesion at an autopsy – 'April 1757. The opening of Genl Herbert's Body. He died suddenly . . . on cutting into the left ventricle, I found it white and callous . . . At the apex it was forming itself into a kind of Aneurism; becoming there very thin. That part was lined with a thrombus, just the shape of the pouch in which it lay.'[36]

RESUSCITATION OF THE DROWNED

In Hunter's time, methods of resuscitation from drowning were wholly unscientific and inadequate. Hickey recounts in his *Memoirs* that in 1775 while he was sailing to Jamaica, the chief mate fell overboard. He was rescued within half an hour – 'The means practised in those days for recovery of drowned persons were then resorted to, one of which was bleeding (which has since been ascertained to be very prejudicial). . . . An incision was therefore made, but no blood followed. The other means, such as friction, the application of salt and strong volatiles were continued two hours without the smallest symptom of returning animation. At the end of that time the blood suddenly spouted out from the arm, . . . then as suddenly stopped, . . . after which the limbs became stiff, . . . and life had evidently fled for ever.'[37]

Hunter presented his paper on the subject to the Royal Society in 1776. It was an excellent scientific appraisal of the problem, based on sound physiological principles and it established the essentials of treatment. He had already conducted experiments on a dog to demonstrate the cardiac embarrassment associated with obstructed respiration (p. 102) and he applied these observations to an understanding of the mechanism of drowning. – 'The loss of motion in drowning seems to arise from the loss of respiration . . . [which] appears . . . to be the first cause, and the heart's motion ceasing, to be the second or consequent; therefore most probably the restoration of breathing is all that is necessary to restore the heart's motion . . .'[38]

Hunter gave details of treatment. The first action should be 'blowing air into the lungs'[39] for which he recommended a special pair of bellows. He advised using electricity to stimulate the heart – 'As the heart is commonly the last part that ceases to act, it is probably the first part that takes on the action of recovery. Electricity has been known to be of service, and should be tried when other methods have failed. It is probably the only method we have of immediately stimulating the heart . . .'[40]

The earliest reports on cardiac resuscitation by the use of electricity are usually attributed to McWilliam (1889),[41] Prevost and Battelli (1900),[42] Beck (1947)[43] and Zoll (1952).[44] However Perman (1978)[45] drew attention to an account of successful cardiac resuscitation by electric shock carried out by Mr. Squires on a patient in 1775,[46] which was reported in the Transactions of the Royal Humane Society. This volume also included a paper by William Henly, FRS[47] strongly advocating the use of electrical stimulation for cardiac resuscitation. John Hunter was one of the first to appreciate the importance of this therapy and advised its application in his paper presented to the Royal Humane Society in 1776.[38]

Hunter recommended using a gastric tube* – 'a hollow bougie, or flexible catheter, of sufficient length to go into the stomach, and convey any stimulating matter into it, without affecting the lungs.'[48] He stated that he 'would by all means discourage bloodletting, which I think weakens the animal principle and life itself . . .'[48]

Hunter concluded by proposing 'that all who are employed in this practice be particularly required to keep an accurate journal of the means used, and the degree of success attending them; whence we may be furnished with facts sufficient to enable us to draw conclusions, on which a certain practice may hereafter be established.'[49]

---

* See also p. 83 on Hunter's method of gastric intubation.

ARTERIES

Hunter was the first to demonstrate the muscularity of arteries. He appreciated that 'in the blood vessels no traces of muscles are distinguishable by mere inspection'[50] and he therefore made experiments on the blood vessels of a dead horse 'by which means the different actions of the muscular and of the elastic powers become easily discernible.'[51] He showed that 'Every part of the vascular system is not equally endowed with muscles; the larger vessels, especially the arteries, being chiefly composed of elastic substances, whilst many parts of the smaller . . . appear to be almost entirely muscular.'[51]

The arterial blood pressure was not considered by Hunter to be of much significance – 'Dr. Hales made an experiment on a horse to ascertain the strength of the arteries, which gives us the power of the left ventricle; but all this explains nothing, for its power is equal to the use wanted.'[52]

Popliteal Aneurysm – John Hunter's operation for popliteal aneurysm is of considerable importance, if only because, over the years, it has been the most common item of all his work for which he is remembered. Popliteal aneurysm was a frequent occurrence in Hunter's time and its surgical treatment was very inadequate. In many cases amputation was the operation of choice.

The aneurysm was believed to be due to a weakness of the coats of the popliteal artery, independent of any actual disease, and the standard operation consisted of a direct approach to the aneurysm, *viz.* ligation of the artery above and below and allowing the sac to heal with suppuration.

Hunter was of the opinion that weakness of the arterial wall alone would not give rise to an aneurysm; he believed that the cause was actual disease of the artery. He therefore set up experiments to support these views – 'One of the carotid arteries of a dog, for an inch in length, was laid bare, and its coats removed, layer after layer, until the blood was seen through the remaining transparent coat, and I had gone as far as I dared; I then left the artery alone for three weeks, when I killed the dog, expecting to find a dilatation of the artery, as had been asserted; but to my surprise the sides of the wound had closed on the artery, and the whole was consolidated to and over it, forming a strong bond of union, so that the whole was stronger than ever.'[53]

The experiments confirmed Hunter's opinion that weakness of

the arterial wall alone did not cause aneurysm, that the aneurysmal artery is the site of disease often extending for some way from the sac and 'that the cause of failure in the common operation arises from tying a diseased artery . . .'[54] Hunter therefore said 'Why not tie it up higher in the sound parts, where it is tied in amputation, and preserve the limb? The circumstances to be regarded chiefly turn upon the collateral branches being sufficient to carry on the circulation.'[55] He was thus led to propose ligation of the femoral artery, well above the diseased part, in the anterior part of the thigh deep to the sartorious muscle at the site which became known for years as 'Hunter's canal'.

Hunter's operation was attended by immediate success. The first patient was forty-five years of age and was submitted to operation in December 1785. He died fifteen months later as the result of a fever and the autopsy showed that the aneurysmal sac was 'somewhat larger than a hen's egg'.[56] Hunter's fourth patient was a coachman aged 36 years who lived for fifty years after the operation. At his death in 1837, Thomas Wormald (President of the Royal College of Surgeons in 1857) obtained the limb which is still to be seen in the Hunterian Museum at the College. Dissection of the specimen in this case showed that '. . . The arteries generally were loaded with calcareous deposit, . . . while the tortuous anastomosing vessels . . . were, comparatively, in their normal state. . . . the aneurysm was represented by a small calcareous tumour about the size of a filbert'.[57]

It is commonly stated that Hunter devised his operation as the result of experiments performed on deer at Richmond Park. The account seems to have originated in statements by Richard Owen in 1879 and in 1881. Owen said that in July 1785 Hunter tied one of the external carotid arteries of a stag in order to study the effect on the growth of the corresponding antler. He noticed that the antler at first became cold and stunted but within a few weeks it resumed its normal growth and temperature. At autopsy it was found that the ligature on the carotid artery was intact and a healthy collateral circulation had developed. An editorial in the British Medical Journal stated that Owen's account was 'founded upon a tradition received by William Clift from his predecessor William Ball [Bell], who assisted John Hunter in injecting and making the preparations which illustrate the phenomena of the successive growth and loss of the antlers of deer.'[58]

This account unfortunately has never been substantiated by any evidence in Hunter's known writings. The experiments described by Hunter and also by Everard Home[59] are confined to delamination of the arteries in dogs. Furthermore Hunter's purpose in ligating the femoral artery was stated to be that 'the force of the circulation being thus taken off from the aneurismal sac, the progress of the disease would be stopped; and he thought it probable, that if the parts were left to themselves, the sac, with its contents, might be absorbed . . .'[60] There is no mention of a collateral circulation. It is remarkable that there is no reference to these experiments on antlers in any of the first four biographies of John Hunter, *viz.* those by Home (1794), Foot (1794), Adams (1817) and Ottley (1835). Indeed Ottley gave a very detailed account of Hunter's contribution to the surgery of aneurysm in which he described the experiments on the carotid artery of the dog but made no mention of the experiment recounted by Owen.[61] It is also of significance that Hunter made no reference to this experiment in discussing the functional increase of size of the external carotid arteries in the stag – 'We find it a common principle in the animal machine, that every part increases in some degree according to the action required. Thus we find muscles increase in size when much exercised; vessels become larger in proportion to the necessity of supply, as for instance, in the gravid uterus: the external carotids in the stag, also, when his horns are growing, are much larger than at any other time.'[62] Nevertheless, Hunter's operation gave a practical demonstration of the development of a collateral circulation adequate to retain the viability of a limb after ligation of its main artery.

John Hunter was 'not the first, as some of his apologists have alleged, to show that collateral circulation, sufficient to preserve the vitality of a limb, may be established after ligature of the main arterial trunk. At most he rediscovered the fact independently for himself, and for some of his contemporaries. The fact itself had long been known. Celsus in the first century, Galen in the second, Aetius in the sixth, Paulus Aegineta in the seventh, and Paré in the sixteenth, each and all recommended the application of the ligature of bleeding blood-vessels, whether on the exposed surface of a wound or in the continuity of a limb. As early as the year 1646 M. A. Severinus and Ioannes Trullius successfully tied the femoral artery for a traumatic aneurism in the thigh, and a few

English and continental surgeons occasionally followed a similar practice. It is nevertheless true that HUNTER was the first to apply a ligature to the femoral artery for spontaneous popliteal aneurism in accordance with distinct scientific principles discovered and demonstrated by the scientific method of observation and experiment.'[63]

VEINS

Air embolus – Hunter conducted a series of experiments to determine the effects of the introduction of foreign materials into the circulation. He made intravenous injections of a great variety of substances, including salt, vinegar, nitric acid, opium and gin. He concluded that 'many substances thrown into the blood produce much more violent effects in this way than when taken into the stomach, and even cause immediate death.' He also found that 'Air killed immediately. We should therefore be very careful in making experiments, when we inject substances into the veins, that air does not enter with the substances, and cause the death which we impute to the latter.'[64]

Phlebitis – John Hunter was the first to appreciate the occurrence of inflammation in veins. Indeed his description of phlebitis is an excellent example of his deductive philosophy. Having established the principles of the pathology of inflammation, he applied this generalisation to the explanation of the changes found in phlebitis – '. . . the inside of veins, as well as of all other cavities, is a seat of inflammation and abscess. . . . in violent inflammations . . . as in compound fractures . . . the coats of the larger veins . . . become also considerably inflamed, and . . . their inner surfaces take on the adhesive, suppurative, and ulcerative inflammations; for in such inflammations I have found in many places of the veins adhesion, in others matter, and in others ulceration.'[65]

Hunter then went on to apply this pathological explanation to clinical cases – 'These circumstances all considered lead us to account for a very frequent complaint, that is, an inflamed arm after bleeding . . . Upon examining the arm of a man who had died . . . I found the veins . . . in many places united by the adhesive inflammation . . . in many parts of the veins that suppuration had begun, . . . and in several other places ulceration had taken place so as to have destroyed that surface next the skin, and a circumscribed abscess was formed.'[66]

Finally Hunter's clear understanding of the pathology of phlebitis led him logically on to an appreciation of the complication of pyaemia – 'In all cases where inflammation of veins runs high, or extends itself considerably, it is to be expected that the whole system will be affected. . . . where no adhesions of the sides of the veins are formed, or where such adhesions are incomplete, pus passing into the circulation may add to the general disorder, and even render it fatal.'[67]

LYMPHATICS

The existence of lymphatics was first demonstrated in 1627 by Aselli[68] but before Hunter's time no recognition had been made of the lymphatics as an absorbent system distinct from the blood capillaries. It was believed that the lymphatics were connected with terminal arterioles and that absorption of tissue fluids was performed by the veins.

John Hunter established the anatomy and physiology of the lymphatics as a separate system by careful dissection and injections and by a series of ingenious experiments on the intestinal lacteals. One of his anatomical preparations demonstrated lymphatic vessels extending from the popliteal fossa up to the inguinal and lumbar nodes and thoracic duct, as well as the lacteals and the receptaculum chyli, all filled with a mercury injection.[69] He isolated a segment of small intestine and demonstrated that milk and fluids coloured with indigo were absorbed by the lacteals but not by the veins. Injections of musk into the intestine showed that the odour was present in the chyle but not in the veins.[70]

The discovery of the correct structure and function of the absorbent system was extremely important and its priority was hotly disputed. Although William Hunter had taught the facts to his classes year after year from 1746, Alexander Monro published a treatise on the subject in 1757, without reference to William Hunter, whose lectures Monro had attended in 1755. The argument between the Hunters and the Monroes went on for several years, but there is no doubt that John Hunter by his dissections and experimental work was primarily responsible for establishing the concept that the absorption of foreign substances from the tissues is by the lymphatic system, a concept that thas since been extended to apply also to the absorption of bacteria.[71]

Absorption – John Hunter was the first to appreciate the

important fundamental principle of absorption of unwanted tissue in the body. Having established this concept by his work on the lymphatics he applied it to the elucidation of a great number of natural and pathological phenomena – 'So far the absorbents have been considered as an active part in the animal oeconomy; but, from a further knowledge of these vessels, we shall find that they are of much more consequence in the body than has been imagined, and that they are often taking down what arteries had formerly built up, thus becoming modellers of the body; and that they are also removing many diseased parts, which were beyond the power of cure . . .'.[72] 'The remote causes of absorption are various. The most simple appears to arise from a part's becoming useless, as the thymus gland, the ductus arteriosus, the alveoli after the teeth drop out, the crystalline lens after couching, the fat of the body in fever, either inflammatory or hectic, all which are removed by the absorbents as useless parts.'[73]

It is not unlikely that his dental work early on in his career first presented Hunter with the concept of the absorption of tissue (p. 82). He wrote – 'Diseases of the Alveolar Processes . . . The first effect which takes place is a wasting of the alveolar processes, which are in many people gradually absorbed and taken into the system . . . Though the wasting of the alveoli . . . are to be considered as diseases, when they happen early in life, yet it would appear to be only on account of a natural effect taking place too soon; for the same thing is very common in old age . . .'[74] And again – 'It is by means of the progressive [absorption] that bones exfoliate and sloughs separate . . . it is somewhat similar to the modelling process in the natural formation of bone. It is this last that removes useless parts, as the alveolar processes when the teeth drop out, or when children are shedding teeth, which allows these to drop out, . . .'[75]

Hunter applied the principle of absorption to an understanding of other natural processes as for example – 'The process of shedding . . . The deer casts his antlers with his hair. . . . I believe that the exfoliation of horns is owing to the first mode of absorption, viz. intestinal absorption; which renders the attached part soft, so as to break easily off.'[76]

John Hunter attached very great importance to the concept of absorption as an explanation of many pathological processes. He wrote – 'A knowledge of the absorbing system, as it is now established, gives us considerable information respecting many of the effects of poisons, and illustrates several symptoms of the venereal disease, in particular the formation of buboes. Prior to this knowledge we find writers at a loss how to give a true and consistent explanation of many of the symptoms of this disease. The discovery of the lymphatics being a system of absorbents has thrown more light on many diseases than the discovery of the circulation of the blood: it leads in many cases directly to the cause of the disease.'[77]

The most important deduction that Hunter made from his established concept of absorption in pathological processes was in its explanation of the ulcerative stage of inflammation – 'The separation of a dead part from a living is performed by the absorbents, which take into the circulation the edges of the sound parts which adjoin to the dead, and thus the dead part being set at liberty drops off. But in order to effect this, inflammation is first produced, and then ulceration or absorption follows: The separation takes place sooner or later, in proportion to the life of the part; hence the skin, muscles, and parts which are nearest the heart, slough readily; tendons and bones slowly; and cellular membrane less readily than the skin.'[78] This concept is especially significant in his detailed observations on the process of sequestration in osteomyelitis (p. 39).

Lymphoedema – Hunter described the condition of idiopathic lymphoedema of the legs [Milroy's disease] – '*Elephantiasis* . . . The legs of young people I have seen so swelled as to be all of a size. It arises from an extravasation of coagulable lymph equally diffused; the parts become firm and similar to dropsy, only there is no pitting: it may be a kind of dropsy, for dropsical swellings often degenerate into this kind of swelling; yet the cause of the two may be very dissimilar: it is most frequent in young people. . . . There is no fixed cure.'[79]

Lymphatics in malignant disease – Hunter appreciated the importance of lymphatic involvement in malignant disease.[80] He wrote: '*Of the Cancerous Testicle* . . . When the testicle has affected the scrotum there may be absorption to the glands of the groin, as in lues; . . . I was at first puzzled to account for the appearance of cancer in the groin, as we know the testicle receives its vessels, etc. from the loins, and therefore the glands in the loins become affected by the disease extending along the course of the cord; but when I recollected that the scrotum was affected, I knew it to be owing to the lymphatics of the scrotum, which pass through the groin.'[81]

In cancer of the breast, John Hunter advised that 'We should examine, for example, the glands in the groin or axilla, to ascertain if they are thickened or swoln, and also the course of the absorbents; for if these are sound and moveable, then the disease may be safely removed. But if any are so deep or fixed as not to admit of removal, then we must consider whether the whole limb can be removed, above the consequent tumours; and if not, we ought to do nothing.'[82] He noted also that '. . . we are apt to be deceived in regard to the lymphatic glands, which often appear moveable, when, on extirpation, a chain of them is found to run far beyond out of our reach, which renders the operation unsuccessful. As this is not easily known, I would, in most cases, where the lymphatic glands are considerably enlarged, advise that the case should be let alone.'[82]

John Hunter was familiar with oedema of the arm associated with enlarged malignant lymph nodes but he also noted that malignant lymphoedema could occur without palpable nodes – 'I have seen the oedema of the arm before there was any tumefaction of the lymphatic glands . . . the oedema above mentioned puzzled me, having never before seen it without the glands being enlarged, and I have never seen another case.'[81]

METABOLISM

Animal and vegetable heat – The correct relation between the production of biological heat and the process of respiration was not established until after Hunter's time* and although his work on animal and vegetable heat included valuable experiments and observations on most of the items associated with the production of heat, it never actually explained the phenomenon.

Hunter appreciated that 'the principle of heat is one of the first principles of action in nature; it is that which unlocks matter . . . It may even be said to compel matter to action.'[83] He discussed various theories of the cause of animal heat and admitted – '. . . I profess, however, not thoroughly to understand it, and the theories hitherto brought forward do not in the least satisfy me . . .'[84]

---

* Oxygen was discovered by Priestley in 1774 and its significance in respiration was demonstrated by Lavoisier in 1789.

In many of his experiments on respiration and observations on the red blood corpuscles, Hunter came close to the correct answer, as for example, in discussing the red blood corpuscles – 'Their use would seem to be connected with strength, for the stronger the animal the more it has of the red globules . . .'[85] And again, he stated that the blood in whales '. . . is . . . similar to . . . quadrupeds, but I have an idea that the red globules are in larger proportion. I will not pretend to determine how far this may assist in keeping up the animal heat, but as these animals . . . live in a very cold climate . . . such as readily carries off heat from the body, they may want help of this kind.'[86]

Hunter was well aware of the vital function of the lungs – '. . . I conceive the Lungs to have two powers, one to receive, the other to give; I should consider them giving to the air what was rendered useless, detrimental, as a constituent part of Life, and exchanging it for that which it had lost, the Essential part.'[87] His experiments on dogs (p. 102) demonstrated a fundamental relation between the function of respiration and the vitality of the blood – '. . . breathing, therefore, seems to render life to the blood . . .'[88] Hunter concluded that 'There is reason to presume that heat has some natural connexion with the respiration of air; for the degree of heat is in proportion to the degree of respiration. From the chemical change produced in the breath, is there not reason to think that one purpose of respiration is to produce a chemical change on the blood? Expired breath is loaded with fixed air or aërial acid [carbonic acid], and this has been proved by the French chemists and by Mr. Muire to be a compound of charcoal [carbon] and vital air [oxygen]. It would appear as if charcoal were an excrementitious part of the blood separated by combining with vital air.'[89]

Hunter's observations on the blood supply to muscles led him to state that '. . . the red blood, in those animals that have it, is of essential use to muscular contraction.'[90] Again he nearly provided the correct answer as he stated – 'What is the connexion of muscular action with respiration? For it is well known that violent exercise excites respiration to a great degree.'[91] It is clear that Hunter had accumulated much of the evidence required to explain the source of animal heat, *viz.* the vital association of respiration and changes in the blood, and the distribution of red blood corpuscles and their importance in muscle activity. That Hunter did not finally interpret the facts correctly may have been due partly to his erroneous deduction about the function of the red blood corpuscles (p. 102). Nevertheless, he 'rather supposed that animal heat was owing to some decomposition going on in the body, and in pretty regular progression, though not the process of fermentation'.[92]

Cold – Hunter made some astute observations on the relation between temperature and body metabolism. He pointed out that cold is associated with a diminution of metabolism – '. . . cold . . . lessens the necessity [of action].'[93] He applied this important principle to clinical cases, e.g. cold air was valuable in debilitated patients suffering from fevers 'by diminishing heat in proportion to the diminution of life, or lessening the necessity of the body's producing its own cold.'[93] In frost-bitten patients it was important not to apply heat rapidly because, the vascular supply being normal ['the powers of action remain as perfect as ever'],[93] a speedy return to normal may result in gangrene. In cases of incipient gangrene of the feet, the vascular supply being deficient ['a diminution of power'], it was necessary to minimise the metabolism ['the action'] – 'to keep the parts cool is proper, and all the applications should be cold.'[94]

Cheyne-Stokes respiration – John Hunter described this condition and cited it to support the opinion that 'the breathing which produces sound is voluntary'. He described a case – 'A gentleman had a singular asthmatic affection, and his breathing gradually stopt and again gradually recovered, but became violent, and this constantly and alternately held two or three minutes; and when the breathing ceased yet he spoke, although but faintly'.[95]

REFERENCES

1 Hunter J. Lectures on the principles of surgery in *The Works of John Hunter*, ed. J F Palmer. London, Longman. 1835, vol. 1, p. 229.

2 Hunter J. A treatise on the blood, inflammation and gun-shot wounds in *The Works of John Hunter*, ed. J F Palmer. London, Longman. 1837, vol. 3, p. 104.

3 Harvey W. On generation in *The Works of William Harvey*, transl. Robert Willis. London, printed for the Sydenham Society. 1847, p. 379.

4 Hunter J. Lectures on the principles of surgery in *The Works of John Hunter*, ed. J F Palmer. London, Longman. 1835, vol. 1, p. 231.

5 Ibid. p. 224.

6 Hunter J. A treatise on the blood, inflammation and gun-shot wounds in *The Works of John Hunter*, ed. J F Palmer. London, Longman. 1837, vol. 3, p. 111.

7 Hunter J. Lectures on the principles of surgery in *The Works of John Hunter*, ed. J F Palmer. London, Longman. 1835, vol. 1, p. 232.

8 Hunter J. A treatise on the blood, inflammation and gun-shot wounds in *The Works of John Hunter*, ed. J F Palmer. London, Longman. 1837, vol. 3, p. 32.

9 Ibid. p. 60.

10 Ibid. p. 356.
11 Ibid. p. 66.
12 Owen R. Preface, *The Works of John Hunter*, ed. J F Palmer. London, Longman. 1837, vol. 4, p. xiii.
13 Hunter J. A treatise on the blood, inflammation and gun-shot wounds in *The Works of John Hunter*, ed. J F Palmer. London, Longman. 1837, vol. 3, p. 57.
14 Ibid. p. 68.
15 Ibid. p. 86.
16 Ibid. p. 77, 78.
17 Ibid. p. 86.
18 Ibid. p. 75.
19 Ibid. p. 74.
20 Ibid. p. 113.
21 Ibid. p. 243.
22 Ibid. p. 119.
23 Ibid. p. 243.
24 Hunter J. Lectures on the principles of surgery in *The Works of John Hunter*, ed. J F Palmer. London, Longman. 1835, vol. 1, p. 520.
25 Hunter J. A treatise on the blood, inflammation and gun-shot wounds in *The Works of John Hunter*, ed. J F Palmer. London, Longman. 1837, vol. 3, p. 254.
26 Ibid. p. 400.
27 Hunter J. Lectures on the principles of surgery in *The Works of John Hunter*, ed. J F Palmer. London, Longman. 1835, vol. 1, p. 504.
28 Ibid. p. 427.
29 Hunter J. A treatise on the blood, inflammation and gun-shot wounds in *The Works of John Hunter*, ed. J F Palmer. London, Longman. 1837, vol. 3, p. 119.
30 Hunter J. A treatise on venereal disease in *The Works of John Hunter*, ed. J F Palmer. London, Longman. 1835, vol. 2, p. 134.
31 Hunter J. A treatise on the blood, inflammation and gun-shot wounds in *The Works of John Hunter*, ed. J F Palmer. London, Longman. 1837, vol. 3, p. 272.
32 Ibid. p. 175.
33 Ibid. pp. 82–84.
34 Ibid. p. 80.
35 Ibid. p. 82.
36 Hunter J. *Case-Book. Transcript by W Clift*. Vol. 3, pp. 20, 21.
37 Hickey W. *Memoirs of William Hickey*, ed. Alfred Spencer. London, Hurst and Blackett. 1913–1925, 5th edn., four volumes, vol. II, p. 19.
38 Hunter J. Proposals for the recovery of persons apparently drowned in *The Works of John Hunter*, ed. J F Palmer. London, Longman. 1837, vol. 4, pp. 168, 169.
39 Ibid. p. 170.
40 Ibid. p. 173.
41 McWilliam J A. Electrical stimulation of the heart in man. *British Medical Journal*. 1889, vol. 1, pp. 348–350.
42 Prevost J L and Battelli F. Les Tremulations fibrillaires et le massage du coeur. *Journal de Physiologie et Pathologie Génerale Paris*. 1900, vol. 2, p. 40. Quoted by H E Stephenson *Cardiac Arrest and Resuscitation*. St. Louis, C V Mosby. 1974.
43 Beck C S, Pritchard W H and Feil H S. Ventricular fibrillation of long duration abolished by electric shock. *Journal of the American Medical Association*. 1947, vol. 135, pp. 985, 986.
44 Zoll P M. Resuscitation of the heart in ventricular standstill by external electric stimulation. *New England Journal of Medicine*. 1952, vol. 247, pp. 768–771.

45 Perman E. Successful cardiac resuscitation with electricity in the 18th century? *British Medical Journal.* 1978, vol. 2, pp. 1770, 1771.

46 Squires Mr. Electricity restored vitality. *Transactions of the Royal Humane Society 1774–1794,* ed. W Hawes. London, Nichols. 1775, p. 51.

47 Henly W. Observations on suspended animation: electricity. *Transactions of the Royal Humane Society 1774–1794,* ed. W Hawes. London, Nichols. 1775, pp. 63–65.

48 Hunter J. Proposals for the recovery of persons apparently drowned in *The Works of John Hunter,* ed. J F Palmer. London, Longman. 1837, vol. 4, p. 174.

49 Ibid. p. 175.

50 Hunter J. Croonian lectures on muscular motion in *The Works of John Hunter,* ed. J F Palmer. London, Longman. 1837, vol. 4, p. 252.

51 Ibid. p. 253.

52 Hunter J. A treatise on the blood, inflammation and gun-shot wounds in *The Works of John Hunter,* ed. J F Palmer. London, Longman. 1837, vol 3, p. 182.

53 Hunter J. Lectures on the principles of surgery in *The Works of John Hunter,* ed. J F Palmer. London, Longman. 1835, vol. 1, p. 544.

54 Hunter J. A treatise on the blood, inflammation and gun-shot wounds in *The Works of John Hunter,* ed. J F Palmer. London, Longman. 1837, vol. 3, p. 597.

55 Hunter J. Lectures on the principles of surgery in *The Works of John Hunter,* ed. J F Palmer. London, Longman. 1835, vol. 1, p. 548.

56 Hunter J. A treatise on the blood, inflammation and gun-shot wounds in *The Works of John Hunter,* ed. J F Palmer. London, Longman. 1837, vol. 3, p. 601.

57 Wormald T. *Hunterian Oration 1857.* London, John Churchill. 1858, p. 15.

58 Editorial, John Hunter and vivisection. *British Medical Journal.* 1879, vol. 1, p. 285.

59 Home E. in *The Works of John Hunter,* ed. J F Palmer. London, Longman. 1837, vol. 3, p. 597.

60 Ibid. p. 598.

61 Ottley D. Life of John Hunter in *The Works of John Hunter,* ed. J F Palmer. London, Longman. 1835, vol. 1, pp. 96–101.

62 Hunter J. A treatise on the blood, inflammation and gun-shot wounds in *The Works of John Hunter,* ed. J F Palmer. London, Longman. 1837, vol. 3, p. 333.

63 Editorial, The Hunterian operation and vivisection. *Lancet.* 1881, vol. 2, p. 636.

64 Hunter J. Lectures on the principles of surgery in *The Works of John Hunter,* ed. J F Palmer. London, Longman. 1835, vol. 1, p. 350.

65 Hunter J. A treatise on the blood, inflammation and gun-shot wounds in *The Works of John Hunter,* ed. J F Palmer. London, Longman. 1837, vol. 3, p. 581.

66 Ibid. p. 583.

67 Ibid. p. 584.

68 Aselli G. *De Lactibus.* Milan. 1627, quoted by J Trueta in *Principles and Practice of War Surgery.* London, Hamish Hamilton. 1946, 3rd edn., p. 53.

69 Hunter J. On absorption by veins in *The Works of John Hunter,* ed. J F Palmer. London, Longman. 1837, vol. 4, p. 309.

70 Ibid. p. 307.

71 Trueta J. *Principles and Practice of War Surgery.* London, Hamish Hamilton. 1946, 3rd edn., p. 53.

72 Hunter J. Lectures on the principles of surgery in *The Works of John Hunter,* ed. J F Palmer. London, Longman. 1835, vol. 1, p. 252.

73 Ibid. p. 420.

74 Hunter J. Treatise on the natural history of the human teeth in *The Works of John Hunter,* ed. J F Palmer. London, Longman. 1835, vol. 2, p. 79.

75 Hunter J. Lectures on the principles of surgery in *The Works of John Hunter*, ed. J F Palmer. London, Longman. 1835, vol. 1, p. 419.
76 Hunter J. *Essays and Observations on Natural History, Anatomy, Physiology, Psychology and Geology*, ed. R Owen. London, John Van Voorst. 1861, vol. 2, p. 137.
77 Hunter J. A treatise on venereal disease in *The Works of John Hunter*, ed. J F Palmer. London, Longman. 1835, vol. 2, p. 354.
78 Hunter J. Lectures on the principles of surgery in *The Works of John Hunter*, ed. J F Palmer. London, Longman. 1835, vol. 1, p. 606.
79 Ibid. pp. 563, 564.
80 Dobson J. John Hunter's views on cancer. *Annals of the Royal College of Surgeons of England*. 1959, vol. 25, pp. 176–181.
81 Hunter J. Lectures on the principles of surgery in *The Works of John Hunter*, ed. J F Palmer. London, Longman. 1835, vol. 2, p. 354.
82 Ibid. p. 627.
83 Hunter J. Lectures on the principles of surgery in *The Works of John Hunter*, ed. J F Palmer. London, Longman. 1835, vol. 1, p. 278.
84 Hunter J. A treatise on the blood, inflammation and gun-shot wounds in *The Works of John Hunter*, ed. J F Palmer. London, Longman. 1837, vol. 3, p. 16.
85 Ibid. p. 68.
86 Hunter J. Observations on the structure and oeconomy of whales in *The Works of John Hunter*, ed. J F Palmer. London, Longman. 1837, vol. 4, p. 364.
87 Hunter J. *Catalogue of the Museum 1800 Gallery*. Royal College of Surgeons of England Library. p. 57.
88 Hunter J. A treatise on the blood, inflammation and gun-shot wounds in *The Works of John Hunter*, ed. J F Palmer. London, Longman. 1837, vol. 3, p. 86.
89 Hunter J. *Essays and Observations on Natural History, Anatomy, Physiology, Psychology and Geology*, ed. R Owen. London, John Van Voorst. 1861, vol. 1, p. 123.
90 Hunter J. Croonian lectures on muscular motion in *The Works of John Hunter*, ed. J F Palmer. London, Longman. 1837, vol. 4, p. 220.
91 Hunter J. *Essays and Observations on Natural History, Anatomy, Physiology, Psychology and Geology*, ed. R Owen. London, John Van Voorst. 1861, vol. 1, p. 125.
92 Hunter J. Lectures on the principles of surgery in *The Works of John Hunter*, ed. J F Palmer. London, Longman. 1835, vol. 1, p. 284.
93 Hunter J. Proposals for the recovery of persons apparently drowned in *The Works of John Hunter*, ed. J F Palmer. London, Longman. 1837, vol. 4, p. 171.
94 Hunter J. A treatise on venereal disease in *The Works of John Hunter*, ed. J F Palmer. London, Longman. 1835, vol. 2, p. 137.
95 Hunter J. A treatise on the blood, inflammation and gun-shot wounds in *The Works of John Hunter*, ed. J F Palmer. London, Longman. 1837, vol. 3, p. 193.

CHAPTER 12

NERVOUS SYSTEM
SPECIAL SENSES

HUNTER showed a great interest in the comparative anatomy of the nervous system, his studies of which extended from the most simple to the most complex forms. He noted the fibrous structure of the brain and observed its distinct characters in cetaceans (p. 144). The anatomy of the nervous system provided Hunter with a basis of classification of animals, one of several such schemes that he evolved in respect of the different systems of the body. His classification of the different types of nervous system in increasing complexity forms an excellent example of an evolutionary series (p. 188).

Hunter recognised six classes of animals according to the structure of the nervous system.[1] In the first two classes he included animals whose brain was not enclosed in a bony skull. The third, fourth, fifth and sixth classes included, respectively, fish, reptiles, birds and quadrupeds. These latter four classes, of course, share the common features of a brain and spinal cord protected by skull and vertebrae, and special senses. It seems remarkable, as Owen pointed out, that Hunter did not base his classification on the great natural grouping of animals into vertebrates and invertebrates, the appreciation of which 'was reserved for the sagacious penetration of Cuvier.'[2] It is tempting to suggest that, in characteristic fashion, Hunter, having too hastily established a classification of six classes of the nervous system, regarded this generalisation as final, from which further opinions on the subject would have to be deduced, while alternative views, even those of greater significance, would not be entertained (p. xiii).

NERVES

Specific response – The doctrine of specific nerve energies enunciated by Müller in 1838 states that '. . . each type of sensation is mediated by a specific type of nerve fibre, that is, one with a distinctive type of end organ.'[3] The subjective response of a sense organ is the same whatever the nature of the stimulus. Thus irritation of the optic nerve by any kind of stimulating agent gives rise to the sensation of light. Hunter's writings include a similar view, which appears to have occurred to him as a result of his demonstration of the nerves of the special senses.

Hunter's paper on the olfactory nerve established the important fact that the special senses are supplied by two sets of nerves, those serving the special sense and those of common sensation. In his dissections Hunter 'found several nerves, principally from the fifth pair, going to and lost upon the membrane of the nose; but suppose that these have nothing to do with the sense of smelling.'[4] He applied this principle to the other special senses – 'Thus we find nerves from different origins going to the parts composing the organ of sight, which are not at all concerned in the immediate act of vision.'[5]

The presence in the organs of special sense of a double nerve supply serving two different purposes immediately suggests the principle of specificity of nerve response. Hunter stated – '. . . upon the same principle, it is more than probable, that every nerve so affected as to communicate sensation, in whatever part of the nerve the impression is made, always gives the same sensation as if affected at the common seat of the sensation of that particular nerve.'[6] And again – 'a blow on the eye often produces light, and on the ear sound. And besides, those senses are subject to diseases, where the sensation often arises without impression from without.'[7]

Referred pain – Hunter was well aware, at an early stage of his career, of the clinical importance of pain occurring at a site remote from the site of disease. In his *Treatise on the Human Teeth*, he described a case of pain in the jaw which he ascribed to 'a nervous affection':

> Of Nervous Pains in the Jaws. There is one disease of the jaws which seems in reality to have no connexion with the teeth, but of which the teeth are generally suspected to be the cause. . . . a tooth is . . . drawn out; but still the pain continues . . . it is then supposed . . . that the wrong tooth was extracted whereupon that in

which the pain now seems to be is drawn, but with as little benefit. I have known cases of this kind where all the teeth of the affected side of the jaw have been drawn out, and the pain has continued in the jaw; . . . Hence it should appear that the pain in question does not arise from any disease in the part, but is entirely a nervous affection.[8]

Hunter does not quote this case as an example of referred pain but it is not unlikely that it was in fact one of pain referred from an unidentified focus of disease. However it demonstrates Hunter's awareness of the principle of referred pain and in a later work he has described this condition. Indeed Hunter was the first to present a satisfactory theory of the mechanism of referred pain, the credit for which is usually given to Martyn (1864).[9] Hunter wrote:

Delusive Symptoms respecting Sensation. – This delusion of the senses makes disease seem where it really is not, from the different seat of the symptoms and of the diseased part. Thus, diseases of the liver are referred to the shoulder, of the testicles to the back, of the hip to the knee. . . . When the trunk of the nerve is injured, the pain is referred to the termination of it, as, after amputation of the leg, pain is felt in the toes. When pressure is made on a large nerve, the most acute sensation will be at some distance below the part pressed on.[10]

Hunter disagreed with the usual view that the principle of 'sympathy' could explain pain located to a site which did not correspond with the site of disease – 'Thus, sensation of pain in the shoulder from disease in the liver has been always supposed to arise from the shoulder sympathizing with the liver. The sensation of the glans penis from a disease or irritation in the bladder has been referred to the same cause. But I believe it is a delusion in the mind; . . .'[11]

Hunter then presents a theory of the mechanism of referred pain which is clear, concise and as authoritative as any that have yet appeared:

We may suppose that when the seat of sensation in the brain only takes on part of the action of sensation in the brain, it may be in this way: Suppose E, (P. XVII.f.3) the brain: A B, two portions of the brain; G H, two nerves; F, communication between these two nerves; C D, two different parts of the body [fig. 7].

The nerve G is inserted into part of the brain A; the nerve H into the other part B. F is a communicating nerve between G and H. A and B are the two parts of the brain to which sensation from C and D

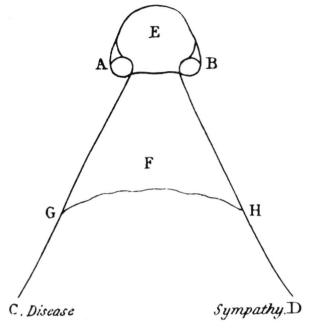

Fig. 7. Copy of John Hunter's original drawing to illustrate his theory of the mechanism of referred pain. (Pl. XVII, fig. 3, in *The Works of John Hunter*, ed. J. F. Palmer, London, Longman, 1837, vol. plates)

is conducted. C is the disease or part impressed. But from the connexion between C and D, by means of the nerves G F H, B will become the seat of action of the nerve G as well as of the nerve H, and the sensation be in part referred to D as well as to C. For if the nerve H is stimulated, in consequence of these connexions, to take up part of the action of the nerve G, and B is sensible of it as well as A is of the sensation of C, then the sensitive principle of the nerves A B is made sensible of both the disease of the part of impression as also of the sympathizer D, which become the two impressions in the sensorium. If anything stimulates G, part of the action is communicated to H; this goes on with the action to B, so that both A and B become sensible of the disease C. If there is disease in C, the mind is made sensible of it, because G always communicates the sense of C to A; but if a small portion of it is brought over to H, and this nerve carries on the action to B, B becomes sensible of it also, and B refers it not to C, but to D, because it is to that point that it has been accustomed to refer all its sensations.[12]

He offers this explanation of 'how we may feel both the disease and the part of sympathy'. But he goes on to question 'How is it in those cases where the sympathizer takes on the whole action, affection, or sensation? In this case we must suppose that not only a part but the whole of the sensation passes by the communicating nerve F to B, and thus the disease appears to be in D only.' Hunter then leads on to the logical conclusion – 'But it is possible that nervous sympathy is not effected by the nerves communicating with one another in the body, but from their connexions in the brain; as from the point B sympathizing with the point A, taking on the whole of its action, and referring its sensation to D.'[12]

Hyperaesthesia – Hunter was familiar with the sign of hyperaesthesia associated with peritonitis – '. . . when an intestine is inflamed . . . it produces somewhat of a soreness, even to the external touch; . . . Thus I have seen complaints in the viscera of the abdomen produce a vast tenderness in the skin of the abdomen.'[13]

PSYCHOSOMATIC DISEASE

Hunter was in no doubt about the very real influence of the mind over the body, an opinion which he expressed on numerous occasions throughout his writings, as for example – '. . . there is not a natural action in the body, whether involuntary or voluntary, that may not be influenced by the peculiar state of the mind at the time. . . . The skin is affected by the feeling of shame; the secretion or even the non-secretion of the testicles takes place under certain states of the mind. Palpitations of the heart and quick respirations are brought on by some states; purging and increased secretions of the urine by others.'[14]

In discussing muscular action, Hunter wrote – 'Those actions which arise from the mind belong mostly to the passions, which affect more muscles of the body than the will; perhaps there is not a muscular fibre in the whole animal machine but is at different times affected according to the different affections of the mind. . . .'[15] He described the act of copulation as 'an act of the body, the spring of which is in the mind . . . Perhaps no function of the machine depends so much upon the state of the mind as this.'[16] Hunter described several cases of loss of virility which he cured by psychological means.

Holland wrote about John Hunter – 'He had always a large belief in the influence of the mind over the body . . . He assured me, . . .

that to one patient in London (I think his own wife) he had prescribed common hot water, allowing it to be so, without any success; but that when he filled Bath bottles with the same water and pretended that they were received by the coach, she, after boiling them, derived all the benefit from them that she had expected from a course of the real waters drunk fresh at the Pump Room.'[17]

In his own case, Hunter was quite satisfied that 'the spasm on my vital parts was very likely to be brought on by a state of mind anxious about any event. . . . Thus . . . I have bees . . . and I once was anxious about their swarming lest it should not happen before I set off for town; this brought it on. . . . The cats teaze me very much by destroying my tame pheasants, partridges, etc. . . . I saw a large cat . . . and was going into the house for a gun when I became anxious lest she should get away before my return; this likewise brought on the spasm. . . .'[18]

SPECIAL SENSES

Eye – Hunter wrote papers on the subjects of accomodation, the choroid pigment, and movements of the eye. The first of these papers was the most valuable. At that time the mechanism of accomodation was not understood. Hunter rejected the two prevalent theories, *viz.* one, that the lens moved forwards and backwards in the eyeball, and the other theory that the eyeball altered its shape. He concluded that accomodation must be performed by a change in shape of the lens – 'I saw no power that could adapt the eye to the various distances . . . unless we suppose the crystalline humour [lens] to be varied in figure.'[19] Hunter suggested that this change in shape of the lens 'can only be effected by a muscular action within itself'[19] and he set up experiments to try and demonstrate muscle fibres in the lens, using the eyes of bullocks. Thus, although Hunter was incorrect in this latter suggestion, he came very near to a correct interpretation of the mechanism of accomodation.

The muscularity of the iris was described by Hunter, a presumption derived from his opinion on the active nature of muscle relaxation (p. 133) – 'The sphincter iridis of the eye contracts when there is too much light, but the radii contract when there is little or no light.'[20]

Ear – Hunter conducted a considerable amount of research on the organ of hearing in fishes and left numerous demonstration specimens in his Museum. He believed for some years that he was the first to describe this organ in fish but in his paper on the subject, written some twenty years after his first discovery, he acknowledged priority to others – 'my claim, even to the discovery of the external opening, is not so strong as I believed it to be.'[21] However, Hunter's account is comprehensive and comparative. He considered the structure of the organ of hearing in fishes as one of a progressive series of varieties in different animals (p. 139).

Hunter made the original observation that the organ of hearing is present in the Molluscs (Cephalopods) and that it is of different construction from that in fishes.[22]

As Hunter suggested, the structure of the ear shows progressive varieties which are transitional between invertebrates and vertebrates. In the former, as evidenced by the Molluscs, there are no semicircular canals. Among the lower orders of fishes, the Cyclostomes, the myxine has one semicircular canal and the lamprey has two. The cartilaginous and bony fishes have three semicircular canals and, as Hunter noted, in the latter the organ of hearing is 'distinct and detached' from the skull while in the former 'the organ is wholly surrounded by the parts composing the cavity of the skull.'[22]

ELECTRIC FISHES

Electric fishes are able to emit electric discharges and to give electric shocks sufficient to stun the recipient. (*Torpere* – to be stiff or numb). The two most common varieties are *Electrophorus* (*Gymnotus*) *electricus* and *Torpedo marmorata*. The former is also known as the Electric Eel from its snake-like shape but it is not related to the eel (Anguilla). It is a freshwater fish of S. America. The Torpedo is also known as the Electric Ray. It is a flat fish which frequents the coast of France and occurs occasionally in British waters. In all electric fishes the electric organ consists of large numbers of disk-like cells called electroplates, each having a nerve connected to one surface but not to the other. The electroplates are arranged in orderly columns, with their innervated sides all facing the same direction.[23] The electric organ of the torpedo is supplied by a large number of nerve fibres which are derived mainly from four nerves which originate from an *electric lobe* of the medulla, with a branch from the trigeminal nerve.[24]

Specimens of the Electric Eel and the Torpedo were presented to

John Hunter by John Walsh, FRS, MP whose researches on these fishes had led him to the conclusion that the shocks delivered by the Torpedo were due to the discharge of electricity. A good account of Walsh's contribution has been given by E. F. Stewart.[25]

Hunter made a careful dissection of the Torpedo and demonstrated the pair of electric organs forming large lateral masses. In describing their extensive nerve supply he noted that the nerves '. . . exceed, compared with the size of the animal, in bulk the nerves in any organ of any other known animal.'[26] Hunter concluded that 'the nerves are subservient to the formation, collection, or management of the electric fluid especially as it appears evident, from Mr. Walsh's experiments, that the will of the animal does absolutely control the electric powers of its body, which must depend on the energy of the nerves. How far this may be connected with the power of the nerves in general, or how far it may lead to an explanation of their operations, time and future discoveries alone can fully determine.'[27] The original specimens are preserved in the Hunterian Museum at the Royal College of Surgeons of England. Hunter presented his observations on the torpedo to the Royal Society in 1773. He later dissected a specimen of the electric eel given to him by James Walsh and presented his findings to the Royal Society in 1775.

Hunter's publications on the electric fishes provided material for two vulgar lampoons of the type which were common in the eighteenth century as a means of criticism of the corruption and follies of wealthy or prominent members of society. They were written by James Perry, an Aberdonian working in London, and one of them was dedicated to Lord Cholmondeley who was well known for his extravagance and dissipation (fig. 8). These publications were entertaining and popular but they were strongly criticised by the Gentleman's Magazine at the time, which said: 'We mention these vermin, merely to caution our readers against them – latet anguis in herba* – and if they should inadvertently touch either of them, they will most certainly receive a shock from which their modesty will not easily recover.'[28]

Recent investigations[23] have confirmed that the electric organ does not function spontaneously and that it is always under the control of the central nervous system, as suggested by Hunter. It

---

* a snake in the grass.

THE

T O R P E D O,

A

P   O   E   M

T O   T H E

E L E C T R I C A L   E E L.

A D D R E S S E D   T O

Mr. J O H N   H U N T E R,   SURGEON:

A N D   D E D I C A T E D   T O

The Right Honourable LORD CHOLMONDELEY.

L O N D O N:

Printed for FIELDING and WALKER, No. 20, Pater-Noster-Row.
MDCCLXXVII.

Fig. 8. First edition of *The Torpedo*, 1777. (Hunterian Society Transactions 1970–1. vol. 29, p. 81)

seems likely that in some cases the electric organ functions as a direction-finding transmitter; the *Gymnarchus niloticus* possesses in its tail tissues corresponding to an electric organ which emit a constant stream of electrical pulses.[29] This observation would have been of great interest to Darwin who admitted that in the establishment of his theory of evolution by natural selection 'the electric organs of fishes offer another case of special difficulty; for it is impossible to conceive by what steps these wondrous organs have been produced'.[30]

REFERENCES

1 Owen R. Preface, *The Works of John Hunter*, ed. J F Palmer. London, Longman. 1837, vol. 4, p. xvi.
2 Ibid. p. xvii.
3 Best C H and Taylor N B. *The Physiological Basis of Medical Practice*. London, Ballière Tindall and Cox. 1955, 6th edn. p. 946.
4 Hunter J. A description of the nerves which supply the organ of smelling in *The Works of John Hunter*, ed. J F Palmer. London, Longman. 1837, vol. 4, p. 189.
5 Ibid. p. 190.
6 Ibid. pp. 190, 191.
7 Hunter J. Lectures on the principles of surgery in *The Works of John Hunter*, ed. J F Palmer. London, Longman. 1835, vol. 1, p. 263.
8 Hunter J. Treatise on the natural history of the human teeth in *The Works of John Hunter*, ed. J F Palmer. London, Longman. 1835, vol. 2, pp. 84, 85.
9 Martyn S. On the physiological meaning of inframammary pain. *British Medical Journal*. 1864, vol. II, pp. 296–298.
10 Hunter J. Lectures on the principles of surgery in *The Works of John Hunter*, ed. J F Palmer. London, Longman. 1835, vol. 1, p. 363.
11 Ibid. p. 332.
12 Ibid. pp. 332, 333.
13 Hunter J. A treatise on the blood, inflammation and gun-shot wounds in *The Works of John Hunter*, ed. J F Palmer. London, Longman. 1837, vol. 3, pp. 291, 292.
14 Hunter J. Lectures on the principles of surgery in *The Works of John Hunter*, ed. J F Palmer. London, Longman. 1835, vol. 1, p. 359.
15 Hunter J. Croonian lectures on muscular motion in *The Works of John Hunter*, ed. J F Palmer. London, Longman. 1837, vol. 4, p. 214.
16 Hunter J. Treatise on venereal disease in *The Works of John Hunter*, ed. J F Palmer. London, Longman. 1835, vol. 2, p. 306.
17 Holland Lord. *Further Memoirs of the Whig Party 1807–1821*, ed. Lord Stavordale. London, John Murray. 1905, pp. 343, 344.
18 Hunter J. Lectures on the principles of surgery in *The Works of John Hunter*, ed. J F Palmer. London, Longman. 1835, vol. 1, p. 337.
19 Hunter J. Some facts relative to the late Mr. J Hunter's preparation for the Croonian lecture by E. Home, Esq. in *The Works of John Hunter*, ed. J F Palmer. London, Longman. 1837, vol. 4, p. 288.
20 Hunter J. A treatise on the blood, inflammation and gun-shot wounds in *The Works of John Hunter*, ed. J F Palmer. London, Longman. 1837, vol. 3, p. 146.

21 Hunter J. An account of the organ of hearing in fishes in *The Works of John Hunter*, ed. J F Palmer. London, Longman. 1837, vol. 4, p. 297.

22 Ibid. p. 294.

23 Keynes R D. The generation of electricity by fishes. *Endeavour*. 1956, vol. 15, pp. 215–221.

24 Parker T J and Haswell W A. *A Text-Book of Zoology*. London, Macmillan. 1962, 7th edn. vol. 2, pp. 271, 272.

25 Stewart E F. John Hunter investigates electricity and receives a shock. *Hunterian Society Transactions*. 1970–71, vol. 29, pp. 69–83.

26 Hunter J. Croonian lectures on muscular motion in *The Works of John Hunter*, ed. J F Palmer. London, Longman. 1837, vol. 4, p. 212.

27 Hunter J. Anatomical observations on the torpedo in *The Works of John Hunter*, ed. J F Palmer. London, Longman. 1837, vol. 4, p. 413.

28 Rudolf C R. Hunteriana Part 3. *Hunterian Society Transactions*. 1952–53, vol. 11, pp. 106–123.

29 Lissmann H W. Continuous electrical signals from the tail of a fish, Gymnarchus niloticus. London. *Nature*. 1951, vol. 167, pp. 201, 202.

30 Darwin C. *Origin of Species*. London, John Murray. 1869, 5th edn, pp. 230, 231.

CHAPTER 13

MUSCULOSKELETAL SYSTEM

HUNTER made an exhaustive study of the muscular system – 'A self-moving power is such a phenomenon as must call up the attention of the thinking mind . . . the mode in which a muscular fibre produces motion has been esteemed an inquiry not unworthy the attention of the greatest philosophers . . .'[1] It is of interest that both Aristotle and Hippocrates were ignorant of the function of the muscular fibre (Owen).[2]

Hunter's observations on muscles were presented to the Royal Society in six Croonian lectures. These were a comprehensive account of all aspects of the anatomy and physiology of muscle in man and animals. He presented intriguing analogies of muscle action with motility in vegetables.

The two most important contributions that Hunter made in his study of muscles were his original observations on elasticity and on relaxation of muscle.

Elasticity – In Hunter's time there was no clear understanding of the difference between the contractility of muscle and the principle of elasticity. Hunter contrasted the unique power of self-action in muscle contraction with the lack of such power in elasticity. He said – 'Elasticity is a property of matter (whether animal or not) which renders it capable of restoring itself to its natural position, after having been acted upon by some mechanical power, but having no power of action arising out of itself. This is exactly the reverse of muscular contraction . . . elasticity in animals does not, like muscular contraction, depend on life, an elastic body possessing that quality as perfectly after death as before . . .'[3]

Relaxation of muscle – It was Hunter's opinion that muscular relaxation is an active process, 'a kind of negative action . . .'[4]

'Relaxation might be supposed to be a simple cessation of action, but I think it is not; it appears to me to be a power as much depending on life as contraction . . .'[5] This observation led Hunter on to the enunciation of the principle of reciprocal innervation of antagonistic muscles – 'Whatever becomes a stimulus to one set of muscles, becomes a cause of relaxation to those which act in a contrary direction; . . .',[6] a principle which was demonstrated a century later by Sherrington.

One of the most important applications of this concept was in its explanation of the movement of peristalsis. Hunter wrote – 'Whatever becomes a stimulus to one part of a muscular canal, where a succession of actions is to take place, becomes also a cause of relaxation in the part beyond it, as in an intestine.'[6]

BONE

John Hunter was among the first to appreciate the significance of bone as an active biological tissue and to demonstrate it by experimental observation.[7] His most important contributions in this field were concerned with the growth and with infection in bone.

Growth of bone

It had been generally assumed that bones increase in size as the result of the deposition of new osseous tissue throughout the bone, as expressed by Hunter – 'new particles put into the interstices of previously formed parts, so as to remove these to a greater distance from each other . . . – as, for instance, if I put a sponge into water, the water getting into all the interstices makes it larger, . . .'[8] Hunter disagreed with this view and considered that bones grow by the addition of new bone on the external surface, associated with the removal of old bone by the absorbents, a process of modelling by which means the bone becomes larger without any great alteration in its shape.

Hunter established his concept of bone modelling by a series of experiments which demonstrated the site and amount of growth by means of bone labelling with madder and with lead shot.

Madder diet. Madder is the colouring principle of the plant *Rubia tinctorum* and has a strong affinity for calcium phosphate. When ingested in the food, madder is deposited with the lime in the formation of bone, giving it a red colour. Hunter fed pigs on madder for a few weeks after which they were killed. The bones showed the red colour to be maximal in the exterior while the interior was much less tinged. Some of the pigs were given additionally a madder-free diet for a few weeks before being killed and in these animals the external parts of the bones were 'of natural colour while the interior was red, demonstrating that new bone was being formed on the exterior while the older bone was being removed on the interior.[9]

Lead shot. Hunter inserted lead shot into two holes bored into the tibia of a pig, one hole near each end with the intervening distance carefully measured. After an increase in the length of the bone had occurred by the growth of the pig, the animal was killed. It was found that the distance between the two lead shots was unaltered, although the bone had grown in length, showing that bone growth occurs at the ends of the bone.[10] These experiments were repeated in fowl and in one such specimen preserved in the Hunterian Museum there had been some increase in distance between the lead shot, suggesting that the middle part of the long bones does increase in length, though in a less degree than the extremities [Owen].[11]

Infection of Bone

Hunter recognized that inflammatory changes in bone are similar in principle to those occurring in the soft parts – '. . . there is no visible difference between suppuration in bones and in the soft parts; for as bones are composed of animal matter with calcareous earth, there is no reason why they should not go through the same process . . . The consequence of suppuration is ulceration . . . There is, I believe, no difference between the ulceration of soft parts and of bone, the adhesive going on with the suppurative in the soft parts; so in the bone we have the ossific going on with the suppurative.'[12]

The pathological details of the formation of sequestra in chronic osteomyelitis were described clearly for the first time by John Hunter. 'Exfoliation. – This is the separation of a dead bone from the living, and is not generally understood. . . . When a piece of bone becomes absolutely dead, it is then to the animal machine as any other extraneous body, and adheres only by the attraction of cohesion to the machine. The first business of the machine, therefore, is to get rid of this cohesion and discharge it. . . .'[13] Hunter then applied his established principles of inflammation to the explanation of the process of extrusion of the bony 'extraneous body', *viz.* an increased blood supply in the living bone adjacent to the dead part, followed by absorption at the line of cohesion of the living and dead bone (p. 39).

Hunter had a clear understanding of the pathological changes associated with compound fractures – '. . . the suppuration is always more or less surrounded by the adhesive inflammation, so that it extends pretty far, and consequently the callus is large. . . . the ends of the bones are sometimes . . . so denuded of their investing membrane as to lose their living principle and to exfoliate, as the dead part must be thrown off before the wound can heal.'[14]

Tumours of Bone

Hunter described spontaneous fracture associated with bone tumours – . . . 'when the tumour is on the inside of the bone, which then appears as if scooped out . . . not exciting ossific inflammation . . . Bones will break from this kind of tumour by very slight causes, such as by turning in bed; . . . This kind of fracture happened to the Archbishop of Canterbury.'[15]

Hunter described a tumour involving the skull which was almost certainly a meningioma. It was a solid tumour situated in the dura mater and it had invaded the skull and the scalp. Hunter regarded it as a demonstration of absorption by pressure – '. . . the tumour . . . had produced the absorbing disposition in that membrane [dura mater] . . . , to the skull which also was absorbed . . . the same disposition was continued on to the scalp . . . the internal parts . . . did not in the least ulcerate . . .'[16]

REFERENCES

1 Hunter J. Croonian lectures on muscular motion in *The Works of John Hunter*, ed. J F Palmer. London, Longman. 1837, vol. 4, p. 195.

2 Owen R. in Hunter's Croonian lectures, *The Works of John Hunter*, ed. J F Palmer. London, Longman. 1837, vol. 4, p. 195.

3 Hunter J. A treatise on the blood, inflammation and gun-shot wounds in *The Works of John Hunter*, ed. J F Palmer. London, Longman. 1837, vol. 3, pp. 149, 150.

4 Hunter J. Croonian lectures on muscular motion in *The Works of John Hunter*, ed. J F Palmer. London, Longman. 1837, vol. 4, p. 250.

5 Ibid. p. 265.

6 Hunter J. A treatise on the blood, inflammation and gun-shot wounds in *The Works of John Hunter*, ed. J F Palmer. London, Longman. 1837, vol. 3, p. 146.

7 Osmond-Clarke, Sir Henry. Base, black ingratitude. *Hunterian Society Transactions* 1968–69, vol. 27, pp. 71–77.

8 Hunter J. Lectures on the principles of surgery in *The Works of John Hunter*, ed.

J F Palmer. London, Longman. 1835, vol. 1, p. 253.

9 Hunter J. Experiments and observations on the growth of bones in *The Works of John Hunter*, ed. J F Palmer. London, Longman. 1837, vol. 4, p. 315.

10 Ibid. p. 317.

11 Owen R. in Hunter's experiments and observations on the growth of bones, *The Works of John Hunter*, ed. J F Palmer. London, Longman. 1837, vol. 4, p. 317.

12 Hunter J. Lectures on the principles of surgery in *The Works of John Hunter*, ed. J F Palmer. London, Longman. 1835, vol. 1, p. 508.

13 Ibid. p. 525.

14 Ibid. p. 509.

15 Ibid. p. 570.

16 Hunter J. A treatise on the blood, inflammation and gun-shot wounds in *The Works of John Hunter*, ed. J F Palmer. London, Longman. 1837, vol. 3, pp. 472, 473.

CHAPTER 14

COMPARATIVE ANATOMY

JOHN Hunter made an exhaustive study of animal structure. Owen stated – 'there is proof that Hunter anatomized at least five hundred different species of animals, exclusive of repeated dissections of different individuals of the same species, . . . Had Hunter published *seriatim* his notes of the structures of the animals which he dissected, these contributions to comparative anatomy would not only have vied with the labours of Daubenton as recorded in the *Histoire Naturelle* of Buffon, or with the Comparative Dissections of Vicq d'Azyr which are inserted in the early volumes of the *Encyclopédie Méthodique* and in the *Mémoires de l'Académie Royale de France*, but they would have exceeded them both together.'[1]

Hunter's interest in anatomy was not merely in the assimilation of facts. In a manuscript, copied by Mr. Clift, relating to a dissection of a turtle, he says, 'The late Sir John Pringle, knowing of this dissection, often desired me to collect all my dissections of this animal, and send them to the Royal Society; but the publishing of a description of a single animal, more especially a common one, has never been my wish.'[2]

It is obvious throughout his work on comparative anatomy that Hunter was concerned especially with four important aspects, *viz.* the anatomical affinities of various animals, the association of structure with function, the classification of animals on the basis of these two factors into series from the most simple to the most complex, and the formulation of general laws. In almost every one of his many papers of anatomical descriptions there will be found numerous references to one or more of these four aspects, richly endowed with pertinent encyclopaedic details collected from his vast experience.

As an example of Hunter's concern with affinities may be quoted part of his paper on the economy of whales:

> In the description of this order of animals I shall always keep in view their analogy to land animals, and to such as occasionally inhabit the water, as white bears, seals, manatees, etc., with the differences that occur . . . Although inhabitants of the waters they belong to the same class as quadrupeds, breathing air, being furnished with lungs and all the other parts peculiar to the oeconomy of that class, and having warm blood; . . .[3]

The association of structure and function is presented repeatedly throughout Hunter's works as for example in his discussion on the various methods of assimilation of food:

> . . . in all granivorous animals there is an apparatus for the mastication of the food, although often differing in construction and situation; but in true carnivorous animals, of whatever tribe, mastication not being so necessary, they have no apparatus for that purpose. The teeth of such quadrupeds as are carnivorous serve chiefly to procure food and prepare it for deglutition; the same thing is performed in the true carnivorous birds by their beaks and talons, whose office it is to procure the aliment and fit it for deglutition, corresponding in this respect with the teeth of the others.[4]

Hunter's concern with the classification of animals on a scale of complexity is well shown in his paper on the organ of hearing in fishes – '. . . I am still inclined to consider whatever is uncommon in the structure of this organ in fishes as only a link in the chain of varieties displayed in its formation in different animals, descending from the most perfect to the most imperfect, in a regular progression.'[5]

The formulation of general laws in comparative anatomy is well exemplified in Hunter's observation in his account of the economy of whales – '. . . we may make this general remark, that in the different classes of animals there is never any mixture of those parts which are essential to life . . .'[6] That is, there is never any combination of the modifications of vital organs characteristic of two different classes of animals in the same species, as of a double heart of the mammal with the branchiae of a fish [Owen].[7]

It is significant that these anatomical features of such special interest to Hunter, *viz.* structural affinities, functional associations, gradations in complexity, and generalisations, all form basic elements in the establishment of the theory of evolution (Chapter 19).

OBSERVATIONS ON BEES

John Hunter made an extensive study of bees over the course of twenty years and it was the subject of the last paper that he himself presented at the Royal Society, on February 23, 1792. He kept bees in specially constructed hives at his establishment at Earl's Court.

Hunter noted that congregated bees maintain a temperature higher than that of the external air – 'Bees are perhaps the only insect that produces heat within itself'.[8] It has since been established, of course, that other social insects behave similarly [Owen][9] but in Hunter's time it was an original observation. He observed the Dance of the Bees – 'We very often see some of the bees wagging their belly, as if tickled, running round and to and fro for only a little way, followed by one or two other bees, as if examining them. I conceived they were probably shaking out the scales of wax, and that the others were ready upon the watch to catch them, but I could not absolutely determine what they did.'[10]

Hunter's most important contribution to the economy of bees was his observation that the wax is formed by the bees themselves. He said 'it may be called an external secretion of oil, and I have found that it is formed between each scale of the under side of the belly.'[11]

A NEW MARINE ANIMAL

This invertebrate animal, *Serpula gigantea* is a marine annelid (annular or segmented worm) which inhabits a tortuous calcareous tube.

The specimen was sent to John Hunter from Barbados by Everard Home. Hunter described the animal and he made the original observation that the animal is able to dispose of its shell by absorption. He stated 'every shellfish has the power of removing a part of its shell, so as to adapt the new and the old together, which is not done by any mechanical power, but by absorption.'[12]

AMPHIBIOUS BIPES

This tailed amphibian, *Siren lacertina*, the Mud Iguana, was transmitted to John Hunter by John Ellis, a prominent natural historian,[13] who had obtained specimens from Dr. Garden, a general practitioner in Charlestown, South Carolina after whom Ellis had named the Gardenia, a pleasant courtesy that he extended to many of his friends.[14]

Hunter's paper was presented to the Royal Society on June 5, 1766 and is of special importance because it was the first of Hunter's many communications to that body to which he was elected a Fellow seven months later. The paper contains no original contribution by Hunter. Indeed his description of the heart was erroneous since Owen subsequently found there to be two auricles instead of the single one described by Hunter.

Siren lacertina is a member of the Order Urodela, which also includes the salamanders and newts, of the Class Amphibia. It is of interest that one of the earliest fossils, discovered in the 18th century, which was originally described as *Homo diluvii testis* (Man, witness to the Deluge) was in fact subsequently shown by Cuvier to have been a salamander. Its importance in the arguments relative to the Flood (p. 176) is emphasised by the verse appended to the original treatise (tr.):

> 'Oh, sad remains of bone, frame of poor Man of sin,
> Soften the heart and mind of recent sinful kin.'[15]

AIR-CELLS IN BIRDS

The communication of the avian pulmonary air-passages with air-sacs in the abdominal cavity was first described by Harvey in 1653 – 'The bronchia or ends of the trachea in birds, moreover, are perforate, and open into the abdomen (and this is an observation which I do not remember to have met with elsewhere), so that the air inspired is received into and stored up within the cells or cavities formed by the membranes mentioned above.'[16]

John Hunter investigated the subject and showed for the first time that the air-containing sacs communicating with the lungs also extended into the bones. He carried out experiments on the hawk and on fowl in which he ligated the trachea and demonstrated that the birds were able to breathe via openings made into the humeri. He discussed various possible functions of the air-sacs. The suggestion that aeration of the bones might assist the act of flying was not supported by the evidence that the ostrich is amply provided with these air-cells. Hunter was inclined to the opinion that the air-cells were accessory organs of respiration – 'I can easily conceive this accumulation of air to be of great use in respiration. . . . the air in its passage to and from these cells must certainly have a considerable effect upon the blood in the lungs, by allowing a much greater quantity of air to pass in a given time than if there was no such construction of parts.'[17] In support of this view he noted the small size of the lungs in birds.

Hunter's opinions come close to modern accepted views on the function of the air-cells. The secondary bronchi open directly into the air-sacs which are formed as dilations of the bronchial mucosa. Most of the inspired air therefore enters directly into the air-sacs and reaches the respiratory tissue finally through recurrent bronchi from the air-sacs so that dead-space is almost eliminated. Aeration of the blood is very complete which provides a high degree of muscle efficiency and heat production enabling birds to sing and fly for long periods without respiratory distress.[18]

OECONOMY OF WHALES

Hunter dissected the porpoise, dolphin ('grampus'), narwhal and the bottle-nosed, baleen (whalebone) and sperm whales.[19,20] He made several original observations which he incorporated, in his usual manner, into the broad framework of comparative anatomy. He wrote – 'It is not, however, intended in this paper to give a particular account of the structure of all the animals of this order which I have had an opportunity of examining: I propose at present chiefly to confine myself to general principles, giving the great outlines as far as I am acquainted with them, minuteness being only necessary in the investigation of particular parts.'[21] Indeed this paper is a model presentation of the subject of comparative anatomy in which Hunter has described the cetacean data not merely as isolated facts, but in relation to other animals, with the emphasis on anatomical affinities, functional comparisons and generalisations.

He described the distribution of fat in whales and compared it with that in land animals of the same class, in fish and in other classes of animal – 'In animals of the same class living on land, the fat is more diffused; it is situated . . . in . . . muscles . . . the viscera; but many parts are free from fat, unless when diseased, as the penis, scrotum, testicle, eyelid, liver, lungs, brain, spleen, etc. . . . In the quadruped . . . in the bird, amphibia, and in some fish, it is contained in loose cellular membrane, as if in bags, . . . in a less degree in the soles of the feet, palms of the hands, and in the breasts of many animals. . . . The fat differs in consistence in different animals . . .'[22]

Hunter recognised that the sperm whale is different from all other animals in its possession of spermaceti oil and although he did not actually describe the spermaceti organ in the whale's snout, he noted that 'As the spermaceti is found in the largest quantity in the head, and in what would appear on a slight view to be the cavity of the skull, from a peculiarity in the shape of that bone, it has been imagined by some to be the brain.'[23]

In a similar way the skin is described with its varieties in different animals and especially in association with different functions – 'The skin is intended for various purposes. It is the universal covering given for the defence of all kinds of animals; and that it might answer this purpose well, it is the seat of one of the senses. . . . In some animals the cutis is extremely thick, and in some parts much more so than in others: where very thick it appears to be intended as a defence against the violence of their own species or other animals. In most quadrupeds it is muscular, contracting by cold, and relaxing by heat. . . . The skin is extremely elastic in the greatest number of quadrupeds, . . .'[24]

The teeth and their development were studied in great detail by Hunter and he pointed out the great difference between them in the whale and in the quadruped. In the latter, the teeth are formed in the jaw while in whales the teeth appear to form in the gum. The jaw grows at its posterior end while the anterior end is constantly being absorbed together with its teeth, so that the teeth are not shed and there is a constant succession of new teeth coming forwards. 'This will make the exact number of teeth in any species uncertain.'[25]

Hunter gave a full account of the baleen (whalebone) plates found in the baleen whales – 'Some genera of this tribe have another mode of catching their food, and retaining it till swallowed, which is by means of the substance called whalebone . . . a substance, I believe, peculiar to the whale, and of the same nature as horn, . . .'[26]

Baleen whales have the numerous horny whalebone plates arranged on the upper jaw with a marginal fringe of bristles forming a sieve for straining the plankton. The bigger species (Right Whales) were the 'right' ones to kill for whalebone since their baleen blades were as long as 15 feet. During the late 19th century heyday of voluminous corsetry, baleen fetched as much as £2000 per ton. It was used also for umbrella ribs and in expensive fabrics guaranteed to 'stand for themselves'.[27]

The extensive ramifications of the cetacean arterial system were noted by Hunter[28] and in particular he recognised that the 'glandulous body' surrounding the medulla spinalis described by Tyson in 1680 [Owen] is in fact composed of a network of arteries acting as a reservoir of arterial blood.[29] Further original observations made by Hunter were the occasional presence of spleniculi – '. . . the spleen . . . is very small . . . There are in some . . . one or two small ones . . . in the epiploon . . . These are sometimes met with likewise in the human body';[30] the fibrous consistence of the brain – '. . . the substance of the brain is more visibly fibrous than . . . in any other animal';[31] and the presence of semicircular canals in the cetacean ear.[32]

REFERENCES

1 Owen R. Preface, *The Works of John Hunter*, ed. J F Palmer. London, Longman. 1837, vol. 4, pp. vi, vii.

2 Ibid. p. vi.

3 Hunter J. Observations on the structure and oeconomy of whales in *The Works of John Hunter*, ed. J F Palmer. London, Longman. 1837, vol. 4, pp. 335, 336.

4 Hunter J. Observations on the Gillaroo trout, commonly called in Ireland the Gizzard trout in *The Works of John Hunter*, ed. J F Palmer. London, Longman. 1837, vol. 4, p. 128.

5 Hunter J. An account of the organ of hearing in fishes in *The Works of John Hunter*, ed. J F Palmer. London, Longman. 1837, vol. 4, p. 293.

6 Hunter J. Observations on the structure and oeconomy of whales in *The Works of John Hunter*, ed. J F Palmer. London, Longman. 1837, vol. 4, p. 336.

7 Owen R. in *The Works of John Hunter*, ed. J F Palmer. London, Longman. 1837, vol. 4, p. 336.

8 Hunter J. Observations on bees in *The Works of John Hunter*, ed. J F Palmer. London, Longman. 1837, vol. 4, p. 427.

9 Owen R. in *The Works of John Hunter*, ed. J F Palmer. London, Longman. 1837, vol. 4, p. 427.

10 Hunter J. Observations on bees in *The Works of John Hunter*, ed. J F Palmer. London, Longman. 1837, vol. 4, p. 434.

11 Ibid. p. 433.

12 Hunter J. Description of a new marine animal, in a letter from Mr. Everard Home to J Hunter, containing anatomical remarks upon the same in *The Works of John Hunter*, ed. J F Palmer. London, Longman. 1837, vol. 4, p. 469.

13 Dobson J. John Hunter's animals. *Journal of History of Medicine and Allied Sciences*. 1962, vol. 17, pp. 479–486.

14 Dobson J. *John Hunter*. Edinburgh and London, Livingstone. 1969, p. 112.

15 Parker T J and Haswell W A. *A Text-Book of Zoology*. London, Macmillan. 1962, 7th edn. vol. 2, p. 432.

16 Harvey W. On generation in *The Works of William Harvey*, trans. Robert Willis. London, printed for the Sydenham Society. 1847, p. 173.

17 Hunter J. An account of certain receptacles of air in birds, which communicate with the lungs and Eustachian tube in *The Works of John Hunter*, ed. J F Palmer. London, Longman. 1837, vol. 4, p. 184.

18 Parker T J and Haswell W A. *A Text-Book of Zoology*. London, Macmillan. 1962, 7th edn. vol. 2, pp. 586–589.

19 Hunter J. Observations on the structure and oeconomy of whales in *The Works of John Hunter*, ed. J F Palmer. London, Longman. 1837, vol. 4, p. 332.

20 Harrison R J. Hunter and his porpoises. *Hunterian Society Transactions.* 1974–75–76, vols. 33, 34, pp. 35–42.

21 Hunter J. Observations on the structure and oeconomy of whales in *The Works of John Hunter*, ed. J F Palmer. London, Longman. 1837, vol. 4, pp. 335–336.

22 Ibid. pp. 344–346.

23 Ibid. p. 346.

24 Ibid. pp. 350, 351.

25 Ibid. pp. 353, 354.

26 Ibid. p. 354.

27 Parker T J and Haswell W A. *A Text-Book of Zoology.* London, Macmillan. 1962, 7th edn. vol. 2, p. 785.

28 Hunter J. Observations on the structure and oeconomy of whales in *The Works of John Hunter*, ed. J F Palmer. London, Longman. 1837, vol. 4, pp. 365, 366.

29 Owen R. in *The Works of John Hunter*, ed. J F Palmer. London, Longman. 1837, vol. 4, p. 366.

30 Hunter J. Observations on the structure and oeconomy of whales in *The Works of John Hunter*, ed. J F Palmer. London, Longman. 1837, vol. 4, p. 363.

31 Ibid. p. 373.

32 Ibid. p. 384.

CHAPTER 15

GUNSHOT
WOUNDS

JOHN Hunter's classic, the *Treatise on the Blood, Inflammation and Gun-shot Wounds,* was published posthumously in 1794, one year after his death. This book included his experiences of military surgery which he had gained over thirty years previously while on active service in the Seven Years War. It is obvious that the Treatise of 1794 was the result of considerable thought and experiment based on Hunter's earlier practical experience, as he acknowledged in his dedication of the Treatise (p. 15).

Prior to the use of gunpowder, the majority of war injuries were due to the sword, lance, dagger or arrow and treatment was relatively simple. Accessible foreign bodies were extracted and various decoctions applied. In nearly all cases suppuration was the usual sequel. Gunpowder was introduced at the end of the thirteenth century and the severity of injuries was greatly increased. Such wounds were so much more complicated by suppuration and tissue necrosis that it was generally believed that these were specific poisonous effects of gunpowder (di Vigo 1514).[1] Cauterisation of gunshot wounds was therefore introduced, using the red-hot iron or boiling oil, in order to counteract the poison. In most cases gunshot wounds were treated by dilatation in order to extract foreign bodies and to cauterise the deeper parts of the wound.

Paré (1545) was one of the first to discard the use of cauterisation and he demonstrated that better results were obtained by the use of non-irritant applications. However, in Hunter's time dilating wounds was still usually practised. John Hunter disagreed with the radical methods of his predecessors. He said dilatation of wounds was usually unnecessary . . . 'this arises, I believe, from the conceit of surgeons who think themselves possessed of powers superior to nature, and therefore have introduced the practice of making sores of all wounds. . . .'[2]

Hunter introduced a conservative regime in the early treatment of wounds. In his experience in Belleisle he had observed that wounds healed more readily without surgical interference. Subsequent military surgeons, especially Guthrie, condemned Hunter's conservative methods and reverted to active surgical procedures. Wounds were probed and dilated but the results in severe injuries were not good and early amputation of injured limbs became popularised by the leading surgeons, especially Larrey.

John Hunter's conservative management of gunshot wounds is still the subject of criticism. In 1963 Whipple stated: 'John Hunter did not mention debriding the wound or removing blood clots. In fact he advised leaving them in the wound. It is surprising that he did not give more attention to these factors, for he was such a keen observer and was seeing and treating wounds in his practice of surgery'.[3] Judged by modern standards, Hunter's conservative management of gunshot wounds would certainly seem to deserve such strong criticism. But it is important to evaluate Hunter's methods in the context of his own time.

A careful study of his *Treatise on Gun-shot Wounds* shows that Hunter had a very clear and accurate understanding of the pathology of gunshot wounds. He fully appreciated the three most important factors involved in wound pathology, *viz.* contamination from the exterior, an impaired blood supply, and the presence of devitalised tissue.

(a) *Contamination from the exterior*

Hunter realised that an external agency, *in* but not *of* the air, was a factor in causing inflammation of wounds. He said:

> . . . as every violence committed from without . . . is exposed more or less to the surrounding air, the applications of this matter to internal surfaces has generally been assigned as a cause of this inflammation; but air certainly has not the least effect upon these parts; . . . In many cases of the emphysema, where the air is diffused over the whole body, we have no such effect, and this air not the purest . . . Nay, as a stronger proof . . . that it is not the admission of air which makes parts fall into inflammation, we find that the cells in the soft parts of birds, and many of the cells and canals of the bones of the same tribe of animals, which communicate with the lungs, and at all times have more or less air in them, never inflame . . . . . . If it was necessary that air should be admitted in

order for suppuration to take place, we should not very readily account for suppuration taking place in the nose from a cold, as this part is not more under the influence of air at one time than at another . . .

And Hunter concludes 'therefore there must be another cause.'[4] These simple cogent arguments could well have been an inspiration to Lister years later.

The concept of an exogenous factor in causing wound infection was given a practical application by Hunter to his treatment of some superficial open wounds by seeking to obtain skin closure as early as possible. He said 'Many wounds ought to be allowed to scab . . .';[2] 'Some compound fractures . . . should be allowed to heal in the same way; for by permitting the blood to scab upon the wound, either by itself, or when soaked in lint, the parts underneath will unite . . .'[2] Nearly a century later, Lister used almost exactly the same words, viz. '. . . in compound fracture . . . if the coagulum . . . is allowed to dry and form a crust, as was advised by John Hunter, all bad consequences are probably averted, and, the air being excluded, the blood beneath becomes organised and absorbed, exactly as in a simple fracture'.[5] Lister's method of treating compound fractures differed from Hunter's method only in the use of antiseptics. Hunter knew nothing of bacterial infection, of course, but it is obvious that he appreciated the importance of exclusion of contamination from the exterior. Furthermore it is important to note that Hunter recommended the closed 'scabbing' treatment only for wounds of superficial type without any deep tissue damage (see below), whereas Lister's faith in the overriding value of antiseptics led him to adopt the closed method of treatment for all open wounds.

(b) *Impaired blood supply*

John Hunter's works abound with references to the importance of a good blood supply in maintaining the natural defences of the body, e.g. 'Blood . . . appears to carry life to every part of the body, for whenever the whole or a part is deprived of fresh blood it very soon dies.'[6] And again: '. . . whenever Nature has considerable operations going on, and those are rapid, then we find the vascular system in a proportionable|degree enlarged.'[7] In discussing the body's resistance to disease, Hunter said – 'Different parts differ very much in their power of resisting diseases, . . . this seems to be according to the strength of the circulation in the part; where there is less the power is less; thus, there is greater power of resistance in a muscle than in a tendon.'[8]

(c) *Devitalised tissue*

The inimical effect of devitalised tissue in the establishment of wound sepsis was fully appreciated by Hunter. He said: 'There is most commonly a part of the solids surrounding the wound deadened, as the projecting body forced its way through these solids, which afterwards is thrown off in the form of a slough, and which prevents such wounds healing by first intention . . .'[9] And again: '. . . when the life of a part has been destroyed by the accident, it must necessarily suppurate; . . .'[10] This completely accurate assessment of the pathology of deep penetrating wounds led Hunter to advise against scabbing of such wounds. He said: '. . . there are cases in which it [scabbing] should be discouraged, as where deep-seated extraneous bodies have been introduced, as in gun-shot wounds, or where deeper-seated parts have been killed; . . .'[11] There could really be no clearer picture of the correct essential pathology of wounds of violence than this one described by Hunter, with its emphasis on devitalised tissue, sloughs and suppuration. He realised that a wound would not heal while devitalised tissue was present – 'it is impossible that such a sore can heal while there is a slough to separate.'[12] The method Hunter advised for this process was the natural one of suppuration and drainage – 'Gun-shot wounds . . . are . . . contused wounds . . . a slough . . . from which circumstance most of them must be allowed to suppurate.'[9]

It is quite clear therefore that Hunter's assessment of the pathological factors to be considered in the treatment of missile wounds was absolutely correct and as acceptable today as it was when he wrote it – indeed he designated suture of the wound as primary and secondary. He wrote: 'In many wounds . . . when we either know or suspect that extraneous bodies have been introduced into the wound, union by the first intention should not be attempted, but they should be allowed to suppurate, in order that the extraneous matter may be expelled. . . . Many operations may be so performed as to admit of parts uniting by the first intention, but the practice should be adopted with great circumspection; the mode of operating with that view should in all cases be a secondary and not a primary consideration, which it has unluckily been too often among surgeons.'[13]

Hunter was fully conversant with the effects of the separation of sloughs as a cause of delayed perforation in abdominal viscera. He said: 'If, for instance, it is a part of an intestine that has received a contusion, so as to kill it, and which is to slough, a new symptom will most probably appear, from the sloughs being separated, the contents of the intestine will most probably come through the wound; and probably the same thing will happen when any other containing viscus is in part deadened . . .'[14]

Hunter described the case of a guardsman who sustained a gunshot wound of the abdomen with a non-penetrating injury of the colon where a faecal fistula developed after ten days. He said '. . . It was not difficult to account for the cause of this new symptom; it was plain that an intestine (the descending part of the colon most probably) had only received a bruise from the ball, but sufficient to kill it at this part, and till the separation of the slough had taken place, both the intestine and canal were still complete, and therefore did not communicate with each other; but when the slough was thrown off, the two were laid into one at this part, therefore the contents of the intestine got into the wound . . .'[15]

It is obvious that Hunter had a sound understanding of the pathology of wound infection, but since he appreciated fully the inimical effects of devitalised tissue, why did he not excise these wounds? Hunter's treatment must be evaluated, not in the context of modern surgery, but in the surgical environment of his time. Operative management of a gunshot wound in Hunter's time was a thoroughly septic procedure, well summarised by Wellington's famous surgeon G. J. Guthrie: 'A military surgeon should never be taught to expect any convenience; his field pannier for a seat for the patient, and a dry piece of ground to spread his dressings and instruments upon, are all that are required.'[16] It could be added that the instruments would be encrusted with stale blood and the ground littered with manure from the battle steeds. It cannot be doubted that, in such a surgical environment, the chances of wound infection must have been considerably less with conservative management than with surgical exploration. Indeed, Hunter said, '. . . the art employed by the surgeon himself may assist in changing the original state of the wound, as the passing of needles and ligatures must always produce suppuration . . .'[17] Under such conditions most modern surgeons would doubtless have chosen conservative treatment for a gunshot wound.

It is maintained, therefore, that *in the surgical environment of his time* Hunter's management of gunshot wounds was quite justified. He fully appreciated the sinister effects of devitalised tissue but he considered that conservative treatment with free suppuration gave better results than the traumatic operative methods available at that time.

Hunter recognised the necessity for surgical interference in certain cases. He wrote – 'It would be absurd for any one to suppose that there is never occasion to dilate gun-shot wounds at all; but it is certain there are very few in which it is necessary.' He then summarises the indications for surgery in gunshot wounds – indications which would be acceptable in modern surgery:

1. . . . a ball or broken bone pressing upon some part, whose actions are either essential to the life of the part or the whole, as some large artery, nerve, or vital part;

2. If an artery is wounded, where the patient is likely to become either too weak, or to lose his life from the loss of blood, then certainly the vessel is to be tied, and most probably this cannot be done without previously opening the external parts, and often freely.

3. In a wound of the head where there is reason to suspect a fracture of the skull, it is necessary to open the scalp, as in any other common injury done to the head where there was reason to suspect a fracture; and when opened, if a fracture is found, it is to be treated as any other fractured skull.

4. Where there are fractured bones in any part of the body, which can be immediately extracted with advantage, and which would do much mischief if left, this becomes a compound fracture wherever it is, and it makes no difference in the treatment whether the wound in the skin was made by a ball or the bone itself, . . .

5. Where there is some extraneous body which can with very little trouble be extracted, and where the mischief by delay will probably be greater than that arising from the dilatation.

6. Where some internal part is misplaced, which can be replaced immediately in its former position, such as in wounds in the belly, where some of the viscera are protruded, . . .

7. When some vital part is pressed, so that its functions are lost or much impaired, such as will often happen from fractures of the skull, fractures of the ribs, sternum, etc., . . .[18]

The practice of formal excision of missile wounds could not be established before the advent of anaesthesia and Listerian surgery. It is in fact an operation of relatively recent origin. Primary excision of wounds of violence as a deliberate operation was first described by Milligan in 1915 in an article with the significant title: 'The Early

Treatment of Projectile Wounds by Excision of the Damaged Tissues.'[19] Milligan described the modern operation of wound excision and he emphasised that, in the prevention of infection, removal of devitalised tissue is far more important than attempted sterilisation of the wound by antiseptics. This article was published in the early years of the first World War and it establishes Milligan as a pioneer of primary excision of missile wounds.

It is a remarkable fact that the introduction of the operation of formal excision of damaged tissue was actually retarded by the enormous initial success of Lister's antiseptic surgery. Lister never advocated excision of wounds because he believed that elimination of exogenous bacterial contamination alone was adequate to prevent wound infection. But antiseptic surgery failed in dealing with wounds of massive tissue destruction and it was in wound excision that Hunterism came to the aid of Listerism by the application to practical surgery of Hunter's clear concept of the pathology of wounds of violence – 'Violence done to parts is one of the great causes of suppuration; . . . a violence attended with death in a part, such as in many bruises, mortifications, sloughs . . .';[20] 'it is impossible that such a sore can heal while there is a slough to separate.'[12] If Hunter's *Treatise on Gun-shot Wounds* had been more carefully studied instead of being so frequently criticised, perhaps the logical operation of excision of wounds of violence might have been evolved before Milligan's time.

The importance of Hunter's fundamental pathological concept of the inimical effect of devitalised tissue in wounds cannot be overemphasised because, in spite of the universally acknowledged priority of elimination of such tissue in the treatment of missile wounds, as exemplified in the brilliant results of wound excision in the second World War, this concept has not yet been generally accepted in the prevention and treatment of surgical wound infection. It is still current practice that in the great majority of cases prevention and treatment of surgical wound infection are based primarily on the employment of bacteriological assay and antibiotics or antiseptics. Indeed the general attitude to the management of wound infection today is comparable to that of the early days of the first World War, when as the result of the enthusiastic acceptance of Listerism, elimination of bacteria from a wound was considered to be the most important, and even the only, aim of treatment. Hunter's clear concept of the pathology of wounds with its emphasis on the deleterious effects of sloughs is applicable not only to missile wounds but equally to tissues damaged by the surgeon's knife or manipulations. The most rigorous sterile precautions may be inadequate to prevent the onset of sepsis in the presence of devitalised tissue, while established infection will persist if there is inadequate drainage of pus or incomplete excision of slough – no antimicrobials, systemic or topical, can sterilise a slough since it has no circulation. The mediaeval surgeons are criticised for pouring boiling oil into gunshot wounds in order to kill the poison which was thought to be present, but there is little difference in principle between this and pouring in antiseptics to kill bacteria. Both methods are inimical to the natural defence mechanisms and neither method removes the basic pathological cause, well recognised by Hunter, the devitalised tissue.

MODERN ATRAUMATIC SURGERY

Halsted was one of the first to appreciate that complete asepsis in surgical wounds is impossible to attain and that sepsis may result from the presence of even the smallest areas of damaged tissue and haematoma.[21] Halsted pointed out that nature was able to deal with bacteria in wounds which did not contain devitalised tissue and foreign bodies, but sepsis was likely to develop when these were present. He showed experimentally that cultures of virulent staphylococci injected into the peritoneum were harmless unless foreign bodies were also included in which case peritonitis developed.[22]

Similar results have been obtained by many other observers, e.g. in human volunteers, intradermal and subcutaneous inocula of more than one million *Staphylococcus aureus* were required to induce infections of the skin, but in the presence of subcutaneous foreign bodies (infected silk sutures) pyogenic reactions occurred with much smaller doses of bacteria (Elek):[23] in experimental gas gangrene infections, the virulence of *Cl. welchii* infections was increased one thousand times by the presence in the wound of crushed muscle, and one million times by having crushed muscle and sterile foreign material (street dirt, cinders, etc.) in the wound (Altemeier *et al.*):[24] subcutaneous injections of bacteria in rabbits produced infections only when the bacterial count exceeded 100,000 bacteria per ml. (Hunt *et al.*).[25]

In a study of the incidence of postoperative wound infection in relation to airborne contamination, Shaw *et al.* found that the wound infection rate varied from one per cent in cardiac operations to fifty per cent in operations on the colon and rectum. They concluded that there is little evidence of exogenous bacterial contamination of wounds in the operating theatre and that the general surgeon's efforts should be directed to the control of endogenous infection of wounds.[26]

It is significant that surgical wounds around the anus yield excellent results, e.g. after excision of haemorrhoids, perianal abscess, or fistula. These wounds are under constant reinfection by faecal bacteria including clostridia and they can never be regarded as any other than grossly contaminated wounds. The excellent results of proctological surgery as well as those of the radical excision of wounds of violence surely emphasise the priority of the endogenous over the exogenous factor in the establishment of wound sepsis.

Halsted's operative technique aimed to minimise tissue damage and to avoid leaving in the wound devitalised tissue, haematomas and foreign material, a technique which may rightly be designated *atraumatic surgery*. It recognises that complete and absolute asepsis in wounds is impossible to obtain and that the best method of avoiding sepsis is to leave a wound with the minimum of devitalised tissue and with a healthy blood supply. It is a common experience of course that the gentle handling of tissues is a characteristic of the technique of all great surgeons, e.g. Wilfred Trotter who wrote: '. . . the art of handling living flesh . . . Hands co-ordinated to smooth, firm and gentle movement are to the sick body the complement of the attentive receptive mind. It yields its secrets to them but denies its secrets to the mutton fist as it does to the beefy mind.'[27] The Queensberry Rules are not for Surgery; the wearing of sterile gloves should give the surgeon no special licence for the infliction of unnecessary trauma. Concentration on the single factor of the avoidance of bacterial contamination may engender a false sense of security leading to the neglect of the two far more important factors in the prophylaxis of wound sepsis, *viz.* maintenance of a good blood supply and elimination of residual devitalised tissue and haematoma.

The cause of wound infection lies more *in* than *on* the surgeon's hands. Antiseptic surgery and aseptic surgery are of secondary importance to atraumatic surgery. Antiseptic surgery aims to kill bacteria but it also injures the tissues; aseptic surgery aims to exclude bacteria but is incapable of full achievement; atraumatic surgery aims to starve bacteria and is the one method capable of control by the surgeon himself. Atraumatic surgery, the art of gentle surgery, is the modern application of Hunter's simple elementary concept that violence is a cause of suppuration in wounds – 'bruises, mortifications, sloughs'[20] – whether the violence is due to a gunshot wound or to surgical trauma. There could be no better text for wound management than Hunter's – '. . . it is impossible that such a sore can heal while there is a slough to separate.'[12]

REFERENCES

1 Di Vigo G. *Practica in Arte Chirurgica Copiosa.* Rome. 1514. Quoted by J Trueta in *Principles and Practice of War Surgery.* London, Hamish Hamilton. 1946, 3rd edn. p. 4.

2 Hunter J. A treatise on the blood, inflammation and gun-shot wounds in *The Works of John Hunter*, ed. J F Palmer. London, Longman. 1837, vol. 3, p. 263.

3 Whipple A O. *Wound Healing and Wound Repair.* Springfield, Ill., Thomas. 1963, pp. 73, 74.

4 Hunter J. A treatise on the blood, inflammation and gun-shot wounds in *The Works of John Hunter*, ed. J F Palmer. London, Longman. 1837, vol. 3, pp. 405, 406.

5 Lister J (Lord). A new method of treating compound fracture, abscess etc. *Lancet.* 1867, vol. 1, pp. 326–329.

6 Hunter J. Lectures on the principles of surgery in *The Works of John Hunter*, ed. J F Palmer. London, Longman. 1835, vol. 1, p. 231.

7 Hunter J. A treatise on the blood, inflammation and gun-shot wounds in *The Works of John Hunter*, ed. J F Palmer. London, Longman. 1837, vol. 3, p. 200.

8 Hunter J. Lectures on the principles of surgery in *The Works of John Hunter*, ed. J F Palmer. London, Longman. 1835, vol. 1, p. 343.

9 Hunter J. A treatise on the blood, inflammation and gun-shot wounds in *The Works of John Hunter*, ed. J F Palmer. London, Longman. 1837, vol. 3, p. 543.

10 Ibid. p. 241.

11 Ibid. p. 263.

12 Ibid. p. 267.

13 Ibid. pp. 258, 259.

14 Ibid. p. 544.

15 Ibid. pp. 565, 566.

16 Guthrie G J. *On Gun-shot Wounds of the Extremities.* London, Longman. 1815, p. 46.

17 Hunter J. A treatise on the blood, inflammation and gun-shot wounds in *The Works of John Hunter*, ed. J F Palmer. London, Longman. 1837, vol. 3, p. 253.

18 Ibid. pp. 550–554.

19 Milligan E T C. The early treatment of projectile wounds by excision of the damaged tissues. *British Medical Journal.* 1915, vol. I, p. 1081.

20 Hunter J. A treatise on the blood, inflammation and gun-shot wounds in *The Works of John Hunter*, ed. J F Palmer. London, Longman. 1837, vol. 3, pp. 404, 405.

21 Finney J M. The founding and influence of a school of surgery. *Hunterian Society Transactions* 1948–49, vol. 7, pp. 47–69.

22 Halsted W S. *Surgical Papers*. Baltimore, Johns Hopkins Press. 1924, vol. 1, p. 102.

23 Elek S D. Experimental staphylococcal infections in the skin of man in *Annals of the New York Academy of Sciences*. 1956, vol. 65, pp. 85–90.

24 Altemeier W A and Furste W L. Studies in virulence of Clostridium welchii in *Surgery*. 1949, vol. 25, pp. 12–19.

25 Hunt T K, Jawetz E, Hutchison J G P and Dunphy J E. A new model for the study of wound infection in *Journal of Trauma*. 1967, vol. 7, no. 2, pp. 298–306.

26 Shaw D, Doig C M and Douglas D. Is airborne infection in operating-theatres an important cause of wound infection in general surgery? in *Bulletin de la Societé Internationale de Chirurgie*. 1974, vol. 33, no. 1, pp. 33–41.

27 Trotter W. Art and science in medicine in *Collected Papers*. London, Oxford Univ. Press. 1941, pp. 85–101.

CHAPTER 16

VENEREAL DISEASE

In 1786 John Hunter published his *Treatise on the Venereal Disease*. At that time the two most common venereal infections, syphilis and gonorrhoea, were known to be transmitted by sexual intercourse, but it was believed by most authorities, including John Hunter, that they were different manifestations of the same infection. It was not until 1838 that Ricord finally established syphilis and gonorrhoea as separate and distinct diseases.[1]

The Treatise is a masterpiece of accurate clinical observation and information on venereal diseases and their complications. In addition there is a large and valuable section on genitourinary surgery. Hunter maintained throughout that syphilis and gonorrhoea were both due to the same 'morbid poison' but although this conclusion was erroneous, it does not detract from the merit of the excellent clinical and pathological aspects of the work, as exemplified by his classic description of the 'Hunterian chancre'. It was a comprehensive and authoritative volume which summarised the surgical knowledge of the subject at that time and it was well received, there being a second edition in Hunter's lifetime and numerous European and American translations of the work.

The main criticism of the Treatise has of course been Hunter's erroneous opinion on the identity of the venereal infections. He said – 'It has been supposed by many that the gonorrhoea and the chancre arise from two distinct poisons; . . . Yet, if we take up this question upon other grounds, and also have recourse to experiments, the result of which we can absolutely depend upon, we shall find this notion to be erroneous. . . . the matter of a gonorrhoea will produce either a gonorrhoea, a chancre, or the lues venerea; and the matter of a chancre will also produce either a gonorrhoea, a chancre, or the lues venerea.'[2]

Hunter formed this opinion largely as a result of deductions from two important principles that he had already established from his work on inflammation. One of these was that 'No two different fevers can exist in the same constitution, nor two local diseases in the same part, at the same time.'[3] He deduced therefore that the not uncommon occurrence of a chancre and gonorrhoea together in a patient proved that the two lesions had a common cause. The other principle was that 'inflammation will in general be in proportion to . . . the nature of the part; . . . as there is a great variety, so must there be in the inflammation.'[4] He applied this concept to venereal infection – '. . . if venereal matter out of the constitution be applied to a living part, it always produces an effect according to the nature of the part, which part may be one of two kinds, either, 1st, a secreting surface, producing then gonorrhoea; or, 2nd, a non-secreting surface, producing then a chancre.'[5] Hunter was thus led on to the conclusion that the same poison gave rise on a soft mucosal surface to the fluid purulent reaction of gonorrhoea and on the hard skin surface to a chancre.

Hunter therefore recognised three clinical types of one venereal disease, *viz.*

'Local kind . . . two sorts, . . . a formation of matter without a breach of the solids, called a gonorrhoea; . . . a breach in the solids, called a chancre . . .'.[6] 'The lues venerea . . . arises in consequence of the poisonous matter being absorbed . . . into the circulation . . . constitutional disease.'[7]

Soon after the publication of the Treatise, in the same year 1786, Jessé Foot wrote a critical commentary on Hunter's work entitled *Observations upon the New Opinions of John Hunter on the Venereal Disease.*[8] Foot later published a *Life of John Hunter* in 1794 soon after Hunter's decease.[9] These two publications by Foot were extremely critical of John Hunter and his work. His criticisms of Hunter's opinions on venereal disease were petty and malicious but the book is of some value in relation to its detailed reference to Hunter's famous allegedly self-inoculation experiment (p. 52). Its publication stimulated an old pupil of Hunter's, Dr. Charles Brandon Trye, to issue a *Review of Jessé Foot's Observations* in which Trye strongly condemned Foot's malicious attacks on his old teacher. John Hunter wrote to Trye – 'I am very much obliged to you for the pains you have taken to laugh at Jessé Foot; he was hardly worth your while; however as you have done it and done it well there can be no reason for not publishing it. Poor Jessé Foot wanted a dinner, and he thought he saw a fine animal he could live on for a while; every animal has its lice.'[10] John Hunter's reference to Jessé Foot as a parasite was very apt since Foot is remembered only as a result of the fame of the subject of his malice.

Farington noted in his Diary dated September 13, 1796: '– Foote, the Surgeon, became rancorous against, John Hunter, because the latter had seemed to describe a Bougie which Foote had invented as not necessary. – To revenge himself He wrote of Hunter with much malignancy & asserted many falsehoods. –'[11]

Hunter's erroneous opinion on the common identity of gonorrhoea and syphilis cannot have been due to any inaccuracy of his observations or experiments but rather to a misinterpretation of their results. He makes numerous observations which would seem to be strongly in favour of a separate aetiology of the two diseases, as in the following:

> Each form of the disease also varies in this respect . . . the gonorrhoea appearing sooner than the chancre.[12]
>
> If a man has a lues venerea and gets either a gonorrhoea or a chancre, or both, neither of them affects the lues venerea, . . . Nor is the cure of either, singly, retarded by the presence of the other . . . a chancre may be cured locally independent of the gonorrhoea . . .[13]
>
> We find, besides, that a gonorrhoea may be cured while there is a chancre, and *vice versa* . . .[14]
>
> . . . I have also observed that mercury has no more power in curing the gonorrhoea than any other medicine . . . but we find that in a chancre it is a specific, and will cure every one . . .[15]
>
> . . . we every day see gonorrhoeas cured by the most ignorant; but in chancre, or the lues venerea, more skill is necessary. The reason is obvious; gonorrhoea cures itself, whilst the other forms of the disease require the assistance of art.[16]

Finally, Hunter had himself established that a gonorrhoeal discharge is not associated with ulceration of the urethra and he contrasted this with a 'venereal' ulcer [chancre] – 'Indeed the method of curing a gonorrhoea might have shown that it could not depend upon a venereal ulcer, for there is hardly any instance of a venereal ulcer being cured by anything but mercury . . . We know, however, that most gonorrhoeas are curable without mercury, and, what is still more, without any medical assistance, which, I believe, is never the case with a chancre.'[17]

It might have been expected that these observations would have led Hunter to the conclusion that the diseases were of different origin but he persisted in his erroneous opinion because of his two already established concepts, *viz.* that different diseases are not active simultaneously and that different tissues react differently to the same stimulus (p. 58). Hunter made the correct observations and experiments on Baconian principles of induction, but instead of accepting the correct and obvious inferences he based his ultimate conclusions on deductions from two concepts, one of which was erroneous, that two different diseases do not occur simultaneously in one subject. Perhaps this is an example of the confusion in Hunter's mind of the inductive and deductive methods of investigation suggested by Buckle (p. xiii). However, Hunter's application of both inductive and deductive methods yielded success in so many other fields of investigation that his erroneous opinion on venereal disease may be blamed not on any failure of his methods but on the insufficient data on which he had promulgated the concept that two different diseases are not active simultaneously.

Hunter's concept that no two diseases can co-exist actively in the same constitution seems to have been widely known and often accepted on the basis of his authority. While in Malta in 1811, Lord Byron wrote to a friend – '. . . Surgeon Tucker . . . administered to me for three complaints *viz.* a *Gonorrhoea* a *Tertian fever*; & the *Hemorrhoides, all* of which I literally had at once, though he assured me the *morbid* action of only one of these distempers could act at a time which was a great comfort, though they relieved one another as regularly as Sentinels . . .'[18] However over the years it became obvious that Hunter's opinion in this matter was erroneous and that two diseases may be active simultaneously in the body.

JOHN HUNTER'S INOCULATION EXPERIMENTS

John Hunter's works record a considerable number of experimental inoculations of venereal matter on patients (p. 49). Indeed it may appear that they were excessively numerous, but he must have had sound reasons for their performance because he did not advocate unnecessary experimentation – 'I think we must set it down as an axiom, that experiments should not be often repeated which tend merely to establish a principle already known and admitted; but that the next step should be, the application of that principle to useful purposes.'[19]

It is just possible that Hunter's persistent inoculation experiments were performed in an attempt to establish a method of immunisation against venereal disease comparable with that in use for smallpox. He was well aware of the immunity against further infection conferred by an attack of a venereal infection. Hunter wrote that after a venereal infection '. . . the parts become less susceptible of the venereal irritation; . . . a man cannot get a fresh gonorrhoea, or a chancre, if he applies fresh venereal matter to the parts when the cure is nearly completed . . . A man . . . having suffered a gonorrhoea, shall have frequent connexions with women of the town, and that for years successively, without being infected.'[20]

In evaluating his experiments he makes frequent allusions to smallpox inoculation e.g. 'Venereal matter must in all cases be the same . . . if the poison can irritate . . . the action will be the same . . . from a strong or weak solution . . . What happens in the inoculation of the smallpox strengthens this opinion . . . let it be . . . applied in a large quantity or a small one, it produces always the same effect.' And Hunter then adds a significant sentence – 'This could only be known by the great numbers that have been inoculated under all these different circumstances.'[21] This statement strongly suggests that Hunter had been studying the effects of a great variety of inoculations, not only of smallpox but also of venereal matter, presumably for some definite purpose. It is unlikely that the chief aim of these experiments was to confirm his opinion that the venereal diseases were all due to the same cause because it is manifest throughout his Treatise that he had no doubt at all on this matter. It is therefore possible that there was another reason for all these experiments, and Hunter's opinion that chancre, gonorrhoea and generalised syphilis (lues venerea) were all due to an identical poison with varying levels of host reaction would have been a very logical concept for the consideration of immunisation by inoculation. Obviously there is no proof for this suggestion but such an experimental programme would have been quite a natural concept for John Hunter's consideration.

GENITOURINARY SURGERY

The Treatise includes a comprehensive account of genitourinary surgery. Urethral stricture, enlarged prostate and urinary retention are described in a practical manner and the work is still well worth studying.

Urethral stricture. Hunter has given a full and accurate account of the management of stricture and its complications, occupying some forty pages in the Treatise.[22] In the treatment of periurethral infections, he says – 'When suppuration takes place, the sooner the abscess is opened externally the better.'[23] On the treatment of fistulae in perinaeo – 'a method should be followed similar to that used in the cure of fistulae in other parts, by laying them freely open to the bottom.'[24]

Non-gonococcal Urethritis and Reiter's Disease. Reiter's disease, a syndrome of non-gonococcal urethritis, polyarthritis and conjunctivitis, was probably first recorded by Stoll in 1776 and described again by Sir Benjamin Brodie in 1818[25] and by Hans Reiter in 1916.[26]

Hunter wrote – '. . . the urethra is subject to inflammation and suppuration from various other causes besides the venereal poison; and sometimes discharges happen spontaneously when no immediate cause can be assigned . . . there is a certain class of symptoms common to almost all diseases of the urethra, from which it is difficult to distinguish the few that arise solely from the specific affection . . .

The urethra is known to be sometimes the seat of the gout; I have known it the seat of the rheumatism. . . . Such a complaint as a discharge without virus is known to exist, by its coming on when there has been no late connexion with women, and likewise by its coming on of its own accord where there had never been any former venereal complaint, nor any chance of infection.'[27]

Peyronie's Disease. The disease was first described by Francois de la Peyronie, Court Physician to Louis XIV, in 1743.[28,29]

Hunter described a condition of chronic induration of the body of the penis with the typical features of Peyronie's disease:

> In many cases the inflammation not only affects the skin of the penis, in which is included the prepuce, but it attacks the body of the penis itself, often producing adhesions and even mortification in the cells of the corpora cavernosa, either of which will destroy the distensibility of those parts ever after, giving the penis a curve to one side in its erections. This sometimes takes place through the whole

cellular substance of the penis, producing a short and almost inflexible stump.

The adhesions of those cells do not proceed from venereal inflammation only; they are often the consequences of other diseases, and sometimes they take place without any visible cause whatever.

A gentleman, sixty years of age, who has been lame with the gout these twenty years past, has for these eighteen months had the penis contracted on the left and upper side, so as to bend that way very considerably in erections, which erections are more frequent than common.

Query: Is the gout the cause of this, by producing adhesions of the cells of one corpus cavernosum, so as not to yield to or allow of the of the influx of blood on that side? And is the irritation of the gout the cause of the frequency of the erections?[30]

Enlarged prostate gland. The work contains a perfect description of senile enlargement of the prostate gland with details of the changes in the urethra associated with an enlarged middle lobe:

From the situation of the gland, which is principally on the two sides of the canal, and but little, if at all, on the fore part, as also very little on the posterior side, it can only swell laterally, whereby it presses the two sides of the canal together, and at the same time stretches it from the anterior edge or side to the posterior, so that the canal, instead of being round, is flattened into a narrow groove. Sometimes the gland swells more on one side than the other, which makes an obliquity in the canal passing through it.

Besides this effect of the lateral parts swelling, a small portion of it, which lies behind the very beginning of the urethra, swells forwards like a point, as it were, into the bladder, acting like a valve to the mouth of the urethra, which can be seen even when the swelling is not considerable, by looking upon the mouth of the urethra from the cavity of the bladder in a dead body. It sometimes increases so much as to form a tumour, projecting into the bladder some inches. This projection turns or bends the urethra forwards, becoming an obstruction to the passage of a catheter, bougie, or any such instrument; and it often raises the sound over a small stone in the bladder, so as to prevent its being felt. The catheter should for this part be more curved than is necessary for the other parts of the urethra.[31]

Hunter describes the principle of the bi-coudé catheter – 'I therefore took a thick bougie, and before I introduced it I bent the point almost double, so that it could not catch at the posterior surface of the urethra, where I supposed the stop to be: this point of the bougie rubbed all along the anterior and upper surface of the urethra, by which means it avoided catching on the posterior surface, and it passed with great ease into the bladder.'[32]

He gives excellent practical advice on the use of a catheter:

> If it is necessary to keep in the catheter a considerable time, it will be the cause of a great deal of slime and mucus being formed in the urethra and bladder; but I believe this is of no consequence. I have known a catheter kept in this way for five months without any inconveniency whatever.
>
> In all cases where it is necessary to keep an extraneous body for a considerable time in the bladder, whether in an artificial passage or the natural one, it will be proper a few days after its first introduction to withdraw it, and examine whether it is incrusting, or filling up in its cavity with the calculous matter of the urine. If, after remaining in the bladder for some days, it has contracted none, we need be under no apprehension of its doing it; but if, as frequently happens, it should have collected a considerable quantity, then it will be necessary to have it occasionally withdrawn and cleaned. The best method probably of doing this is to put it in vinegar, which will soon dissolve the stony matter.[33]

Chronic Urinary Retention. John Hunter used the word 'suppression' as synonymous with 'retention' but he did know the mechanism by which retention was caused.[34] He gave an accurate description of the changes in the bladder resulting from chronic retention with trabeculation, diverticula and stones:

> I have seen the muscular coats of the bladder near half an inch thick, and the fasciculi so strong as to form ridges on the inside of that cavity; . . . This appearance was long supposed to have arisen from a disease of the viscus; but upon examination I found that the muscular parts were sound and distinct, so that they were only increased in bulk in proportion to the power they had to exert, and that it was not a consequence of inflammation, for in that case parts are blended into one indistinct mass.
>
> I have also seen the fasciculi very thin, and even wanting in some parts of the bladder, so that a hernia of the internal coat had taken place between the fasciculi and formed pouches . . . This is perhaps the cause of the stone being often found in a pouch formed in the bladder: for the bladder in cases of stone is often very strong, which arises from the violent contraction of that viscus, caused by the irritation of the stone on the sides of it; and also from the stone being often opposed to the mouth of the urethra in the time of making water.[35]

Hunter described the autopsy appearances in a case of suppression of urine with a large prostate and middle lobe.[36]

REFERENCES

1 Goodman H. *Notable Contributors to the Knowledge of Syphilis.* New York, Froben Press. 1944, p. 88.

2 Hunter J. A treatise on venereal disease in *The Works of John Hunter,* ed. J F Palmer. London, Longman. 1835, vol. 2, pp. 143–145.

3 Hunter J. A treatise on the blood, inflammation and gun-shot wounds in *The Works of John Hunter,* ed. J F Palmer. London, Longman. 1837, vol. 3, pp. 3, 4.

4 Ibid. p. 301.

5 Hunter J. Lectures on the principles of surgery in *The Works of John Hunter,* ed. J F Palmer. London, Longman. 1835, vol. 1, p. 258.

6 Hunter J. A treatise on venereal disease in *The Works of John Hunter,* ed. J F Palmer. London, Longman. 1835, vol. 2, p. 154.

7 Ibid. p. 381.

8 Foot J. *Observations upon the New Opinions of John Hunter on the Venereal Disease.* London, T Becket. 1786.

9 Foot J. *The Life of John Hunter.* London, T Becket. 1794.

10 Rudolf C R. Hunteriana Part 4. *Hunterian Society Transactions.* 1957–58, vol. 16, pp. 141–166.

11 Farington J. *The Farington Diary,* ed. J Greig. Second edn. London, Hutchinson. 1922, vol. 1, p. 165.

12 Hunter J. A treatise on venereal disease in *The Works of John Hunter,* ed. J F Palmer. London, Longman. 1835, vol. 2, p. 160.

13 Ibid. p. 394.

14 Ibid. p. 164.

15 Ibid. p. 332.

16 Ibid. pp. 163, 164.

17 Ibid. p. 159.

18 Marchand L A. *Byron: A Biography.* New York, Alfred A Knopf. London, John Murray. 1957, vol. 1, p. 276.

19 Hunter J. Some observations on digestion in *The Works of John Hunter,* ed. J F Palmer. London, Longman. 1837, vol. 4, p. 86.

20 Hunter J. A treatise on venereal disease in *The Works of John Hunter,* ed. J F Palmer. London, Longman. 1835, vol. 2, p. 165.

21 Ibid. p. 142.

22 Ibid. pp. 229–272.

23 Ibid. p. 266.

24 Ibid. p. 269.

25 Brodie B C. *Pathological and Surgical Observations on Diseases of the Joints.* London, Longman, Hurst, Rees, Orme and Brown. 1818.

26 Editorial. Reiter's disease. *British Medical Journal.* 1971, vol. 3, p. 386.

27 Hunter J. A treatise on venereal disease in *The Works of John Hunter,* ed. J F Palmer. London, Longman. 1835, vol. 2, pp. 161, 162.

28 Smith B H. Peyronie's disease – sequel to VD or to urethritis? *World Medicine.* 1969. Feb. 25. p. 41.

29 Odiase V O N and Whitaker R H. Peyronie's disease in a district general hospital. *Postgraduate Medical Journal.* 1980, vol. 56, pp. 773–776.

30 Hunter J. A treatise on venereal disease in *The Works of John Hunter,* ed. J F Palmer. London, Longman. 1835, vol. 2, pp. 326, 327.

31 Ibid. pp. 278, 279.
32 Ibid. p. 282.
33 Ibid. p. 298.
34 Riches Sir Eric. Hunterian milestones. *Hunterian Society Transactions* 1968–69, vol. 27, pp. 7–19.
35 Hunter J. A treatise on venereal disease in *The Works of John Hunter*, ed. J F Palmer. London, Longman. 1835, vol. 2, p. 299.
36 Hunter J. *Case-Book. Transcript by W Clift.* Vol. 3, pp. 76, 77.

CHAPTER 17

PATIENTS

JOHN Hunter kept careful notes of his cases and fortunately many have been preserved. They consist of Cases in Surgery; Accounts of the Dissections of Morbid Bodies; Cases and Observations; and Cases and Dissections, giving a total of over 700 different records of cases in his practice.[1] Many of them are unidentified and described as 'a Gentleman', or 'a Lady', or 'a Nobleman'. In some cases, however, their identity has been established, largely as the result of Clift's industry in transcribing the manuscripts.[2] The records include a great variety of medical and surgical cases, and they must be representative of most of the diseases common in Hunter's time. The following cases are of some interest.

The *Duke of Queensberry* was attended by John Hunter when he ruptured his Achilles tendon:

> It is impossible for a patient with a fracture of the tendo Achillis to act with the gastrocnemius and soleus muscles, if he were to try to do so. When the Duke of Queensberry broke his tendo Achillis he was immediately aware of what had happened, and pointed out to me the broken ends. He readily submitted to my reasoning: walked about his room as well as he could, and found it impracticable to contract the gastrocnemius muscle. Some surgeons thought the tendon could not be broken, because he was walking about his room; but in such a case the patient has no more power to contract his gastrocnemius and soleus muscles than to jump over St. Paul's.[3]

General Murray developed an empyema following a chest wound. In discussing the treatment of this condition Hunter stated – '. . . wounds have been made into the cavity of the thorax, suppuration has taken place, and yet the patient has got well; but how this has been brought about I cannot tell. General Murray, to whom I have often expressed a wish to peep into his chest, has been twice wounded in this way.'[4]

William Hickey (1749–1830), the peripatetic diarist, was attended by John Hunter in 1776 at Margate. While staying at the home of a friend, a Mr. Cane, Hickey sustained a badly burned foot –

> . . . my friend Cane was beyond measure distressed. He instantly dispatched an express to London to summon Mr. Robin Adair* to come and attend me, but that gentleman happening to be at Bristol at the time, Mr. John Hunter, who had undertaken to act for him during his absence, instantly left town and came to me. After meeting the Margate surgeon and inspecting my foot he at once declared no ill consequence would arise, and that a few days' quiet, keeping my leg in a horizontal position, and frequently applying an embrocation which he ordered, would completely cure the hurt. And so it proved; in a week I was perfectly recovered, but during that period I was kept upon chicken broth, and not allowed a drop of wine, lest fever should ensue.[5]

Sir Joshua Reynolds (1723–1792) developed cirrhosis of the liver and was attended by John Hunter who also performed an autopsy, as described by Ottley:

> Hunter, with Sir G. Baker and Mr. Home, attended Sir J. Reynolds in his last illness, the nature of which was very obscure, and is said not to have been understood until a fortnight before his death, when it was ascertained to depend on enlargement of the liver. The following is a copy of the *post mortem* examination, the original of which is in the possession of my friend Mr. Palmer, the great-nephew of Sir Joshua, and editor of the present edition of Hunter's works.
>
> 'In examining the body of the late Sir Joshua Reynolds, we found no marks of disease in the cavity of the breast, except only a slight adhesion of the lungs to the surrounding membrane on the left side.
>
> 'In the cavity of the belly the only diseased part was the liver, which was of a magnitude very uncommon, and at least double of what is natural: it weighed eleven pounds, and was of a consistence which is usually called scirrhous. It had lost its natural colour, and become of a pale yellow.
>
> 'We found the optic nerve of the right side shrunk, and softer than natural. There was more water in the ventricles of the brain than what is generally found at so advanced an age.
>
> G. Baker,
John Hunter,
E. Home.[6]
>
> 24th Feb. 1792.

---

* Robert Adair (1711–1790), best known perhaps as the subject of the ballad, was Inspector-General of Hospitals and in 1760 granted John Hunter his Army commission. When Adair died in 1790 Hunter succeeded him in that appointment.

Joseph Haydn (1732–1809) was on friendly terms with John and
Anne Hunter (p. 21). He consulted Hunter about a nasal polyp for
which he had already undergone inadequate surgery. Haydn's
letters include a reference to these consultations – '. . . He had
inspected my polyp and offered to free me of this nuisance. I had
half agreed, but the operation was put off and at last I thought no
more of it. Shortly before my departure, Mr. H. asked me to come
and see him about some urgent matters. I went there. After the first
exchange of greetings, a few brawny fellows entered the room,
grabbed me and wanted to force me into a chair. I yelled, kicked
and hit until I had freed myself and made clear to Mr. H., who
already had his instruments ready for the operation, that I did not
want to undergo the operation. He was very astonished at my
obstinancy, and it seemed to me that he pitied me for not wanting to
undergo the happy experience of enjoying his skill. I excused
myself, saying that there was not time because of my forthcoming
departure, and took my leave of him.'[7]

Dr. William Hunter (1718–1783) suffered for many years from
recurrent urinary symptoms, probably due to stones. The description of his terminal attack suggests that he developed uraemia. His
case history, dated June 1783, is recorded in John Hunter's
Case-Books, and although no name is given there is an additional
note in William Clift's handwriting and initialled by him – 'This
Case is without a name, but is undoubtedly that of Dr. William
Hunter, who died March 30th 1783. . . . W.C.'[8]

Samuel Foote (1720–1777), the celebrated actor and playwright,
suffered the loss of a leg through an accident and wrote himself parts
to suit his infirmity, as in *The Lame Lover* (1770).[9] John Hunter
refers to him in his lectures on surgery – '. . . the late Mr. Foote,
who was not able to command his attention to more than one action
or circumstance at a time: thus, if he took his snuff-box out of his
pocket and held it in his hand, it was all very well, until he
attempted another action, such as taking a pinch of snuff out of it,
and then the box fell immediately out of his hand; . . .'.[10] 'Mr.
Foote was cured of a violent pain in his head by amputation of his
leg; but he afterwards died with a different complaint in his
head . . .'[11]

Lieut.-General Desaguliers died from haemorrhage resulting from
spontaneous rupture of the spleen. John Hunter's records state –
'He was only ill for a few days: had something like an Ague, . . .

the last fit in which he died, . . . he felt a violent pain in his two buttocks. He was opened thirty-three hours after death. March 3rd 1780.'[12] Autopsy showed 'Two pints and a half of extravasated blood loose among the bowels. Spleen a mere pulp, with its coat separated from its substance. The coat had burst and the blood had escaped by that opening.'[13]

Mr. Chaworth was stabbed by his cousin, Lord Byron, the fifth Baron and great-uncle of the poet, in 1765.[14] John Hunter noted 'violent vomitings and retchings, but no blood. Pain all over the belly . . . He died twelve hours after the accident.'[15] Autopsy showed that 'The Stomach was wounded and a tendency for universal inflammation all over the Peritoneum . . .'[16]

Lord Byron, 6th Baron (1788–1824), the poet, was born with a caul (amniotic membrane over the head and supposed by sailors to be a lucky charm against drowning), and a right club-foot (talipes equinovarus). John Hunter was consulted and 'recommended a special shoe that he thought would enable the boy, when old enough, to walk without difficulty, though he offered no hope of an actual cure.'[17]

Indeed Hunter's treatment may have been of some value since in 1805 'Byron's foot had so far improved that he could now wear a common boot over a corrective inner shoe,' but he still had difficulty in running',[18] and in that year, aged 17, he was in the Harrow school cricket team against Eton, while in 1810 he swam the Hellespont, a distance of more than 4 miles.[19]

In childhood Byron was inoculated for smallpox by John Hunter – 'On Monday I inoculated Master Byron in both arms. On the Tuesday the wounds were very much inflamed; also a space round them broader than a halfpenny. This alarmed me, as I suspected that it showed too great a disposition for the irritation. On the Wednesday, the surrounding inflammation was gone off, and only that of the Wounds; which was less than the preceding day.'[20]

David Hume (1711–1776), the great historian and philosopher, died of cancer after a year's illness.[21] In a letter to his brother he described a consultation with John Hunter – '. . . Dr. Gusthart proposed that I should be inspected by him: He felt very sensibly, as he said, a Tumor or Swelling in my Liver; and this Fact, not drawn by Reasoning, but obvious to the Senses, and perceived by the greatest Anatomist in Europe, must be admitted as unquestionable.'[22]

This letter, dated '10 of June 1776', was written by Hume from Bath where he was spending a few weeks on medical advice. The consultation arose from '. . . John Hunter . . . coming accidentally to Town . . .' There can be no doubt therefore that John Hunter was staying at Bath, in June 1776 so that it is very likely that one of his most severe attacks of cardiac disturbance, described by himself (p. 48) occurred in the spring of 1776 (p. 41).

Adam Smith (1723–1790), the political economist and author of the *Wealth of Nations*, travelled up from Edinburgh in 1787 in order to consult John Hunter about his failing health.[23] Unfortunately his case notes have not been found but at the time of the consultation 'he was wasted to a skeleton'[24] and his condition deteriorated slowly until his death in 1790. Dugald Stewart states that his illness arose from a chronic obstruction of the bowels.[25]

Joseph Farington (1747–1821), the celebrated landscape painter, had a cyst removed from his back by John Hunter in 1792. In his diary Farington noted, on October 17th 1793 – 'Much concerned at an account in the newspaper of the death of John Hunter, the eminent Surgeon, to whom I was greatly obliged in the course of last summer for his advice etc., on account of an incested tumour on my back, which he removed . . . He mentioned to me once that he had some obstruction or complaint about his heart which he was well assured would cause his death suddenly at some period.'[26]

The *Marquis of Rockingham* (1730–1782), twice Prime Minister, sustained an injury while horse-riding in 1759, after which he suffered chronic abdominal pain. John Hunter's Case-Books state – 'Every Physician and Surgeon in Europe, of any Note, was consulted; and various were the opinions of the Cause of this pain . . . As this Case had called forth the attention of almost every Physical (Medical?)* man in London, and nothing had ever been made out, the appearance after death became an object of inquiry, and many were anxious to be present at the examination, which was attended by Dr. William Hunter, Dr. Warren, Mr. Bromfield, and opened by J. Hunter.'[27]

The results of the autopsy were inconclusive – 'Considerable quantity of water in Thorax, right side nearly 3 pints – in the left above a pint and a half – of clear serum. Lungs perfectly sound.'

---

* This insertion in the *Case-Book* was probably made by Clift in transcribing the manuscript.

The abdomen was 'in a sound state'. The account of this case appears in Hunter's Case-Book under the title of 'Hydrops Pectoris'.[28]

Thomas Gainsborough (1727–1788) died with a cancerous tumour in his back for which John Hunter had been consulted. Farington stated in his Diary on October 29, 1794 – 'Gainsborough Dupont called. . . . He told me his uncle, Gainsborough, had completed his sixty-first year when he died. The tumour in his neck which proved cancerous and caused his death, he had been conscious of five or six years, but when he occasionally mentioned it he was led by others to believe it only a swelled kernel. A cold he caught at Hastings trial caused it to inflame. He applied to Dr. Heberden [Gainsborough's next door neighbour] who treated it lightly and said it would pass away with the cold. He applied to John Hunter, who advised salt water poultices, which greatly increased the inflammation and a suppuration followed. There seems to have been a strange mistake or neglect both in Heberden and Hunter – Gainsborough was ill for six months.'[29]

Sir Patrick Crawford came under the care of John Hunter whose notes state '. . . observed a fullness . . . in his left side . . . it appeared to be the Spleen . . . he lost flesh very considerably.'[30] The autopsy report records that – 'On opening the belly, . . . the spleen . . . occupied almost the whole of the left side of that cavity; . . . about twelve times its natural size.'[31]

Lady Mary Coke, daughter of the Duke of Argyll, was a wealthy widow whose letters and journals provide an excellent account of court and social life in the eighteenth century. There are numerous references to Dr. William Hunter especially in relation to the patients in his fashionable obstetric practice. An entry in her Journal records that on 23rd July 1772 Lady Mary Coke was attended by John Hunter at her home, Notting Hill House – '. . . I had appointed Mr. Hunter, the Surgeon at my House, to bleed me: . . . Mr. Fox [an apothecary] who I now consult, advised me to be blooded in my foot. I accordingly was, and sat with my foot up till I went to Bed. . . .'[32]

Thomas Secker (1693–1768), Archbishop of Canterbury, sustained a spontaneous fracture of the femur, described by Hunter as being due to a tumour of the bone (p. 136). This occurrence is recorded in Lady Mary Coke's Journal where it is stated that the Archbishop died in 1768 as the result of a broken thigh, '. . . the bone being rotten, . . . it being impossible for the bone to nit . . .'[33]

The *Earl of Morton* died as the result of a perforated duodenal ulcer, demonstrated by Hunter at autopsy (p. 87).

REFERENCES

1 Dobson J. John Hunter's practice. *Annals of the Royal College of Surgeons of England.* 1966, vol. 38, pp. 181–190.
2 Dobson J. Some of John Hunter's patients. *Annals of the Royal College of Surgeons of England.* 1968, vol. 42, pp. 124–133.
3 Hunter J. Lectures on the principles of surgery in *The Works of John Hunter*, ed. J F Palmer. London, Longman. 1835, vol. 1, p. 439.
4 Ibid. pp. 443, 444.
5 Hickey W. *Memoirs of William Hickey*, ed. Alfred Spencer. London, Hurst and Blackett. 1913–1925, 5th edn. four volumes, vol. II, p. 87.
6 Ottley D. Life of John Hunter in *The Works of John Hunter*, ed. J F Palmer. London, Longman. 1835, vol. 1, p. 121.
7 Landon H C Robbins. *Haydn in England 1791–1795*. London, Thames and Hudson. 1976, pp. 178, 179.
8 Hunter J. *Case-Book. Transcript by W Clift.* vol. 1, pp. 173–175.
9 *Chambers's Encyclopaedia.* London, George Newnes. 1950, vol. 5, p. 786.
10 Hunter J. Lectures on the principles of surgery in *The Works of John Hunter*, ed. J F Palmer. London, Longman. 1835, vol. 1, p. 336.
11 Ibid. p. 401.
12 Hunter J. *Case-Book. Transcript by W Clift.* vol. 1, pp. 112, 113.
13 Ibid. vol. 3, p. 193.
14 Dobson J. John Hunter and the Byron family. *Journal of History of Medicine and Allied Sciences.* 1955, vol. 10, pp. 333–335.
15 Hunter J. *Case-Book. Transcript by W Clift*, vol. 2, p. 115.
16 Ibid. vol. 3, p. 107.
17 Marchand L A. *Byron: A Biography.* New York, Knopf and London, John Murray. 1957, vol. 1, pp. 25, 26.
18 Marchand L A. *Byron: A Portrait.* London, John Murray. 1971, p. 33.
19 Ibid. p. 82.
20 Hunter J. *Case-Book. Transcript by W Clift.* vol. 2, p. 3.
21 *Chambers's Encyclopaedia.* London, George Newnes. 1950, vol. 7, p. 287.
22 Greig J Y T. Ed. *The Letters of David Hume.* Oxford, Clarendon Press. 1932, vol. 2, pp. 324, 325.
23 Rae J. *Life of Adam Smith.* London, Macmillan. 1895, p. 402.
24 Ibid. p. 404.
25 Stewart D. The life and writings of Adam Smith in *The Collected Works of Dugald Stewart*, ed. W Hamilton. Edinburgh, T and T Clark. 1877, vol. 10, p. 73.
26 Farington J. *The Farington Diary*, ed. J Greig. Second edn. London, Hutchinson. 1922, vol. 1, pp. 6, 7.
27 Hunter J. *Case-Book. Transcript by W Clift.* vol. 1, pp. 224–226.
28 Ibid. vol. 3, p. 217.
29 Farington J. *The Farington Diary*, ed. J Greig. Second edn. London, Hutchinson. 1922, vol. 1, p. 75.
30 Hunter J. *Case-Book. Transcript by W Clift.* vol. 2, pp. 134, 135.
31 Ibid. vol. 3, pp. 213, 214.

32 Home J A. Ed. *The Letters and Journals of Lady Mary Coke.* Bath, Kingsmead Reprints. 1889–1896, vol. 4, p. 102.
33 Ibid. vol. 3, p. 273.

ADDITIONAL BIBLIOGRAPHY

Abel A Lawrence. John Hunter's Patients. *Hunterian Society Transactions.* 1961–62, vol. 20, pp. 55–84.
Pasmore S. John Hunter in Kensington. *Hunterian Society Transactions.* 1976–78, vols. 35, 36, pp. 69–97.
Wright A D. Venereal disease and the great. *British Journal of Venereal Disease.* 1971, vol. 47, pp. 295–306.

CHAPTER 18

GEOLOGY AND PALAEONTOLOGY

In Hunter's time knowledge of geology and palaeontology was unscientific and based essentially on the Scriptures. The Mosaic account of the Creation was incorporated into the Bible and given a scientific value by the Church, a concept which was not finally discredited until Darwin's work. In the eighteenth century there were very few people who did not sincerely accept the Scriptural views about the age of the earth, the occurrence of the Flood and the Creation. The Geological Society of London was founded only in 1807 and the Palaeontographical Society of Britain in 1847. The position of these subjects at that time is well summarised by Gillispie:

> . . . around 1790, the origin of fossils was no longer a matter of serious debate. These curiosities were recognized as the residues of living creatures, but they were not the object of any particular attention, scientific or otherwise. Noah's flood probably accounted for their presence in the mountain tops, and there the matter rested. There was no question about the historical reality of the flood. When the history of the earth began to be considered geologically, it was simply assumed that a universal deluge must have wrought vast changes and that it had been a primary agent in forming the present surface of the globe. . . . The accepted time span since creation was still around six thousand years, though there was beginning to be some doubt whether this was long enough. Whenever the question arose, however, it was supposed that this chronology might be referred to the deluge rather than to the origin of the world. In any case, the earth was allowed no very great antiquity. The antiquity of animal life depended on whether one postulated a single, all-sufficient act of creation or a series of special creations as the necessity arose for new forms of life. Both views were held, and the latter reserved mankind for a comparatively recent beginning. Animal and vegetable species, of course, were absolutely immutable and permanent, each created in its present image. . . .[1]

Hunter, as might be expected, held views in geology and palaeontology which were strongly opposed to Orthodoxy and his contributions to these subjects were considerable. As regards the Flood, Hunter considered that 'Forty days' water overflowing the dry land could not have brought such quantities of sea-productions on its surface; nor can we suppose . . . that it remained long . . .; therefore there was no time for their being fossilised; . . .' He then makes the suggestion that . . . 'it would appear that the sea has more than once made its incursions at the same place; for the mixture of land- and sea-productions now found on the land is a proof of at least two changes having taken place.'[2] These words were written around 1790, more than thirty years before Professor William Buckland wrote his famous 'Reliquiae Diluvianae' (1823) in which he presented geological evidence supporting the reality of the Flood.[3]

Dr. William Buckland (1784–1856), father of Frank Buckland (p. 195) was Professor of Geology at Oxford and the leading geologist of his time. His numerous contributions giving scientific support to Scriptural geology probably helped considerably towards his appointment as Dean of Westminster. He died in 1856 as a result of tuberculosis of the cervical spine and his son Frank had an autopsy performed and presented the specimen to the Hunterian Museum of the Royal College of Surgeons of England.

The age of the earth was another geological aspect on which Hunter expressed an unorthodox view. In discussing the preservation of fossils, he wrote: '. . . many . . . retain some of the their form for many thousand years, . . .'[4] It is often stated that Hunter referred to many thousand *centuries* rather than *years*. However, reference to the manuscript, in Clift's handwriting, shows that in fact Hunter used the word *years*.[5] It seems that Hunter had originally written *centuries* but he altered it on the advice of Major James Rennell, FRS,[6] a copy of whose letter to Hunter is appended to the manuscript. In the printed edition of Hunter's manuscript, published in 1859, the word *years* has been altered to *centuries*.[7] There is no satisfactory explanation of this alteration, but it probably accounts for the apocryphal story that Hunter had submitted his treatise to the Royal Society but withdrew it when they requested him to make the alteration from *centuries* to *years*. There is no record of the paper having been received by the Royal Society[6] and Major Rennell was never an officer of the Society although he received the Copley Medal in 1791 for his distinguished work in geography.[8] The erroneous idea that Hunter refused to make the alteration from centuries to years is frequently quoted as an example of his strict independence of opinion in all scientific matters. The evidence provided by Rennell's letter suggests that Hunter had in fact already made this alteration in an earlier undisclosed MS. It is very likely that this evidence influenced the editors of the printed edition in making the alteration from the existing MS, from *years* to *centuries*, in the belief that Hunter had originally written *centuries*. It is doubtful that Hunter could have regarded the alteration from centuries to years as a serious matter of principle. It is obvious that Hunter disagreed with the biblical chronology which determines the age of the earth as some 6,000 years, and he implied that an enormous span of time would have been necessary for the occurrence of recognised geological events.

Hunter makes frequent references to the great age of the earth. In his description of the fossil bones of Anspach he said: '. . . difference in the state of the bones . . . there was probably a succession of them for a vast series of years . . . between the . . . last and the present time . . . many thousand years. And . . . to be as far decayed as some others are, it will require many thousand years.'[9]

Hunter's opinions in geology were well ahead of his time. He held quite modern views on the importance of water as a major agent in geological changes. '. . . the motion of the waters . . . with the power of solution, appear to be the regulators of the formation of the surface of this globe.'[10] He gave numerous examples of the changes in distribution of land and water. His earliest observations were made when he was in the Army in Portugal in 1762 where he observed that 'the extensive flat tract of land . . . called Alentejo' showed evidence 'of the sea having once covered this tract, and afterwards having left it gradually.'[11]

Hunter appreciated the constant cycle of changes in the land due to erosion by water and its rejuvenation by upheavals. 'The waters are continually carrying away the land from one situation, and depositing it in another, taking down continents, and leaving the ocean in their place; whilst at the same time they are raising continents out of the sea.'[12] Like James Hutton (1726–1797), his contemporary, he explained former changes on the earth's surface by natural agencies instead of by catastrophic occurrences. Indeed, he was a pioneer of uniformitarianism, a geological concept that only received its due acknowledgement half a century later, after Lyell's *Principles of Geology* had been published.

A great variety of causes had been proposed to explain geological phenomena. The *neptunists* believed that such physical changes were brought about by the agency of water. The *vulcanists* and *plutonists* proposed an igneous origin of geological formations. The *catastrophists* considered that physical changes resulted from sudden and violent disturbances of nature. The *diluvialists* regarded geological processes as the result of a deluge or flood such as the Noachian Flood. The *uniformitarians* attributed geological phenomena to the continuous uniform action of natural forces over a vast period of time; that Hunter held this view is obvious from his writings.

The collection of fossils was one of Hunter's great interests (p. 67) and his letters to Jenner include repeated demands for as many fossils as possible, e.g.

> . . . Send me all the Fossels you find. What I meant by Bones, was all the Bones that are found any depth under the surface of the Earth, . . . send me some of them, and if any History can be given send it also . . .[13]

> . . . I have but one order to send you which is send every thing you can get either animal vegetable or mineral, and the compound of the two *viz* either animal or vegetable mineralised.[14]

A fundamental principle of geology and palaeontology is the significance of fossils in determining the relative age of geological strata. The establishment of this principle is usually ascribed to William Smith in 1816[15] – indeed he is often called the 'father of British geology'. But John Hunter had made this observation several years before. In discussing the causes of 'the operations that must have taken place on the surface of this Globe', he said, '. . . all of which we should have been unable to consider if we had not preserved parts of sea-animals, . . . The Fossils of sea-animals inform us of the change of place in the waters, otherwise we could not have supposed it; just as we would trace the remains of former actions in any country by the monuments left, judging of past from the present.'[16]

This observation of the relation of fossils and geological strata was of prime importance in the establishment of biological evolution, as expressed by Whewell –

But the study of geology opens to us the spectacle of many groups of species which have, in the course of the earth's history, succeeded each other at vast intervals of time; one set of animals and plants disappearing, as it would seem, from the face of our planet, and others which did not before exist, becoming the only occupants of the globe. And the dilemma then presents itself to us anew: – either we must accept the doctrine of the transmutation of species, and must suppose that the organized species of one geological epoch were transmuted into those of another by some long-continued agency of natural causes; or else, we must believe in many successive acts of creation and extinction of species, out of the common course of nature; acts which, therefore, we may properly call [miraculous.[17]

It is remarkable that there is no reference in the literature to Hunter's collection of fossils which must have been the largest in the country in the eighteenth century. Von Zittel's classic work on the *History of Geology and Palaeontology* (1901) states that prior to the nineteenth century there was no general work on fossils except John Woodward's collection in Cambridge (1695).[18]

Hunter has had little recognition in the fields of geology and palaeontology, to which he contributed so much. Undoubtedly the chief reason for this was that Hunter's most important geological and palaeontological work, *Observations and Reflections on Geology*, although written in 1791 or 1792, was not published until 1859.[19] The reasons for this delay are obscure and they have been discussed by Wood Jones (1953).[6] The two parts of the original manuscript were sequestrated, along with other Hunterian manuscripts, by Everard Home after Hunter's death in 1793. The first part of the manuscript was eventually returned to the Royal College of Surgeons in 1839 by Home's son, Capt. E. Home, R.N. However, Clift had made copies of both parts of the manuscript soon after Hunter's decease and there is no evidence that these copies were ever removed from the College. But even if Clift's copies had not existed, the treatise could have been published in 1839 when it was returned to the College. There can be no doubt that the Council deliberately delayed publication of this important work until December 1859.

It is not at all difficult to account for the Council's procrastination in this matter. Hunter's manuscript was a logical scientific treatise of geology which completely discredited the Scriptures. Its contents must have antagonised most of the members of the Council because orthodox biblical views were still almost universally held. The great majority of scientists and theologians sincerely believed in the Mosaic account of a universal deluge and had the powerful support of Cuvier and Buckland whose theory of Diluvialism, which vindicated the Noachian Flood, dominated geological opinion of the time. Members of the Council could hardly be blamed for holding the sincere orthodox opinions of their time, but even if the Council had been prepared to accept the responsibility of publication of Hunter's heretical views, the College would undoubtedly have suffered considerable embarrassment and criticism. The date of publication of Hunter's treatise is significant. It was published hurriedly at the end of the year in which the *Origin of Species* appeared. It is very suggestive that it was only after the advent of this crucial influence on scientific thought that the Council felt able to publicise Hunter's unorthodox views.

There is another aspect concerning the delay in publication of the manuscript – why did not Hunter publish it himself? There can be only one answer to this question, that Hunter actually did not dare to publish a work which contained opinions which in those days would have been regarded as heretical. It is not easy to appreciate the strength of feeling with which any attack on orthodox Christian teaching was rejected in Hunter's time. The doctrine of philosophical materialism caused serious offence to the vast majority and its adherents were persecuted violently. 'In virtually every branch of knowledge, repressive methods were used: lectures were proscribed, publication was hampered, professorships were denied, fierce invective and ridicule appeared in the press. Scholars and scientists learned the lesson and responded to the pressures on them. The ones with unpopular ideas sometimes recanted, published anonymously, presented their ideas in weakened forms, or delayed publication for many years.'[20] Even Darwin in his *Origin of Species*, nearly a century after Hunter, did not dare to publish his views on the origin of man and merely stated that 'In the distant future . . . Light will be thrown on the origin of man and his history,'[21] and he gave vent to his beliefs, only when he could hide them no longer, in the *Descent of Man*, in 1871.[22]

An Act passed in 1698 (still unrepealed) penalised such as 'shall deny the Christian religion to be true, or the holy scriptures of the Old and New Testament to be of divine authority', the penalties being, for the first offence, incapacity for any office or employment, ecclesiastical, civil, or military, an incapacity removable by renunciation of the error; for the second offence, perpetual outlawry, and three years' imprisonment without bail.[23]

John Hunter must have been acutely aware of the many pioneers who had been persecuted for their unorthodox views, not only in the past such as Bruno (1548–1600), Copernicus (1473–1543), Kepler (1571–1630), Galileo (1564–1642), Descartes (1596–1650), and Newton (1642–1727), but even among his own contemporaries, including Buffon, Diderot and Gibbon.[24]

Buffon (1707–1788) advocated the antiquity of the globe and the great and gradual changes which its surface had undergone. His views were censured by the Faculty of Theology at the Sorbonne and Buffon made a declaration that he abandoned everything in his book respecting the formation of the earth that might be contrary to the narration of Moses.[25] Lyell stated that 'The grand principle which Buffon was called upon to renounce was simply this, – "that the present mountains and valleys of the earth are due to secondary causes, and that the same causes will in time destroy all the continents, hills and valleys, and reproduce others like them." Now, whatever may be the defects of many of his views, it is no longer controverted that the present continents are of secondary origin . . . and that the land now elevated above the level of the sea will not endure for ever . . .'[26] John Hunter made this important geological observation in his Treatise on the Blood (p. 58).

Diderot (1713–1784) supported religious tolerance and decried supernatural revelation for which he suffered imprisonment and suppression of his monumental encyclopaedia.[27]

Gibbon (1737–1794) expressed heretical views in his *Decline and Fall* but he had to adopt a stylistic artifice of irony in order to avert persecution.[28]

There were thus good reasons why Hunter could very well be forgiven for not wishing to publicise his own heretical views. In addition to the risk of outraging the public, in his position as Surgeon-General to the Army Hunter owed allegiance to the King who was Head of the English Church. Indeed Hunter dedicated his Treatise on Gun-shot Wounds to the King. He certainly could not have dedicated his Observations on Geology to the Sovereign. Hunter must have realised that he would have risked his position, his livelihood and perhaps even his life by the publication of this work and, if this speculation is correct he could hardly be blamed for not wishing to antagonise the orthodox doctrines of his age.

REFERENCES

1 Gillispie C C. *Genesis and Geology.* Cambridge, Harvard University Press. 1969, p. 42.
2 Hunter J. *Observations and Reflections on Geology.* London, Taylor and Francis. 1859, p. 10.
3 Buckland W. *Reliquiae Diluvianae* or *Observations on Organic Remains, attesting the Action of a Universal Deluge.* London, John Murray. 1823.
4 Hunter J. *Observations and Reflections on Geology.* MS. Royal College of Surgeons of England Library. c. 1792, p. 5.
5 Qvist G. Hunterian Oration 1979. Some controversial aspects of John Hunter's life and work, Part 5, Geology and Palaeontology. *Annals of the Royal College of Surgeons of England.* Vol. 61, pp. 381–384.
6 Jones F Wood. John Hunter as a geologist. *Annals of the Royal College of Surgeons of England.* 1953, vol. 12, pp. 219–245.
7 Hunter J. *Observations and Reflections on Geology.* London, Taylor and Francis. 1859, p. 3.
8 Robinson N H. (Librarian, Royal Society). Personal communication. 1978.
9 Hunter J. Observations on some fossil bones of Anspach in *The Works of John Hunter,* ed. J F Palmer. London, Longman. 1837, vol. 4, p. 473.
10 Hunter J. *Observations and Reflections on Geology.* London, Taylor and Francis. 1859, p. 22.
11 Ibid. p. 16.
12 Hunter J. A treatise on the blood, inflammation and gun-shot wounds in *The Works of John Hunter,* ed. J F Palmer. London, Longman. 1837, vol. 3, p. 15.
13 Editorial. Letters from the past. *Annals of the Royal College of Surgeons of England.* 1974, vol. 55, p. 255.
14 Ibid. vol. 54, p. 260.
15 Smith W. *Strata Identified by Organised Fossils.* Printed by W Arding for the Author. 1816.
16 Hunter J. *Observations and Reflections on Geology.* London, Taylor and Francis. 1859, pp. 1, 2.
17 Whewell W. *History of the Inductive Sciences.* London, John Parker. 1837, vol. 3, p. 574.
18 von Zittel K A. *History of Geology and Palaeontology,* transl. Maria M Ogilvie-Gordon. London, Walter Scott. 1901, p. 127.
19 Hunter J. *Observations and Reflections on Geology.* London, Taylor and Francis. 1859.
20 Gruber H E and Barrett P H. *Darwin on Man. A Psychological Study of Scientific Creativity.* London, Wildwood House. 1974, p. 203.
21 Darwin C. *Origin of Species.* London, John Murray. 1869, 5th edn. pp. 577, 578.
22 Gould S J. *Ever Since Darwin. Reflections in Natural History.* Burnett Books and Andre Deutsch. 1978, p. 25.
23 Gordon A. *Heresy: Its Ancient Wrongs and Modern Rights In these Kingdoms.* Essex Hall Lecture 14 May 1913. London, The Lindsey Press. 1913, pp. 32–34.
24 White A D. *The Warfare of Science with Theology.* London, Arco. 1955, p. 15.
25 Woodward H B. *History of Geology.* London, Watts & Co. 1911, p. 15.
26 Lyell C (Sir Charles). *Principles of Geology.* London, John Murray. 1853, Ninth edn. p. 40.
27 *Encyclopaedia Britannica.* London, Ency. Br. Ltd. 1957, 14th edn. vol. 7, pp. 343–345.
28 Ibid. vol. 10, pp. 330–332.

CHAPTER 19

EVOLUTION

ONE of the most wondrous features of animate Nature must surely be the perfect harmony existing between structure and function, as shown for example by the woodpecker's tongue and beak so admirably suited to capture insects under the bark of trees, by the structure of many flowers in such forms as to facilitate the collection of their nectar by bees, and by the mistletoe plant in its specific relationship to certain trees, birds and insects.

This harmonious combination of structure and function may be explained either by a Divine Act of Creation, a static concept with fixed immutable species, or by a process of evolution, a dynamic physiological concept with transmutation of species.

In Hunter's time, in the eighteenth century, the theory of Creation was almost universally held and although a Scale of Nature was recognised on the basis of a gradation of structural complexity, it was believed that the different species of fauna and flora were immutable, there was no phylogenetic relationship between them, no evolutionary transformation and no species became extinct. Even as late as 1860, it was stated that 'The opinion amongst naturalists that species were independently created, and have not been transmuted one from the other, has been hitherto so general that we might almost call it an axiom'.[1]

Evidence for evolution accumulated over the years until in 1859 it was collated by Charles Darwin into the Theory of Evolution, with an explanation of its mechanism by Natural Selection.[2] John Hunter's name is rarely associated with the history of evolution and yet his contributions to comparative anatomy, embryology, geology and palaeontology contain most of the salient facts on which Darwin's theory of evolution was founded. Hunter had no doubt about the mutability of species. He wrote:

To attempt to trace any natural production to its origin, or its first production, is ridiculous; for it goes back to that period, if ever such existed, of which we can form no idea, *viz.* the beginning of time. But, I think, we have reason to suppose there was a period in time in which every species of natural production was the same; there then being no variety in any species; but the variations taking place on the surface of the earth, such as the earth and water changing situations, which is obvious; . . . The varieties [so produced] . . . are still existing in what may be called the 'Natural' Animal. Also civilization has made varieties in many species, and without number, which are the 'Domesticated'.[3]

In this statement Hunter has expressed the principle of physical and biological evolution subsequently elaborated by Lyell and Darwin.

It is of interest, therefore, to note the contributions that Hunter made to the various principles on which Darwin established the theory of biological evolution.

1. *Unity of type*

Darwin stated 'By unity of type is meant that fundamental agreement in structure which we see in organic beings of the same class, and which is quite independent of their habits of life. On my theory, unity of type is explained by unity of descent . . .'[4] 'The similar framework of bones in the hand of a man, wing of a bat, fin of the porpoise, and leg of the horse, – the same number of vertebrae forming the neck of the giraffe and of the elephant, – . . . at once explain themselves on the theory of descent with slow and slight successive modifications.'[5]

John Hunter said, '. . . everything in Nature has a relation to or connexion with some other natural production . . . each is composed of parts common to most others but differently arranged.'[6]

2. *Biogenetic law*

The stages of development of the embryo of a species show a resemblance to the succession of stages in the phylogenetic history of the species (ontogeny repeats phylogeny). This law is usually associated with the name of Ernst Haeckel but Hunter described it a century previously . . . 'if we were capable of following the progress of increase of the number of the parts of the most perfect animal, as they first formed in succession, from the very first, to its state of full perfection, we should probably be able to compare it with some one of the incomplete animals themselves, of every order of animals in the creation, being at no stage different from some of those inferior orders; or, in order words, if we were to take a series of animals from the more imperfect to the perfect, we should probably find an imperfect animal corresponding with some stage of the most perfect.'[7]

The concept that ontogeny (the development of the individual) repeats phylogeny (the evolution of the race) is not strictly correct.[8,9,10] The embryonic stages are a recapitulation of the *embryo* forms of the phylogenetic series, not of the *adult* forms, as for example the gill-pouches of the mammalian embryo resemble those of the *embryo* fish and not of the *adult* fish. A more accurate statement might be that ontogeny repeats embryonic phylogeny.

3. *Time span*

The concept of a greatly extended time scale of the age of the earth was a vital element of the theory of evolution. Darwin acknowledged that his appreciation of the time factor in nature was a major step towards his theory of evolution. He said: 'He who can read Sir Charles Lyell's . . . Principles of Geology, . . . yet does not admit how vast have been the past periods of time, may at once close this volume.'[11] But Hunter's investigations in geology and palaeontology show that he fully appreciated the great age of the earth.

It is not unlikely that, in developing this scientific geological assessment, Hunter had the great advantage of a lack of formal religious indoctrination that left him completely free of any bias in favour of the biblical description, whereas Lyell, Huxley and others, and even Darwin in his early years, were in fact handicapped by a rigid orthodox education which made it difficult for them to accept the drastic unorthodox views inevitably associated with a vastly increased time scale and indeed, in all of them except Darwin, delayed their acceptance of the theory of evolution.

4. *Law of succession*

Darwin's law of succession of types expressed the view that, geographically, existing animals have a close relation in form with extinct species – 'In each great region of the world the living mammals are closely related to the extinct species of the same region.'[12] Both Darwin and Wallace used this idea as a strong demonstration of evolutionary links. It was based largely on the observation, made by William Clift, that the fossil mammals in Australia were closely related to the living marsupials,[13] and similarly those found in South America include a high proportion of

Edentata possessing a bony armour analogous to that of the armadillos which are peculiar to that continent.[14] But long before these discoveries were made John Hunter had already made this observation, as was pointed out by Owen. In discussing the geographical distribution of animals relating to fossils, Hunter said: '[Fossil] Bones of animals'. . . one would have naturally supposed to consist chiefly of those of one class or order in every place, . . .'[15]

5. Extinction of species

The concept that species could·become extinct was an important argument in favour of the theory of evolution. It is evident that Hunter held this view. He said: '. . . very few Fossils correspond with the recent, though very similar, . . . but if they are really different species, then we must suppose the old are lost; . . .'[16] '. . . that many are actually lost is, I think, plainly shown, by the remains of land-animals that are now not known. Yet how they became extinct is not easily accounted for . . .'[17]

In describing the fossil bones of Anspach he said: 'The bones . . . belonging to the white bear; . . . the heads . . . differ from the present white bear . . . some of them, when compared with the recent white bear, would seem to have belonged to an animal twice that size . . .'[18]

6. Descent of man

The most bitter opposition to Darwin's theory of course arose from its uncompromising but logical inference that man had descended from an ape-like ancestor and its complete rejection of the divine act of creation. It is obvious that Hunter had no doubts about the physical relationship of man to the animal kingdom. He said: '. . . man is the most complicated part of the whole animal creation.'[19] And again: 'The monkey in general may be said to be half beast and half man; it may be said to be the middle stage.'[20]

Hunter recognised only one vital principle throughout animate Nature; he said '. . . although life may appear very compounded in its effects in a complicated animal like man, it is as simple in him as in the most simple animal, . . .'[21] Hunter was indeed fortunate that none of his contemporary critics had him denounced as a heretic.

7. Variations among species

Varieties among species had, of course, been noted for many years, but their significance in producing new species had been minimised and they were regarded as acting only within restricted limits in the species. Hunter made numerous observations on this problem of the development of new species from varieties. He said: 'it is evident . . . that there is in a great number of species a considerable variety . . . and . . . it becomes a doubt . . . whether any one of them are original, or none of them . . .'[22] And again: '. . . many appearances . . . owe their birth to changes that have taken place in the productions of Nature by Time . . .'[22]

Like Darwin, Hunter appreciated the importance of deviation in nature: '. . . every species has a disposition to deviate from Nature in a manner peculiar to itself.'[23] Indeed, he came very near to Darwinism: '. . . in the individuals of each species varieties are every day produced in colour, shape, size and disposition. Some of these changes are permanent with respect to the propagation of the animal, becoming so far a part of its nature, as to be continued in the offspring.'[24] Darwin said: '. . . variations . . . if they be . . . profitable to the individuals of a species . . . will tend to the preservation of such individuals, and will generally be inherited by the offspring.'[25] Alas, modern geneticists have undermined this simple Darwinian concept, but at least Hunter was in good company in this matter.

Recent research has been presented in support of the theory that in fact acquired characteristics may be inherited by offspring. It has been shown that an acquired ability to tolerate grafts of foreign tissue induced experimentally in certain mice may be inherited by some of their progeny. The mechanism could depend on the transfer of altered genes from the body to the germ cells so that an acquired characteristic might thus be incorporated into the recognised mechanisms of inheritance. It is known that changes in genes may occur in the acquisition of immunity and also that there are viruses capable of transferring genetic information from one cell to another.[26]*

It was principally on the study of variations among species that Darwin and Wallace independently founded their theory of the mechanism of evolution. Prior to Darwin and Wallace, the concept of the struggle for existence was considered of significance only in

---

* Repetition of these experiments by other workers more recently has failed to confirm these results (Brent *et al*. Supposed Lamarchian inheritance of immunological tolerance. *Nature* 1981, vol. 290, pp. 508–512; McLaren *et al*. Immune reactivity of progeny of tetraparental male mice. *Ibid*. pp. 513, 514).

its relation to established species. It received general acceptance as an explanation of the survival of the individuals of a species, but it did not seek to explain the development of new species. Darwin and Wallace independently applied the principle of the struggle for existence to the behaviour of varieties as an explanation of the mechanism of evolution. They applied the principle of survival of the fittest not just to established species but to varieties of species competing for establishment. They added a dynamic physiological element to the static anatomical view of the significance of varieties. They coordinated function with structure, physiology with anatomy, in the dynamic process of adaptation among varieties. Hunter came close to an enunciation of the concept of adaptation. He noted the relation between the size of the organs of special sense and their functional activity – '. . . parts of animals . . . are generally in size in proportion to the . . . size of the animal; but those that . . . concern external matter, . . . such as eyes, ears, nose, etc, bear not the same proportion but relate to the way of life that each animal is adapted to. Some small animals, for example, have large ears, and *vice versa*: the same of the eyes . . .'[27]

The Darwinian theory was that evolution is essentially an ongoing physiological process – the natural selection of successful physiological varieties from among the mass of spontaneous anatomical variations. Now that of course is exactly the principle demonstrated in the Hunterian Museum. It is not just a collection of cold static anatomical specimens to be viewed in isolation. The specimens in the Museum represent a dynamic series of physiologically successful varieties of the various body systems linked together in an evolutionary scale, from the most simple to the most complex. Hunter's message is not just *in* the specimens but *between* the specimens. It is more than a museum of comparative anatomy or even of comparative physiology – it is a museum of evolution.

The basic pattern of evolution is demonstrated typically in the specimens of the central nervous system and of the heart and circulation. It must have been apparent in Hunter's original arrangement of the fossil specimens in relation to recent associated forms. A most significant example of the evolutionary trend in Hunter's work is included in the famous portrait by Reynolds (frontispiece), where the centre-piece of the background is the folio of drawings demonstrating Hunter's concept of the evolutionary series associated with the head and hand of man (fig. 9).

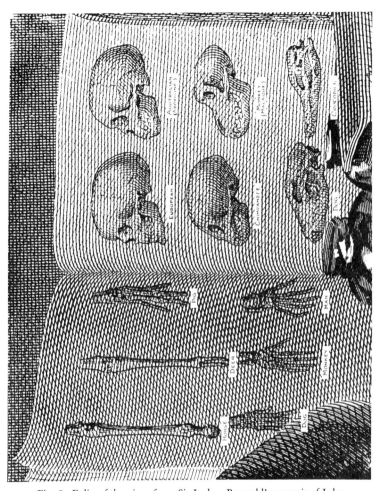

Fig. 9. Folio of drawings from Sir Joshua Reynold's portrait of John Hunter (see frontispiece), demonstrating the evolutionary series associated with the human head and hand (Hunterian Museum).

The significance of this folio was first noted by Sir Anthony Carlisle who wrote – 'In Sir Joshua's picture of John Hunter: he has intelligibly pourtrayed his pursuits by the two exposed plates; the one displays a series of fore limbs, from the simplest *foot* to the human *hand*. – In the opposite plate he ranges the human skull first, and descends to the Quadruped with least *brains* . . .'[28] This important folio has never been discovered and was no doubt among the Hunterian manuscripts sequestered by Everard Home, so that its inclusion in the portrait by Reynolds is of unique and inestimable value.

The skull series extends from that of a European through Australian aborigine, chimpanzee, Macaque monkey and dog down to the crocodile, while the forelimb series runs up from the hand through monkey, dog, pig and deer up to the horse. Hunter regarded the 'hand' of the horse, a single digit, as the most specialised and most highly evolved of the mammalian series; this indeed is an excellent example of Hunter's concern with the demonstration of evolution on the physiological basis of successful functional adaptation – the quintessence of Darwinism.

There can be little doubt that Hunter arranged his museum on an evolutionary basis because this would have been the only obvious way for him. Throughout all his work on natural history there is discernible this basic concept of an evolutionary process in Nature – for example: 'On the Origin of Species – Does not the natural gradation of animals, from one to another, lead to the original species? And does not that mode of investigation gradually lead to the knowledge of that species? Are we not led on to the wolf by the gradual affinity of the different varieties in the dog? Could we not trace out the gradation in the cat, horse, cow, sheep, fowl, etc., in a like manner?'[29] This was written at least seventy years before Darwin's *Origin of Species*, at a time when immutability of species was the established concept; it will be recalled that even Lyell, Huxley and Hooker abandoned this concept only after Darwin's work was published in 1859.

Hunter was a Darwinian in outlook, a century ahead of his contemporaries. He couldn't have expressed so many views explicable only on evolution in all branches of natural history, without being an evolutionist. The language of evolution was his ABC, his dictionary. He therefore arranged his museum on a fundamentally evolutionary basis, in a way comparable to a modern physicist who would automatically use relativity in solving his mathematical problems. Darwin described and established the principle of biological evolution but Hunter demonstrated it.

John Hunter's place in the establishment of the theory of evolution has been well expounded by Atkins. In an authoritative discourse, he discussed the question of priorities between Newton and Kepler in the discovery of the laws of gravity and between Darwin and Hunter and others in establishing the theory of evolution. He came to the conclusion that the attribution of credit should go to 'the man who not only had the inspiration but possessed the diligence, the industry and the basic knowledge to work out and present the concept in all its detail in a manner that no reasonable man thereafter could, within the available evidence of the day, challenge it.'[30] There can be little disagreement with Atkins' conclusion that pride of place in establishing the theory of evolution should go to Darwin, but the Hunterian Museum is a powerful practical demonstration of John Hunter's sincere appreciation of the principle of evolution.

REFERENCES

1 Wollaston T V. *Annals and Magazine of Natural History*. 1860, vol. 5, p. 133. Quoted by A Ellegärd in *Darwin and the General Reader: The Reception of Darwin's Theory of Evolution in the British Periodical Press, 1859–1872*. Göteborg, Almqvist. 1958, p. 14.

2 Darwin C. *Origin of Species*. London, John Murray. 1869, 5th edn.

3 Hunter J. *Essays and Observations on Natural History, Anatomy, Physiology, Pyschology and Geology*, ed. R Owen. London, John Van Voorst. 1861, vol. 1, p. 4.

4 Darwin C. *Origin of Species*. London, John Murray. 1869, 5th edn, p. 253.

5 Ibid. p. 567.

6 Hunter J. *Essays and Observations on Natural History, Anatomy, Physiology, Psychology and Geology*, ed. R Owen. London, John Van Voorst. 1861, vol. 1, p. 9.

7 Ibid. p. 203.

8 Garstang W. The theory of recapitulation: a critical restatement of the biogenetic law. *Journal of the Linnean Society, London, Zoology*. 1922, vol. 35, pp. 81–101.

9 De Beer G R. *Vertebrate Zoology*. London, Sidgwick & Jackson. 1966, p. 416.

10 Romer A S. *The Procession of Life*. London, Weidenfeld and Nicolson. 1968, p. 12.

11 Darwin C. *Origin of Species*. London, John Murray. 1869, 5th edn., p. 348.

12 Darwin C. *The Descent of Man and Selection in Relation to Sex*. London, John Murray. 1871, 2 vols. vol. 1, p. 199.

13 Clift W. On the fossil bones found in the bone-caves and bone-breccia of New Holland. In *Edinburgh New Phil. Journal*. 1831, p. 394.

14 Darwin C. *Origin of Species*. London, John Murray. 1869, 5th edn, pp. 414, 415.

15 Hunter J. Observations on some fossil bones of Anspach in *The Works of John Hunter*, ed. J F Palmer. London, Longman. 1837, vol. 4, p. 475.

16 Hunter J. *Observations and Reflections on Geology*. London, Taylor and Francis. 1859, p. 7.

17 Ibid. p. 8.

18 Hunter J. Observations on some fossil bones of Anspach in *The Works of John Hunter*, ed. J F Palmer. London, Longman. 1837, vol. 4, pp. 474, 475.

19 Hunter J. Lectures on the principles of surgery in *The Works of John Hunter*, ed. J F Palmer. London, Longman. 1835, vol. 1, p. 220.

20 Hunter J. *Essays and Observations on Natural History, Anatomy, Physiology, Psychology and Geology*, ed. R Owen. London, John Van Voorst. 1861, vol. 1, p. 43.

21 Hunter J. Lectures on the principles of surgery in *The Works of John Hunter*, ed. J F Palmer. London, Longman. 1835, vol. 1, p. 221.

22 Hunter J. *Essays and Observations on Natural History, Anatomy, Physiology, Psychology and Geology*, ed. R Owen. London, John Van Voorst. 1861, vol. 1, p. 3.

23 Hunter J. An account of an extraordinary pheasant in *The Works of John Hunter*, ed. J F Palmer. London, Longman. 1837, vol. 4, p. 45.

24 Hunter J. On the colour of the pigmentum of the eye in *The Works of John Hunter*, ed. J F Palmer. London, Longman. 1837, vol. 4, p. 277.

25 Darwin C. *Origin of Species*. London, John Murray. 1869, 5th edn, p. 72.

26 Gorczinski R M and Steele E J. Inheritance of acquired immunological tolerance to foreign histocompatibility in mice. *Proceedings of the National Academy of Sciences of the United States of America*. 1980, vol. 77, pp. 2871–2875.

27 Hunter J. *Essays and Observations on Natural History, Anatomy, Physiology, Pyschology and Geology*, ed. R Owen. London, John Van Voorst. 1861, vol. 2, pp. 2, 3.

28 Keith A (Sir Arthur). The portraits and personality of John Hunter. *British Medical Journal*. 1928, vol. 1, pp. 205–209.

29 Hunter J. *Essays and Observations on Natural History, Anatomy, Physiology, Psychology and Geology*, ed. R Owen. London, John Van Voorst. 1861, vol. 1, p. 37.

30 Atkins Sir Hedley. Hunterian Oration. The attributes of genius from Newton to Darwin. *Annals of the Royal College of Surgeons of England*. 1971, vol. 48, pp. 193–218.

EPILOGUE

John Hunter died on October 16, 1793 at the age of 65, while attending a Board meeting at St. George's Hospital. The records show that there were only five attending the meeting. John Hunter's name is not entered.[1] The others present were the Reverend James Clarke, Dr. Pearson, Dr. Robertson, Dr. Matthew and Mr. Walker. It has often been asserted that Hunter's death was to be blamed on his colleagues at the Board meeting, for example Peachey stated – 'Between him [Dr. Matthew] and William Walker rests the responsibility of having flatly contradicted Hunter at the meeting, and on one of them lies the opprobium of being the immediate cause of John Hunter's death.'[2]

It is doubtful that many would agree with this opinion. Dobson's account is more realistic:

> There is no precise evidence of any argument or contradiction: the only resolution noted is 'that Mr. Hunter's letter to the Board relating to two of the surgeons' pupils, who were received this day, be preserved for future consideration', which makes it appear that possibly this matter was not even discussed. . . . William Clift, who presumably would have heard any comments on the matter of his master's death, has nothing to say on this point nor did any further information come to light about the incident. The only ones who would be in a position to know the true facts were those present at the meeting, or the members of his family and close friends, but no accusation was ever made against any one person at the meeting who might have argued with or contradicted Hunter.

The assertion that John Hunter was in frequent disagreement with his colleagues at St. George's Hospital is certainly not supported by the significant fact that he was presented with a gold watch by them, during the active period of his career. The watch, now the property of the Hunterian Society, is inscribed '*Presented to John Hunter by the staff of St. George's Hospital'*. On the inner case is inscribed 'Left to my friend Charles James Fox MP 1793', but little is known of the friendship between them.[3]

John Hunter's death provoked little comment at the time, especially as the public were so deeply concerned with the horrors of the French Revolution. But to William Clift it was a sad historic moment and he wrote in his account book:

JOHN HUNTER ESQ. FRS.
*Surgeon General to the Army, and
Inspector General of Hospitals;
Surgeon to St. Georges Hospital;
Surgeon Extraordinary to the King;
&c   &c   &c*
DIED OCTOBER 16TH, 1793.
*On the same day, and perhaps hour,
that the unfortunate Marie Antoinette
Queen of France was beheaded in
Paris.*

W. CLIFT.[4]

An autopsy was performed by Everard Home, in the presence of Matthew Baillie, David Pitcairn and William Clift. It demonstrated the cause of death to be atherosclerosis involving the arteries of the brain and heart (p. 45). In later years Clift made a critical comment about the examination: 'It is to be regretted that Mr. Hunter's wish, so often expressed to many persons, respecting the preservation of his tendo achillis and his heart, should not have been complied with . . . Mr. Hunter often expressed himself very warmly on this head, with imprecations on those who should open his body if they did not preserve his heart and his tendo achillis, yet neither were preserved. In the situation of the union in Mr. Hunter's Tendo Achillis was a firm bony deposit of about two inches in length felt but not examined.'[5]

John Hunter was buried on October 22, 1793 at the Church of St. Martin-in-the-Fields. Clift wrote: 'It was a very private burying for there was only a Hearse and two coaches besides Mr. Hunter's chariot, but nobody rode in that; my cloaths was not made soon enough to go to the burying and none of the servants went to the burying but I was acquainted with the undertaker and so I went to

the church and he put me into the vault with him – none of our
people saw me there, I believe, and I did not want them to.'[6]
John Hunter's coffin remained in the crypt of St. Martin's
Church until 1859 when as the result of a determined effort by
Frank Buckland it was removed and reinterred at Westminster
Abbey.

Frank Buckland (1826–1880) was one of the greatest authorities
in natural history of the nineteenth century. His father was William
Buckland Dean of Westminster and a pioneer of geology (p. 176).
Frank Buckland took a keen interest in the curiosities of Nature and
his books and articles made him the most popular writer on natural
history of his time. In 1859 he applied himself to searching for the
coffin of John Hunter in the crypt of St. Martin-in-the-Fields,
where it had been placed in 1793. Buckland examined nearly three
thousand coffins during the search which occupied him from
January 26 until February 22 on which day he discovered John
Hunter's coffin. It was found to be in excellent condition with the
inscription on the brass plate clearly decipherable: JOHN HUN-
TER, ESQ. died October 16th 1793, aged 64.[7,8] The error in the
engravement of his age (he was actually aged 65) possibly epitomises
the meagre and parsimonious arrangements of what was close to
being a pauper's funeral. A similar error in his age was made by
John Hunter's own brother-in-law Everard Home – 'At the time of
his death he was in the 65th year of his age . . .'[9] and also by
Ottley.[10]

John Hunter's coffin was reinterred at Westminster Abbey on
28th March, 1859[11] and on 14th February, 1952 a Memorial Tablet
was unveiled at St. Martin's Church to commemorate the original
resting place of John Hunter's body.[12]

JOHN HUNTER'S MANUSCRIPTS

At the time of Hunter's death a large number of his manuscripts
remained unpublished. These were kept at the house at Castle Street
under the care of William Clift. In December 1799 they were
transferred to Sir Everard Home's residence by his order. 'He
merely said that these papers, being a very large proportion of them
loose fasciculi, were not fit for the public eye; and therefore he
should take them into his keeping, for the purpose of using them in
describing the collection ' (Clift, quoted by Paget).[13] The manuscripts remained in the possession of Everard Home from 1800 to

1823. On numerous occasions the trustees of the Hunterian Collection requested Home to write a catalogue of the collection, but Home never produced it nor did he allow Clift or anyone else to write a catalogue. In July 1823 Home destroyed Hunter's unpublished manuscripts.

It was fortunate that Clift had had the foresight to copy a large number of the manuscripts during the seven years up to 1800 when he had charge of them at Castle Street. Clift said:

> He had a kind of presentiment that if they were removed to his house some accident might befall them, and even then feeling their value, I copied for my own use and information a considerable proportion of them (Thank God), never having been forbidden from so doing . . . I wrote out the different memoirs and dissections that most interested me on such scraps of paper as were within my power (7/- a week not affording me much means) – and I worked night and day when I found I was probably to lose them altogether . . . When I began to forethink what might possibly happen when I saw that every day Mr. Hunter's memory and labours were gradually sinking and less and less noticed – my eyes began to open to the reality.[14]

There was a very large number of manuscripts. Clift stated that 'Mr. Hunter had for many years two or three persons almost constantly employed as amanuenses and consequently the quantity of manuscript at his death was enormous, as he appeared to me to preserve every thing whether published or not . . .'[15]

Various motives have been presented to explain Home's conduct. Sir Arthur Keith offered a charitable view of Home's behaviour when he wrote:

> Home burned Hunter's original manuscripts, the usual explanation being that he had pilfered from them. A close study of the conventional character of Sir Everard Home and of the circumstances which surround this infamous act of vandalism have convinced me that the accepted explanation is not the true one. Home shared implicitly in the religious beliefs of his time and never doubted that by destroying all evidence of Hunter's heretical convictions he was performing an act of piety on behalf of the world in general and for the memory of his brother-in-law in particular.[16]

This generous view proposed by Keith cannot be supported by the large amount of available evidence. Dobson made a careful study of the subject and concluded that 'There seems to be little doubt that Hunter's papers were destroyed, as Clift suspected, in order to conceal the fact that Home had systematically used their contents as a basis for his own writings . . . Home abstracted practically the whole of Hunter's unpublished work and, after minor rearrangement, reproduced it as his own.'[17] This conclusion is obvious from a consideration of the following evidence:

(a) Comparison of Hunter's paper on the Oeconomy of Whales published in 1787 with one on the same subject by Home published in 1814 shows numerous passages which are almost identical, e.g.

> Some genera of this tribe have another mode of catching their food, and retaining it till swallowed, which is by means of the substance called whalebone. Of this there are two kinds known; one very large, probably from the largest whale yet discovered; the other from a smaller species.
>
> *Oeconomy of Whales.* John Hunter. 1787[18]
>
> Some genera of this tribe have another mode of catching their food, and retaining it till swallowed, by means of the substance called whalebone. Of this there are two kinds known; one very large, probably from the largest whale yet discovered, the great balaena mysticetus; the other from a smaller species, the piked-whale.
>
> *On the Teeth of the Whale Tribe.* E. Home. 1814[19]

(b) In a copy of one of Hunter's manuscripts made by Clift before it was removed by Home, there are numerous marginal notes inserted by Clift indicating passages where Hunter's observations are identical with passages in Home's *Lectures on Comparative Anatomy*.

(c) Sir Benjamin Brodie mentions in his *Autobiography* that he recognised passages in Home's later works purporting to be original but which were in fact taken from Hunter's unpublished manuscripts with which Brodie was very familiar.

(d) Home had repeatedly stated that he was the only person suitable to prepare the museum catalogues requested by the trustees, but in fact he never produced the catalogues. A good reason for this procrastination could well have been that he was plagiarising Hunter's writings, since many of Home's publications were on subjects in which it was known that Hunter was interested.

(e) During the period between Hunter's death in 1793 and the destruction of the manuscripts in 1823, Home published 92 papers in the Philosophical Transactions alone. Indeed, 'Sir Everard Home contributed more papers to the Royal Society than any other single Member of that distinguished Body since its foundation.'[20] Between 1814 and 1823 Home published his *Lectures on Comparative Anatomy* which comprised five large volumes and included reports of numerous dissections. It would have been impossible for any one individual, even John Hunter himself, to produce such a large volume of original work in that relatively short period of time considering that, in addition, Home was actively engaged in his large surgical practice and had also many other commitments, especially in association with the Royal College of Surgeons of which he became President in 1821.*

(f) Home destroyed Hunter's manuscripts in 1823, only a few days after he had received from the printers the final proofs of his *Lectures on Comparative Anatomy*.

There can be little doubt that Home made use of Hunter's work freely and without acknowledgement. Indeed Home stated, after Hunter's decease, that he was preparing to use Hunter's lecture material for his own publications – 'In the year 1792, Mr. Hunter found that his course of lectures took up so much of his time . . . He therefore gave it up to me . . . The materials of these lectures having come into my hands; that they may not be entirely lost to the public, I mean to avail myself of them, and am preparing my arrangements for that purpose.'[21]

HUNTER'S LEGACY

John Hunter's life and work have been the subjects of numerous biographies, orations, lectures and articles but in spite of this manifest acknowledgement of his genius, Hunter's name is not associated with any single great discovery. The names of Harvey, Lister and Jenner are immediately remembered for their respective contributions to medical science but the products of Hunter's greatness are not so easily identified.

Hunter's contribution to science is to be found, not in the form of a single discovery, however important, but rather in the establishment of numerous basic principles from which other discoveries have been derived. His interests were essentially germinal but it was especially in his methods that he demonstrated his originality and genius. He brought the experimental method of investigation to the study of living tissues, a method which he applied to his work on growth, inflammation, blood, lymphatics, transplantation and

---

* The Royal Charter under which the title of Master was changed to President was dated 13th February 1822.

other subjects. Thus John Hunter was the founder of scientific
surgery.

Hunter's publications include observations and research in all
branches of natural and physical science (p. 58). His numerous
contributions to comparative anatomy were gleaned from the whole
range of the animal kingdom and many of his original observations
have been quietly incorporated into standard zoological description. His studies in physiology formed the basis of his scientific
methods and were essentially of a practical clinical significance as
for example in his demonstration of the growth of bone, the
function of the lymphatics and the interrelation of the heart and
lungs during respiration.

Hunter's study of disease processes was based on a sound
understanding of anatomy and physiology. In his careful investigations into the causes of disease, Hunter inevitably uncovered the
basic principles of pathology. His work on inflammation alone was
a landmark in the understanding of disease phenomena and its basic
principles have been assimilated unobtrusively into modern pathology. John Hunter was thus the founder of surgical pathology.

In geology and palaeontology Hunter's observations were revolu-
tionary but for various reasons many of the most important of these
were not revealed until, years later, others had reached similar
conclusions (p. 179).

In biological science Hunter 'revolutionised the outlook, shifting
emphasis from the Linnean or taxonomic viewpoint to the "physiological" i.e. to the exploration of the animal machine in an
attempted understanding of the operation of the vital processes'
(Cave).[22] This change in emphasis from a static to a dynamic
concept was fundamental to the establishment of Darwin's theory
of evolution and Hunter's contributions to the theory have never
been fully appreciated. His works abound with observations in
comparative anatomy, embryology, geology and palaeontology
which cover almost all the aspects on which the theory of evolution
is based, while his Museum is a lasting monument expressive of the
theory.

REFERENCES

1 Dobson J. *John Hunter*. Edinburgh and London, Livingstone. 1969, p. 347.
2 Peachey G C. *A Memoir of Williams and John Hunter*. Plymouth, William
  Brendon. 1924, pp. 220, 221.

3 Rudolf C R. Hunteriana. *Hunterian Society Transactions* 1950–51, vol. 9, pp. 84–93.

4 Finlayson J. Account of a ms. volume, by William Clift, relating to John Hunter's household and estate; and to Sir Everard Home's publications, *British Medical Journal*. 1890, vol. 1, pp. 738–740.

5 Clift W. *MSS. Catalogue of the Pathological Collection, Wet Preparations*. No. 129. Quoted by J Dobson in *John Hunter*. Edinburgh and London, Livingstone. 1969, p. 349.

6 Dobson J. *John Hunter*. Edinburgh and London, Livingstone. 1969, p. 350.

7 Burgess G H O. *The Curious World of Frank Buckland*. London, John Baker. 1967, p. 79.

8 Buckland F J. John Hunter's Coffin. *Lancet*. 1859, vol. 1, p. 252.

9 Home E. A short account of the author's life in Hunter's *A Treatise on the Blood, Inflammation and Gun-shot Wounds*. London, G Nicol. 1794, p. 62.

10 Ottley D. Life of John Hunter in *The Works of John Hunter*, ed. J F Palmer. London, Longman. 1835, vol. 1, p. 133.

11 Editorial. Reinterment of John Hunter. *Lancet*. 1859, vol. 1, pp. 350, 352, 353.

12 Gordon-Taylor Sir Gordon. Unveiling of memorial tablet to John Hunter. *Hunterian Society Transactions* 1951–52, vol. 10, pp. 134–141.

13 Paget S. *John Hunter*. London, T Fisher Unwin. 1897, p. 251.

14 Dobson J. *William Clift*. London, Heinemann. 1954, p. 21.

15 Ibid. p. 68.

16 Keith A. *British Masters of Medicine*, ed. d'A Power. London, Medical Press and Circular. 1936, p. 51.

17 Dobson J. *William Clift*. London, Heinemann. 1954, pp. 59–62.

18 Hunter J. Observations on the structure and oeconomy of whales in *The Works of John Hunter*, ed. J F Palmer. London, Longman. 1837, vol. 4, p. 354.

19 Home E. On the teeth of the whale tribe in *Lectures on Comparative Anatomy*. London, G and W Nicol. 1814, vol. 1, p. 262.

20 Ottley D. Life of John Hunter in *The Works of John Hunter*, ed. J F Palmer. London, Longman. 1835, vol. 1, p. 153.

21 Home E. A short account of the author's life in Hunter's *A Treatise on the Blood, Inflammation and Gun-shot Wounds*. London, G Nicol. 1794, p. 36.

22 Cave A J E. Personal communication 1977.

ADDITIONAL BIBLIOGRAPHY

Dobson J. John Hunter's statue. *Annals of the Royal College of Surgeons of England*. 1959, vol. 24, p. 209.

Editorial. John Hunter, Ben Johnson and Wilkie. *Lancet*. 1859, vol. 1, p. 399.

APPENDIX

GENERAL BIBLIOGRAPHY

Abel A Lawrence. Bleeding through the Ages. *Hunterian Society Transactions* 1968–69, vol. 27, pp. 79–96.

Abernethy J. *Hunterian Oration 1819*. London, Longman.

Adams J. *Memoirs of the Life and Doctrines of the late John Hunter, Esq*. London, J Callow and J Hunter. 1817. Second edn. 1818.

Atkins Sir Hedley. Hunterian Oration 1971. The attributes of genius from Newton to Darwin. *Annals of the Royal College of Surgeons of England*. vol. 48, pp. 193–218.

Buckle H T. *History of Civilization in England*. London, Parker Son and Bourn. 1861, vol. 2, pp. 535–577.

Butler F H. John Hunter. *Encyclopaedia Britannica*. Edinburgh, Adam and Charles Black. 9th edn. 1881, vol. 12, pp. 385–391.

Cohen Sir Henry (Lord). Reflections on the Hunterian method. *Hunterian Society Transactions* 1955–56. vol. 14, pp. 80–95.

Dobson J. *William Clift*. London, Heinemann. 1954.

Dobson J. *John Hunter*. Edinburgh and London, Livingstone. 1969.

Foot J. *The Life of John Hunter*. London, T Becket. 1794.

Gloyne S Roodhouse. *John Hunter*. Edinburgh, E & S Livingstone. 1950.

Home E. A short account of the author's life in Hunter's *A Treatise on the Blood, Inflammation and Gun-shot wounds*. London, G Nicol. 1794.

Horder Lord. The Hunterian tradition. *Hunterian Society Transactions* 1936–37, vol. 1, pp. 66–78.

Hunterian Museum Guide. Royal College of Surgeons of England ed. E Allen. 1974.

Jones F Wood. John Hunter as a geologist. *Annals of the Royal College of Surgeons of England*. 1953, vol. 12, pp. 219–245.

Keith Sir Arthur. The portraits and personality of John Hunter. *British Medical Journal*. 1928, vol. 1, pp. 205–209.

LeFanu W R. The Hunter-Baillie manuscripts. *Hunterian Society Transactions* 1953–54, vol. 12, pp. 88–101.

Norbury L E C. The Times of John Hunter. *Hunterian Society Transactions* 1954–55, vol. 13, pp. 49–70.

Ottley D. Life of John Hunter in *The Works of John Hunter*, ed. J F Palmer. London, Longman. 1835, vol. 1.

Paget S. *John Hunter*. London, T Fisher Unwin. 1897.

Peachey G C. *A Memoir of William and John Hunter*. Plymouth, William Brendon and Son. 1924.

Qvist G. Hunterian Oration 1979. Some controversial aspects of John Hunter's life
and work. *Annals of the Royal College of Surgeons of England.* vol. 61,
pp. 138–141, 219–223, 309–311, 381–384, 478–483.
Riches Sir Eric. Example is the School of Mankind. *Hunterian Society Transactions*
1966–67, vol. 25, pp. 66–91.
Royal College of Surgeons of England. *Letters from the past. From John Hunter to
Edward Jenner.* 1976.
Rudolf C R. Hunteriana. *Hunterian Society Transactions* 1950–51, vol. 9, pp. 84–
93; Part 2, 1951–52, vol. 10, pp. 120–133; Part 3, 1952–53, vol. 11, pp. 106–
123; Part 4, 1957–58, vol. 16, pp. 141–169.
Rudolf C R. The Hunter-Baillie MSS*. *Hunterian Society Transactions* 1964–65,
vol. 23, pp. 88–112; Part 2, 1966–67, vol. 25, pp. 92–119.

---

* The Hunter and Baillie families (fig. 1) preserved a vast mass of correspondence
that passed through their hands in several generations. The collection was arranged
by Miss Helen Hunter-Baillie, great-great-niece of John Hunter, and the bulk of it
presented by her to the Royal College of Surgeons of England, around 1925. The
residual part of the collection, containing more intimate correspondence, was
generously presented to the Hunterian Society, in about 1963, by Mr. Patrick
Hunter Jobson, FRCS, John Hunter's great-great-great-great-nephew.

INDEX